SOCIAL WORK VALUES AND ETHICS

ELAINE P. CONGRESS

Fordham University

SocialWork
VALUES
AND
ETHICS

Identifying and Resolving Professional Dilemmas

Nelson-Hall Publishers / Chicago

Project editor: Dorothy J. Anderson
Design: Jane Rae Brown
Cover: "High Load Blue" by Diane Cooper
Typesetter: Skripps and Associates
Manufacturing: Book-mart Press, Inc.

The *NASW Code of Ethics* reprinted on pages 157–179 by permission of the National
Association of Social Workers, Washington, DC.
Copyright 1996, National Association of Social Workers, Inc.

Library of Congress Cataloging-in-Publication Data

Congress, Elaine Piller.
  Social work values and ethics, identifying and resolving professional dilemmas /
Elaine P. Congress
    p.   cm.
  Includes biblioographical references and index.
  ISBN 0-8304-1492-4 (alk. paper)
  1. Social workers—Professional ethics—United States   2. Social service—Moral and
ethical aspects—United States   I. Title.
  HV10.5.C64   1998   98-27940
  174'.9362—DC21   CIP

Manufactured in the United States of America

10   9   8   7   6   5   4   3   2

The paper used in this book meets the
minimum requirements of American
National Standard for Information
Sciences—Permanence of Paper for
Printed Library Materials. ANSI
Z39 48-1964

CONTENTS

FOREWORD   vii
by Dennis Saleebey, University of Kansas

PREFACE   ix

CHAPTER 1   **Introduction and Overview**   1

CHAPTER 2   **The NASW Code of Ethics**   7

CHAPTER 3   **Values and Social Work Principles**   17

CHAPTER 4   **Social Work Dilemmas
              and the ETHIC Decision-Making Model**   29

CHAPTER 5   **Ethical Dilemmas in Mental Health**   39

CHAPTER 6   **Ethical Dilemmas in Child Welfare**   53

CHAPTER 7   **Ethical Dilemmas in Health Care**   69

CHAPTER 8   **Ethical Dilemmas
              in Group and Family Work**   81

CHAPTER 9   **Ethical Dilemmas in Aging**   95

CHAPTER 10   **Ethical Dilemmas for the Professional
              Social Worker: Dual Relationships and
              Impaired Colleagues**   105

CHAPTER 11   **Ethical Dilemmas in Interdisciplinary
              Collaboration**   117

CHAPTER 12   **Ethical Dilemmas Relating to HIV and AIDS** 129

CHAPTER 13   **Ethical Dilemmas in Supervising and
              Managing**   141

CHAPTER 14   **The Future of Social Work Ethics**   151

              APPENDIX: The NASW Code of Ethics   157

              REFERENCES   181

              INDEX   189

Dennis Saleebey, DSW, LMSW
School of Social Welfare, University of Kansas

We live in a society in which the moral and ethical environment is changing rapidly. Whether it is technological tinkering with the human genome, the rapidly widening gulf between rich and poor in this country and the world, the privatization of formerly public concerns and institutions, the dismantling of the welfare state, the frenzied expanding influence of large corporations in public affairs, or the rampant polluting and destruction of natural resources, the issues that confront us as a society, a world, and a profession seem ever more urgent and more daunting. The era when we could simply rely on a few timeless moral prescriptions seems quaint in comparison. Although the ways that we define the sins to which the flesh is heir probably haven't changed much and the pitfalls to living a life well would be known to a Plantagenet, Assyrian, or taxi driver in the Bronx, the scope of the ethical dimensions of the challenges and changes we face today is beyond the ken, it seems, of most of us.

Social workers are citizens, and the changing moral and ethical environment also affects us. But as social workers we face particular challenges to our professional values and ethics as well. The moral and social environment of practice is unstable, whirling about us with great force and dynamism, and it kicks up dust in almost every field of social work practice. Welfare reform is putting thousands of families and individuals on the streets; downsizing and outsourcing is putting thousands of workers out of jobs; privatizing services is directly challenging the ethical foundations of many fields of practice; and the increasing influence of the medical/psychiatric/insurance/pharmaceutical cartel is dramatically shaping the dimensions, pace, and character of practice in the health field. These and other forces require that we, as professionals, do some serious thinking about the nature of our professional ethics and their relationship to practice and how, as professionals, we should respond to some of the shifts and changes in values characteristic of the environments in which we practice.

This book could not have come at a more opportune time. Dr. Congress has devoted much of her academic and professional career to understanding the play of values in our practice decisions and activities, and the role of ethics in shaping and forming principles and technologies of professional practice. As a scholar, teacher, and practitioner she is supremely qualified to bring to an audience of students and practitioners ideas about the interplay between ethics and practice, between the dimensions and scale of clients' lives and the responsibilities and perplexities of an ethical and competent professional social worker.

The singular virtue of this book is that it is about practice. This is no tome articulating high-flown and removed philosophical and ethical principles, no tract forwarding effete musings about the moral and ethical high ground to be taken. No. This is a book about ethical social work practice, about facing the emergent and enduring ethical dilemmas confronting practitioners working with families and children, working with elders, dilemmas that challenge practitioners who work in health and mental health, and very importantly, in this day and time, practitioners who work with those who are facing HIV/AIDS.

Dr. Congress moves beyond fields of practice to discuss other important relationships and activities of the professional social worker that have ethical dimensions, consequences, and ambiguities. These include contending with the questions and concerns that impaired colleagues may provoke; finding a suitable ground for competent and ethical interdisciplinary collaboration (a reality that will surely intensify with the spread of managed care); and exploring the ethical contours and claims of supervisory and administrative practice. In chapters devoted to these topics and fields of practice, Dr. Congress amply illustrates and instructs with case examples and other learning devices.

The grounding of this book is the NASW Code of Ethics. Professional ethical codes accomplish at least four things: they are a part of the socialization of practitioners to professional culture; they inform professionals on the character of appropriate ethical practice and conduct; they set the stage for judgments about professional accountability in various fields of practice; and they provide impetus and a basis for continuing interpretation and articulation of ethical codes as practitioners face difficult ethical quandaries (and these may become the basis for subsequent changes in the code). The NASW Code also recognizes something that Dr. Congress highlights as well:

> A code of ethics cannot guarantee ethical behavior. Moreover, a code of ethics cannot resolve all ethical issues or disputes, or capture the richness and complexity involved in striving to make responsible choices with a moral community. Rather, a code of ethics sets forth values, ethical principles, and ethical standards to which professionals aspire and by which they can be judged. (NASW Code of Ethics, 1996)

That is to say, often enough ethical issues and challenges are deceptive, murky, and require a degree of thoughtfulness, consultation, intellectual alacrity, and study that will render them more tractable in practice. This reality must be a part of any discussion about morals and ethics, and Dr. Congress, throughout the book, encourages this kind of thinking.

Dr. Congress also invites thought and perspective about the very important relationship between values (personal, societal, client, and agency) and ethics. This is not always a direct or compatible relationship. Social work practitioners must become clear about the interaction, for example, between their own personal values, agency values, and what the client needs and wants. Finally, at the outset (chapter 4) and as a heuristic device, Dr. Congress presents and discusses four models of ethical decision making and then presents her own, which she names with the acronym ETHIC. She provides clear examplars about the application of her model and ample justification for its use.

The student or practitioner who has read and studied from this text will, in my mind, be well prepared to face and manage the stupefying array of ethical and moral uncertainties and challenges that await the concerned, competent, and ethical professional social worker. Dr. Congress is to be congratulated for providing such a learning experience.

This book has been one year in writing, but many years in unfolding. I first became interested in the study of ethics when, as a doctoral student at Hunter College School of Social Work, Dean Harold Lewis became my faculty advisor. After I completed an independent study project with him, Dean Lewis mentored my dissertation on ethical decision making among field instructors in social work education. After many years of experience in outpatient mental health, I was keenly aware of the many ethical dilemmas that social workers face in their practice.

When I first joined the faculty at Fordham University Graduate School of Social Service, I developed a master's level course on ethics and co-taught a doctoral ethics course with Dr. Ursula Gerty, who helped increase my understanding of philosophical issues and social work ethics. Now, after ten years of teaching social work ethics to graduate students, I have become increasingly aware of how useful case vignettes are in helping students identify and resolve ethical dilemmas. Thus, this book contains many vignettes that will be helpful to those who teach ethics in the classroom or in the field. As director of the doctoral program, I am very aware of the importance of educating students, as well as professionals, about social work values and ethics to promote ethical practice in the future.

In my professional involvement, first as chair of the NYC NASW Ethics Committee and now as president of the NYC NASW chapter, I know how often professional social workers struggle with ethical dilemmas and require a clear, straightforward approach to resolve them. This concern led to the development of the ETHIC model of decision making, which appears for the first time in this book.

I would like to acknowledge several people who helped to make this book possible. I want to thank Dean MaryAnn Quaranta for her ongoing support during this undertaking. I am particularly aware of how she continually demonstrates social work values in her interactions with faculty, students, staff, and others in our social work community. I would also like to thank the much published Dr. Albert Roberts, who has been an important role model and mentor to me in my publishing endeavors. I received important input from NYC NASW ethics committee members, especially Eileen Ain, who provided research on the history of the Code of Ethics. Finally, I especially appreciated the support and encouragement of my husband, Judge Robert T. Snyder, throughout the writing of this book.

After writing numerous articles on social work ethics, I am pleased to have had the opportunity to write this timely, user-friendly book on ethics. I hope that you will find it helpful in your work as a social work practitioner, educator, or student.

ABOUT THE AUTHOR

Elaine P. Congress, DSW, is director of the doctoral program and professor at Fordham University Graduate School of Social Service. She is president of the New York City chapter of the National Association of Social Work and chair of the Ethics and Professional Standards Committee. Her articles on social work ethics have appeared in *The Clinical Supervisor, Journal of Teaching in Social Work, Journal of Social Work Education, Journal of Multicultural Social Work, Social Work in Education, Journal of Social Work with Groups*, and *Currents*, a publication of the NYC chapter of NASW. Congress, who also writes about cultural diversity, developed the culturagram, a family assessment tool for use with culturally diverse families, and authored the book *Multicultural Perspectives in Working with Families* in 1997.

CHAPTER 1

Introduction and Overview

Social workers' concern about values and ethical issues is not new. Values have long been considered "the major substance of social work" (Gordon, 1965, p. 20). But the nature of ethical issues has shifted over the years, and a concern has been raised that social work does not have a permanent, unchanging value base (Meinert, Pardek, and Sullivan, 1994). One example of this was the emphasis on client morality in the early years of the profession. While social workers once primarily looked at client deficits and problems, they now stress client strengths and empowerment.

This book focuses on social work values and ethics as delineated in the 1996 Code of Ethics established by the National Association of Social Workers (NASW). The three following case vignettes relate to current practice issues. They all present dilemmas in which the social worker must decide the most ethical course of action.

Bob, a certified social worker in a group counseling center, has been seeing the Boyds for marital therapy for the last month. They have been continuously fighting ever since their youngest son left for college. As the parents of four children they have spent their last twenty years involved with child-rearing issues. Now suddenly they are alone. Every topic, even what to eat for dinner, becomes a subject of conflict. Bob applies a cognitive-behavioral model of treatment, and both Bob and the Boyds are pleased by the latter's progress.

Bob's son comes home for a family party and tells Bob that he has a new girlfriend whom he wants them to meet. Bob discovers that she is Terry Boyd, the daughter of his clients.

Should Bob tell the Boyds that his son has a personal relationship with their daughter? Should Bob tell his son that he has been seeing his girlfriend's parents for marital therapy? Should Bob continue to see the parents for therapy?

Everyone at the Carolina Children and Families Service Agency knows that Susan drinks too much. Her colleagues notice that she often does not come in on Mondays, and that she smells of alcohol after lunch. She even passed out at the office Christmas party. Andrea is particularly aware of the problem, because her office is next to Susan's. She knows that Susan often misses appointments with clients because she "made a mistake in her schedule." No one, however, wants to "get her into trouble." One reason that Andrea and others from the agency do not want to take any action is that as the single mother of two young children, Susan really needs the job. Tomorrow afternoon Susan is scheduled to drive two children upstate to a new foster home.

Should Andrea take action about Susan's drinking? Is Susan's contact with clients impaired because of her drinking? Will her clients be in danger if she drives after lunch?

Maria, a professional social worker, is employed in a small mental health agency. Because of cutbacks in government funding the agency is struggling to keep afloat. Two social workers hired earlier this year have just been laid off. Recently, Maria provided crisis-intervention services to Christine, a rape victim, who needs further treatment, and had submitted a report to the managed-care company that was paying for Christine's treatment. A clerk from the managed-care company calls to say that they never received the report and that therefore they are going to disallow the claim. Maria could fax the report to them immediately so that the agency could be paid.

Keeping in mind issues of confidentiality, should Maria fax the report to the managed-care company? If so, how detailed should the report be? What could be the consequence of faxing this report?

Case vignettes one and two relate to new provisions in the NASW Code of Ethics. Until 1993 the Code of Ethics did not specifically address dual relationships and impaired colleagues. While social workers have believed for many years that there should be a clear boundary between the professional and the personal, social work was one of the last professions to delineate specifically the prohibition against dual relationships in its code of ethics (NASW, 1993; NASW, 1996).

The third vignette involves confidentiality. While preserving confidentiality has always been an important value in social work, fax machines and computers bring new challenges to confidentiality.

Previously, case information was located in the written or typed case record, but now it is often stored on the computer and sent via fax machines, exposing it to many people other than the one for whom it was intended. Managed care presents additional challenges to confidentiality. Often a report intended for one purpose is shared with another professional and used for something else (Scarf, 1996). Also, the type and length of treatment are often decided by someone other than the professional who has responsibility for the care.

Social work practice continually presents ethical dilemmas to the clinician, who must decide between two often conflicting positions. The preceding examples describe ethical dilemmas in which the social worker must choose between two alternative courses of action. If one way is clearly wrong and the other clearly right, then an ethical dilemma does not exist. For example, the agency administrator does not have an ethical dilemma about whether to use child welfare grant money for his or her vacation to Florida, because this is clearly wrong.

Social work values can be defined as the relatively enduring beliefs of the profession. Social workers are continually translating their values into action; abstract values have been described as having importance only if they are moved into practice (Perlman, 1975). Social work ethics involves putting values into practice. However, when social work values are implemented, ethical dilemmas often emerge. For example, few would debate the relevance of such social work values as the provision of client service and maintaining confidentiality. However, as the third case vignette shows, values in practice often conflict. Consequently, as Pumphrey (1959), an early author on social work ethics, has suggested, values should not be studied in isolation but rather in pairs. This book presents a model for understanding and addressing ethical dilemmas that may arise because of conflicting values.

I am honored that Dr. Dennis Saleebey has written the Foreword for this book on social work ethics. Our social work values are very much rooted in the strengths perspective, an area in which Dr. Saleebey has written extensively. His professional work repeatedly demonstrates his commitment to philosophical and ethical issues in social work practice and education.

The first chapter sets the goal of helping social work students and practitioners become more familiar with the values and ethics of the social work profession as they are presented in the new NASW Code of Ethics. It also outlines how the book will address these issues.

Chapter 2 discusses the development of the Code of Ethics into its current form. Although social workers may sometimes use other codes in specialized areas, the NASW Code of Ethics remains the main code for the profession. A questionnaire with answers is presented to familiarize readers with the current code.

Chapter 3 focuses on values and ethical principles as defined in the NASW Code of Ethics. Professional values as well as personal values, societal values, client values, and agency values are illustrated through a case example. Social workers need to understand value differences, but professional values should prevail. A value exercise is presented to increase readers' sensitivity to values in professional practice.

Chapter 4 discusses different models of ethical decision making and presents the ETHIC model. This model uses the following five steps:

1. *Examine* relevant personal, social, agency, client, and professional values.
2. *Think* about what ethical standard from the NASW Code of Ethics might apply to the situation as well as about relevant laws and case decisions.
3. *Hypothesize* about different courses of action.
4. *Identify* who will benefit and who will be harmed in view of social work's commitment to the most vulnerable.
5. *Consult* with supervisors and colleagues about the most ethical choice.

A case example is used to illustrate the application of the ETHIC model to practice.

Chapter 5 focuses on current ethical issues in the mental health field. Ethical dilemmas posed by managed care and advanced technology are addressed in terms of promoting client interests and maintaining confidentiality. Discussions of mental health issues that may threaten client autonomy and confidentiality, including the duty to warn, privileged communication, the use of DSMIV, and involuntary hospitalization, are also included. Ethical challenges for the private practitioner, such as fees, bartering, and recording, are discussed and illustrated through case examples.

Chapter 6 centers on ethical challenges in child welfare. The conflict of interest paradigm of foster parent–child–birth parent is examined by applying the ETHIC model to a case example. Also, the timely issue of opening adoption records is addressed and illustrated through a case vignette.

Chapter 7 addresses current ethical issues in the health field. Technological advances, including renal dialysis, transplants, and genetics, have created new ethical dilemmas for the social worker. End-of-life decisions about severely disabled newborns and the terminally ill raise concerns for social workers. The NASW policy on end-of-life decisions is demontrated through a case example. Timely issues about euthanasia and assisted suicide are discussed. The chapter concludes with a discussion about culturally sensitive ethical practice in the health field.

Chapter 8 concentrates on ethical issues and dilemmas in group and family work. Increasingly, social workers work with clients on other than a one-to-one basis; thus the new code includes a section on group and family work. Maintaining confidentiality in task and treatment groups is discussed and illustrated through case examples. Ethical issues in family work, including conflicting values, confidentiality, and conflict of interest, are demonstrated through a case vignette.

Chapter 9 focuses on older people, a growing but often neglected group in our youth-oriented society. Different theories on aging—disengagement, activity, and substitution—are discussed, as is the emerging problem of elder abuse. Case examples are used to illustrate ethical dilemmas in protecting client autonomy while ensuring the safety of older clients.

In chapter 10 two important themes of professional practice—dual relationships and impaired colleagues—are discussed. The new Code of Ethics advises social workers to avoid dual relationships, especially of a sexual nature, and obliges them to take action when confronted with impaired and incompetent colleagues. Ethical practice for social workers is illustrated through case examples.

Chapter 11 focuses on an emerging issue in social work ethics—interdisciplinary consultation. For the first time the NASW Code of Ethics includes a section on this subject. Case examples from a school, a child welfare agency, and a hospital are included to illustrate interdisciplinary consultation and the use of ethics committees to promote ethical collaboration.

Chapter 12 discusses ethical practice with people with HIV/AIDS. Issues of stigmatization, mandatory testing, and confidentiality are discussed, and a case example is used to illustrate ethical practice. Conflicts relating to service delivery and dilemmas for supervisors/administrators are also addressed.

Chapter 13 focuses on ethical practice for supervisors and administrators. This topic is most timely because it is estimated that most graduating social workers will be supervisors within two years. For the first time the new code includes a section on ethical practice for supervisors and administrators. Distributive justice issues regarding cutbacks to programs and staff are addressed. Supervisory dilemmas relating to workload assignments and dual relationships are discussed and illustrated through case examples.

Chapter 14 concentrates on emerging issues for social work ethics brought about by current social and economic trends. Recent developments in technology and managed care are discussed as well as their implications for ethical social work practice and education in the twenty-first century.

The NASW Code of Ethics

Like other professions, social work developed a code to set forth its basic values, principles, and standards. According to Lowenberg and Dolgoff (1996), professional codes are essential to:

1. Guide practitioners in resolving ethical dilemmas that arise in practice.
2. Protect the public from incompetent practitioners.
3. Ensure self-regulation rather than governmental control.
4. Enable professional colleagues to have set standards for interaction.
5. Protect professionals from litigation.

The practice of social work, however, preceded the development of the first code. In 1915 the Flexner Report raised the concern that social work could not be considered a profession unless it had a code. Mary Richmond is credited with developing the first experimental Code of Ethics for case-workers in 1920; the first Code of Ethics developed by a chapter of the American Association of Social Workers (the organization that preceded NASW) originated in Toledo, Ohio (Lowenberg and Dolgoff, 1996).

In 1955 the National Association of Social Workers emerged through the joining of the American Association of Group Workers, American Association of Medical Social Workers, American Association of Psychiatric Social Workers, American Association of Social Workers, Association for the Study of Community Organization, National Association of School Social Workers, and Social Work Research Group. Five years later a code for the National Association of Social Workers that was very different from the current code appeared. One page in length, the 1960 NASW Code of Ethics consisted of fourteen abstract and idealistic state-ments that described the social worker's responsibilities to the profession. In 1967 the Code of Ethics was amended to include a nondiscrimination clause that coincided with national issues about civil rights.

The NASW Code of Ethics did not even begin to resemble the current code until 1979, when a ten-page document was developed that included provisions about social workers' conduct and comportment and their responsibility to clients, colleagues, the profession, and society. Also, for the first time the code began to be enforceable, as social workers were "required to cooperate in its implementation and abide by any disciplinary rulings based on it." The next change, in 1990, eliminated the prohibition against soliciting colleagues' clients and added that social workers should not exploit relationships with clients for personal advantage or accept anything of value for making a referral. These changes came about because of legal discussions with the Federal Trade Commission.

In 1993 two important amendments were added that dealt with responsibility to impaired colleagues and the prohibition of dual relationships. In adding these amendments, social workers were responding to a growing concern about the importance of monitoring professional behavior.

Development of the Current Code

Social workers have frequently raised concerns about the usefulness of a code in resolving difficult ethical dilemmas. The NASW code, like other codes, is most helpful in dealing with clear-cut ethical issues but is less helpful in dealing with the more ambiguous situations that social workers often encounter (Lowenberg and Dolgoff, 1996).

There are many advantages of the new code, however, over previous codes. A criticism of previous Codes of Ethics had been that they applied primarily to direct-service practitioners rather than to supervisors, administrators, educators, or trainers. Yet 30 percent of NASW social workers are engaged in other than direct practice (Gibelman and Schervish, 1997). Also, although an increasing number of social workers deal with groups and/or families, previous codes focused primarily on work with individual clients. Furthermore, the code minimally considered such issues in agency practice as interdisciplinary consultation, although 80 percent of social workers report agency practice as their primary function (Gibelman and Schervish, 1997). Finally, timely topics of concern to social workers, including confidentiality and technology, sexual harassment, managed care, cultural competency, and dual relationships, were not addressed in earlier codes.

In 1994 NASW formed a committee of social work educators and leaders in the field of ethics and charged it with developing a new Code of Ethics. After gathering input from social workers across the country, the committee arrived at the current code, which is more comprehensive than any previous code. The code was presented and approved by the Delegate Assembly in the summer of 1996 and became effective January 1, 1997. (This code is reprinted in the Appendix.)

The current code sets forth the following six main purposes:

1. Identify core values on which social work's mission is based.
2. Summarize broad ethical principles that reflect the profession's core values and establish a set of specific ethical standards that should be used to guide social work practice.
3. Help social workers identify relevant considerations when professional obligations conflict or ethical uncertainties arise.
4. Provide ethical standards to which the general public can hold the social work professional accountable.
5. Socialize practitioners new to the field to social work's mission, values, ethical principles, and ethical standards.
6. Set standards that the social work profession can use to assess whether social workers have engaged in unethical conduct. Violations of standards can lead to formal NASW adjudication proceedings. (NASW, 1996, p. 2)

The code is not "meant to provide a set of rules that prescribe how social workers should act in all situations" and states that social workers must always apply the code in the context in which practice occurs (NASW, 1996, pp. 2–3). The principles (values) section will be discussed in greater detail in chapter 3. Ethical standards that are the focus of this chapter are divided into six main areas in the current code—social workers' ethical responsibility to clients and to colleagues, in practice settings, as professionals, to the social work profession, and to the broader society. Some principles are seen as aspirational, while others are enforceable guidelines for professional conduct.

Although in some ways the new code is similar to previous codes, there are important differences which are summarized in the following ten points:

1. **Limits to confidentiality**. While the earlier Code of Ethics merely prohibited the disclosure of information except for "compelling professional reasons," the new code explains what these compelling professional reasons are (NASW, 1993, p. 4; NASW, 1996, p. 10). Social workers are advised to maintain confidentiality except when doing so would cause serious, foreseeable, and imminent harm to a client or other identifiable person or when laws or regulations require disclosure without a client's consent. Social workers are advised that confidentiality can be breached in order to report child abuse, because laws mandate reporting. Also, social workers may violate confidentiality when a client is suicidal or homicidal.

2. **Confidentiality in a technological age.** For the first time, social workers are advised to protect confidentiality while using computers, electronic mail, fax machines, and telephone answering

machines. Disclosure of identifying information should be avoided whenever possible.

3. **Confidentiality—family and group work.** A criticism of previous NASW codes was that they focused primarily on work with individual clients. The new code addresses confidentiality issues in group and family work. An important provision about confidentiality states that social workers should seek agreement with all parties about the importance of confidentiality but should inform participants that confidentiality cannot be guaranteed.

4. **Managed care.** While managed care is not cited specifically in the new code, sections that relate to informed consent and confidentiality advise social workers to inform clients of limits to services because of the requirements of third-party payers.

5. **Cultural competence.** For the first time, the new code includes a section on cultural competence and social diversity. Social workers are now expected to understand culture and its function in human behavior, with an emphasis on the strengths perspective. Social workers also need to understand their clients' cultures and demonstrate competence in providing services to people from different cultures. Finally, social workers now are required to pursue education related to diversity and oppression by reason of race, ethnicity, national origin, color, sex, sexual orientation, age, marital status, political belief, religion, and physical and mental disability.

6. **Dual relationships.** Social workers should avoid dual relationships in which there is risk of exploitation or potential harm to clients. When the primary relationship is therapeutic, social workers should not enter social, business, or educational relationships with clients. When dual relationships cannot be avoided, the responsibility is on social workers to set appropriate limits.

7. **Sexual relationships, physical contact, and sexual harassment.** The new code has several provisions on sexual relationships. While the previous code only addressed the avoidance of sexual relationships with current clients, the new code forbids sexual contact with former clients, future clients, clients' relatives, or clients' close friends. Social workers should not engage in physical contact with clients when there is the possibility of psychological harm. The responsibility rests with the social worker to set boundaries. The code also prohibits the sexual harassment of clients and colleagues.

8. **Impairment and incompetence of colleagues.** While the 1993 code advised social workers who knew that a colleague's effectiveness was impaired because of personal problems, psychosocial distress, substance abuse, or mental health difficulties to consult with that colleague, the new code extends the responsibility of the social

worker to the impaired colleague. If after consultation the colleague refuses to address the issue and seek help for the problem, the social worker should take action through employers, agencies, and NASW as well as through licensing and regulatory bodies.

9. **Education and training.** For the first time, the new Code of Ethics specifically addresses educational and training issues. Social work educators are advised to provide instruction only in their areas of competence and to base this instruction on the most current knowledge and information. Although the issue is complex, especially regarding employment relationships with graduate students (Congress, 1996), social workers are advised to avoid dual relationships with students. An important new provision codifies the increasingly acknowledged practice of informing clients when students provide services.

10. **Application to administrators.** While previous NASW codes were criticized for their primary focus on direct-service practitioners, the new code includes a section specifically on administration, stating that social work administrators should advocate for resources in and outside agencies to meet clients' needs. They should pursue resource allocations that are open and fair. When clients' needs cannot be met, administrators should develop an allocation procedure that is nondiscriminatory. The need to provide adequate staff supervision and to maintain a working environment consistent with the Code of Ethics is also enumerated.

Quiz on the 1996 NASW Code of Ethics

Taking the following quiz will help you assess your knowledge of the new Code of Ethics.

1. **Social workers are advised to inform clients of**
   a. Ethical challenges of managed care.
   b. Limits to services because of requirements of third-party payers.
   c. Diagnosis and prognosis in terms of treatment.
   d. Advantages of following a treatment plan.

2. **The provision on cultural competency states that social workers should**
   a. Have an ethnic background similar to that of clients.
   b. Consider how diagnosis is affected by ethnic background.
   c. Understand their clients' culture.
   d. Always arrange to have interpreters available.

3. **Which statement best describes the provision on dual relationships?**
   a. Social workers should not engage in dual relationships with clients.
   b. Social workers should never engage in dual relationships with current or former clients.
   c. If dual relationships occur, clients are responsible for setting limits.
   d. Whenever possible, social workers should avoid dual relationships with current or former clients.

4. **In the new code, confidentiality**
   a. Should be maintained under all circumstances.
   b. Should be maintained except to prevent harm to a client or another.
   c. Should be maintained except as required by law.
   d. Both b and c are correct.

5. **The new code includes the following provision for those who work with groups and families:**
   a. Social workers should assure participants that confidentiality will be protected.
   b. Social workers should inform participants that no guarantees can be made that all participants will honor confidentiality.
   c. Social workers should only discuss agency's policy on confidentiality.
   d. Social workers will share with the group or family what individual members have discussed.

6. **The new code states that confidentiality**
   a. Does not apply to dead clients.
   b. Applies only to oral and written reports.
   c. Should be protected while using computers and fax machines.
   d. Prevents the use of case materials for educational purposes.

7. **Which statement best describes the new code's position on sexual relationships with clients?**
   a. Social workers should avoid sexual relationships with current clients.
   b. Social workers should avoid sexual relationships with current and former clients.
   c. Social workers should avoid sexual relationships with relatives of current clients and future clients.
   d. Statements b and c are correct.

8. **The following provision is new in the 1996 Code of Ethics:**
   a. Social workers should never engage in physical contact with clients.
   b. Bartering is appropriate whenever clients request it.
   c. Sexual harassment of clients and colleagues is prohibited.
   d. Social workers may accept a referral fee.

9. **In the new Code of Ethics the provision on impaired colleagues states that**
   a. Social workers should consult with colleagues whose impairment interferes with their practice and take additional steps if necessary.
   b. Social workers should advise colleagues to seek professional help.
   c. Social workers should report concerns about impairment to their supervisors.
   d. Social workers should first report concerns about impairment to the state licensing board.

10. **In the new Code of Ethics**
    a. Supervisors are limited in the number of supervisees they can have.
    b. Evaluations must be conducted annually.
    c. Administrators should avoid reducing social work positions.
    d. Administrators and supervisors are responsible for providing continuing education for their staff.

Answers to Quiz and Discussion

1. b.   Under the informed consent section of the new code, social workers are asked "to inform clients of the purpose of the services, risks related to the services, limits to services because of the requirements of a third-party payer, relevant costs, reasonable alternatives, client's right to refuse or withdraw consent, and the time frame covered by the consent" (NASW, 1996, p. 8). Whether to include the term *managed care* was discussed at the Delegate Assembly, but in the final draft of the code *managed care* does not appear (response a). In terms of treatment, *diagnosis* and *prognosis* are medical rather than social work terms and do not appear in the new code (response c). Advantages of following a treatment plan are not discussed in the provision about informed consent (response d).

2. c.   Social workers are now expected to have or to develop a knowl-

edge base of their clients' culture. The provision on cultural competency is new to the 1996 Code of Ethics. Having an interpreter present may not always be possible (response d), but social workers are advised to use interpreters, especially when they are trying to ensure informed consent (see Section 1.03c). The more medically linked response b is not in the new Code of Ethics. Response a, which would be impossible to ensure and might involve segregation, is also not included in the new Code of Ethics.

3. d. The new code explicitly states that social workers should avoid dual relationships with current or former clients. Response a does not capture the new code's provision about former clients. Response b uses the word *never* and thus does not include the code's statement that at times dual relationships may be unavoidable. Social workers from rural areas with small populations often face dilemmas of dual relationships. Social workers, *not* clients, have the responsibility of setting limits in dual relationships (response c).

4. d. For the first time, the Code of Ethics enumerates what are compelling professional reasons to break confidentiality, that is, to prevent harm to the client or another or when required by law. Including these exceptions is important, especially because social workers in all fifty states are required to report child abuse. This new code provision gives social workers the right to violate confidentiality in cases of child abuse. Response a is not accurate; a social worker soon learns that there are many situations in which breaking confidentiality is necessary. Taken individually, responses b and c are not inclusive enough.

5. b. For the first time, the Code of Ethics addresses issues important to the group worker and family therapist. The social worker is advised to "seek agreement among the parties involved concerning each individual's right to confidentiality and obligation to preserve the confidentiality shared by others, [but] social workers cannot guarantee that all participants will honor such agreements" (NASW, 1996, p. 11). Response a would be unrealistic, because the social worker cannot guarantee to all members that confidentiality will be protected. Social workers are asked to explain "the social worker's, employer's, and agency's policy" concerning the disclosure of confidential information; thus, response c is not complete. Response d would be a violation of confidentiality provisions of the code.

6. c. The new code addresses current issues for the social work practitioner in a technological era. It contains a provision that relates to the protection of confidentiality when using computers, electronic mail, fax machines, telephones, and telephone answering machines. The new code also protects the confidentiality of dead clients; thus response a is incorrect. The current code's provisions on confidentiality are very extensive (three pages) and cover many situations; thus response b is too limited. The new code forbids disclosing identifying information when using case materials for educational purposes but does not state that case materials cannot be used (response d).

7. d. The new code prohibits sexual relationships with current clients, former clients, relatives of clients, and future clients; thus, response d is correct. Answer a would have been correct for the previous code, which included only current clients. Answers b and c together are correct but separately are not inclusive enough.

8. c. The new code specifically prohibits sexual harassment of both clients and colleagues. It prohibits physical contact only when such contact might cause psychological harm. Thus not all instances of physical contact are prohibited (response a). For example, it might be acceptable for a social worker to put an arm around a child to console him on the death of his mother because rather than causing psychological harm, such physical contact would be supportive and therapeutic. In the new code, bartering by accepting goods or services as payment for professional services is discouraged except under very specific circumstances. The new code enumerates these circumstances: in communities where bartering is an accepted practice, "when it is considered essential for the provision of service, when it is negotiated without coercion, when it is initiated by the client and has the client's informed consent" (NASW, 1996, p. 14). Response b does not enumerate these circumstances. The new code as well as the previous code prohibits social workers from receiving referral fees (response d).

9. a. The new code advises the social worker to consult with an impaired colleague. If he or she resists getting help, the social worker should take action with employers, agencies, NASW, and licensing and regulatory boards. Response b would have been correct for the previous code, but the new code instructs the social worker to take issues regarding impaired colleagues to another level if the colleague is not willing to seek professional help.

Responses c and d enumerate choices that the social worker should follow only after he or she has first consulted with the colleague.

10. d. The new code mandates that supervisors and administrators strive to provide continuing education for their staff. This provision is particularly important for the profession at a time when social services face diminished resources, especially for education and training. While the new code addresses specific issues for social work supervisors and administrators, it does not specify how many supervisees they can have (response a) and the time limits for evaluations (response b). The new code considers resource allocation primarily in terms of client needs rather than needs of social workers; thus, there is no provision that social work positions cannot be cut (response c).

CHAPTER 3

Values and Social Work Principles

Sabrina Lopez, a professional social worker employed in a family counseling center, has recently been assigned Anne McNamara and her seventeen-year-old daughter, Lisa. Sabrina learns that mother and daughter have been fighting for the last year about Lisa's boyfriend, a high school dropout who works part-time at a gas station. Before her involvement with Rick, Lisa was an A student, but this last year her grades plummeted. The crisis that brought the family into treatment, however, is Lisa's pregnancy. Lisa wants to leave school, move in with her boyfriend, have the child, and marry next year when she turns eighteen. Although Anne was brought up in a very religious Irish Catholic home, she wonders if an abortion might not be the best option so that Lisa can continue her schooling and not feel the need to solidify her relationship with Rick.

Although Sabrina knows that as a professional social worker she should not let her personal values interfere with her work with clients, she really believes that abortion is wrong. In fact, she has in the past distributed leaflets for a pro-life association. Sabrina is particularly against abortion now that she herself is having such a difficult time becoming pregnant. She and her husband had planned to have a child when she finished social work school five years ago, but so far she has not become pregnant.

The preceding example highlights the types of values that enter the social worker-client relationship and how differing personal and professional value systems may conflict. Values can be defined as our beliefs about what is right and correct (Lowenberg and Dolgoff, 1996). The personal values of Lisa and Anne differ, as do the values of Anne and Sabrina. Lisa believes that having a close relationship with her boyfriend is most important and that having a child will unite them as a family. Anne believes that adolescents are too young to marry and that they should stay in school. Sabrina, on the other hand, believes that abortion is a sin and that adoption might be a good alternative for pregnant adolescents.

Personal values usually develop out of familial, cultural, and societal values. Families often have very strong beliefs about education, work, and other life activities. Members of the McNamara family have disparate values about education. Personal values are also strongly affected by religious/cultural values. While Anne has turned away from her family values about abortion, Sabrina's Catholic Hispanic religious/cultural values about the sanctity of life have remained constant. Sabrina's personal values have also been shaped by her personal circumstances, that is, her own difficulty in getting pregnant.

Societal values influence our personal values. While fifty years ago a young woman's decision to live with her boyfriend would have been rare and brought shame on the family, now more than three million unmarried couples live together, and many have children (U.S. Bureau of the Census, 1993). Because raising a child born out of wedlock was considered scandalous, often an unmarried pregnant young woman chose to have her child secretly and place the child for adoption. Before 1967 abortion was illegal; thus the prevailing societal value was that abortion was not a feasible alternative to unplanned pregnancy.

The rights and privileges of adolescents are also subject to societal values. While some may believe that Lisa is still an adolescent and that her mother should have the right to decide for her, others believe that an adolescent, especially one over sixteen, should have the right to make important life decisions.

Agency values also come into play. Child welfare agencies often articulate the value of preserving the family. This may conflict with another, often expressed value of such agencies— promoting the best interests of the child. Catholic and Orthodox Jewish agencies may not believe that abortion should be presented as a possible alternative. Also, the mission of the agency can influence its value orientation. For example, if the goal is to place children for adoption, the agency may have the value that adoption is often the best alternative for an unplanned pregnancy. The values of the agency, however, are transmitted through individual workers, and as a condition of employment workers often make a tacit agreement to accept the value base of the agency.

When social workers discuss different value systems, they often fail to mention client values, despite the social worker's emphasis on clients' self-determination and autonomy. Clients' values may stem from family, religious/cultural, and societal values. In the case example described above, Lisa has the value that spending life with Rick is the most important, while Anne believes that pursuing education is preferable. Sometimes clients' and social workers' values can be very disparate, especially in the criminal justice field. The client's values may sanction robbing the elderly, which the worker feels is abhorrent. A classic discussion of such conflicting values can be found in Hardman's article about a social worker who tries to promote the client's self-determination until it becomes evident that the client is sexually interested in the social worker's daughter (Hardman, 1975). To work more effectively with the client, the social worker should try to understand what values motivate the client, even though he or she might not subscribe to them.

The main focus of this book is on professional values. Professional values have been seen to differ from personal values (Horner and Whitbeck, 1991). Future social workers are schooled in professional values (Congress, 1992; Joseph, 1991; Lewis, 1987), although the difficulty in teaching values has long been acknowledged (Noble and King, 1981; Pumphrey, 1959).

A fundamental question is: What are professional values? The 1996 Code of Ethics delineates certain values as key to social work and describes some ethical principles based on these values. The six values and principles are outlined in figure 3.1.

FIGURE 3.1 Professional Values and Ethical Principles

Values	Ethical Principles
Service	Social workers' primary goal is to help people in need and to address social problems.
Social justice	Social workers challenge social injustice.
Dignity and worth of the person	Social workers respect the inherent dignity and worth of the person.
Importance of human relationships	Social workers recognize the central importance of human relationships.
Integrity	Social workers behave in a trustworthy manner.
Competence	Social workers practice within their areas of competence and develop their professional expertise.

Values Described in the 1996 Code of Ethics

Perhaps the most fundamental value in social work is to provide service to those in need. The social worker must place service above self-interest. The focus should be on helping the client, not on promoting the well-being of the social worker. For example, if a stockbroker consults a social worker about a marital problem, the social worker should not use the stockbroker to get stock tips.

Social workers are also encouraged to volunteer professional and other services. Conflicts often arise about the social worker's commitment to service. How much pro bono service is expected? This may be especially problematic when a managed-care plan permits a client only a limited number of sessions. What happens when the social worker believes that the client needs additional treatment? Should the social worker provide free or almost-free sessions? Should self-interest always be construed as negative? How can social workers pay their own living expenses if they provide free clinical services? Often social workers develop fees based on sliding scales to help balance the value of service to clients with that of the need to survive.

Another major value of social work is to promote social justice. Since the beginning of the profession, social workers have been committed to combatting social injustice and oppression. Early social workers worked in settlement houses to bring needed services to vulnerable immigrants, and members of the profession have continued to be sensitive to issues of discrimination and oppression. The Council of Social Work Education requires that all accredited social work programs teach students about oppression and diversity. In the previous example, Sabrina knows that her client is from a different culture and that she must be sensitive to this difference. Still, conflicts arise. The daughter and mother are from the same culture, but they have different values. This often occurs when children are more acculturated than their parents (Congress, 1994).

Being culturally sensitive and providing culturally competent services is in keeping with the value of promoting social justice. This value has special relevance, as the United States becomes increasingly culturally diverse (U. S. Bureau of the Census, 1988). Cultural sensitivity for the school social worker (Congress and Lynn, 1994), the health care social worker (Congress and Lyons, 1992), and the social work educator (Congress, 1993, 1996) has been seen as essential. Furthermore, culturally sensitive and competent practice is stressed in the new Code of Ethics (NASW, 1996). However, does cultural sensitivity always involve sanctioning the beliefs and behaviors of other cultures? For example, corporal punishment for children may be condoned by other cultures but may result in charges of child abuse in the United States. Such ethical dilemmas are not easily resolved by professional social workers.

The value of respecting the inherent dignity and worth of the person is taught to all students of social work early in their education. Yet this value may be difficult to carry out in practice, especially if a client's values and belief systems are very different from the social worker's. A young woman social worker found it very difficult to work with a male client who had been charged with raping his twelve-year-old daughter. Another beginning social worker was reluctant to interview a homeless schizophrenic man who had not bathed in a month. The consequence of this value, that is, promoting client self-determination, may be equally challenging. In the preceding case, does the teenage girl have a right to self-determination even if her mother and the social worker believe that keeping the child may detrimentally affect her life forever? It is often a struggle for a social worker to promote a client's self-determination if the client seems to be acting in a self-destructive way, such as when a battered woman chooses to return to live with her spouse. The woman should be permitted to self-determine, even though she is returning to an abusive situation. However, if a client is threatening to harm himself or others, there may be a need to limit self-determination. Thus a client who threatens to kill his wife or jump in front of a train cannot be permitted to self-determine.

The value of strengthening human relationships enters into all social work. Whether they are working with individuals, families, groups, or communities, social workers strive to improve their relationships and connections with others. Thus, in the previous example, Sabrina should work to improve the relationship between Anne and her daughter, Lisa.

Trustworthiness is another crucial value for social workers. In fact, the social worker's fiduciary responsibility to a client is a legal one similar to that of other professions (Kutchins, 1991). The development of a trusting relationship is especially important because the client is often vulnerable (Lewis, 1972). In the preceding example, Sabrina must act in a trustworthy manner toward both clients. She must tell each client what type of information she will and will not share. Suppose Lisa had told Sabrina that she did not want her mother to know about her pregnancy. What would be Sabrina's responsibility in keeping this information from Anne? Chapter 8 on families and groups further describes some dilemmas that may arise when the social worker tries to act in a trustworthy manner toward clients who have conflicting interests.

A final value of social work relates to competence; that is, social workers should always practice within their areas of competence and always strive to improve their professional skills. It is assumed that all graduates of accredited social work programs have a general ability to work with clients. However, social workers with little experience in working with adolescents may want to take additional courses to enhance their skills in dealing with this population.

Value Exercise

Understanding what values may influence a social worker's decisions in working with clients is a first step toward practicing ethical social work. The following exercise will help you assess what personal, societal, agency, client, and professional values can impact on the practice of social work. For each example, think of which values might influence your choice of a particular answer. Then decide which response is the most correct in the context of the above discussion on professional values.

1. Mrs. Smith has been your client for the last two years. She confides that she has decided to return to her estranged spouse in an attempt to save her marriage. Her alcoholic husband has physically abused her several times; the last time she required treatment for a broken hand. Last month she separated from her husband and moved into a shelter for battered women. Which intervention is best?
    a. Advise Mrs. Smith to remain in the shelter, because she may be abused again if she returns to her husband.
    b. Discuss the consequences of Mrs. Smith's returning to her spouse versus remaining in the shelter but allow her to make her own decision.
    c. Tell Mrs. Smith that she should return to her spouse if this is her wish.

2. A homeless woman known only as Mary lives on a street near your agency. Sometimes staff members buy her coffee and bring her food. Although it is summer, she continues to wear multiple layers of clothing. You have spoken to her about entering a shelter, but she is reluctant to leave her street. What should you do?
    a. Advise the police to bring Mary to a shelter or psychiatric hospital because her life is in danger.
    b. Tell Mary that she must go to a shelter.
    c. Inform Mary about housing options but ultimately allow her to make her own decision about whether to remain homeless.

3. John, your client in a mental health clinic, is very depressed after breaking up with his girlfriend. He has not been going to work and wonders whether living is worthwhile. He tells you that he has been hoarding sleeping pills and that he plans to swallow them today. What should you do?
    a. Refer John to the psychiatrist for involuntary hospitalization.
    b. Allow John to make his own decision about whether to take his own life.
    c. Discuss with John the option of voluntary hospitalization.

4. Mrs. Barrow has been trying to raise her four children alone since her husband abandoned her six months ago. Recently she has been very upset because her landlord is demanding rent and her welfare check has not yet come through. Further, plaster falling from the ceiling of the bedroom threatens the safety of her children, but the landlord refuses to make repairs. She confides to you that she has purchased a gun and that she will use it on the landlord if he hassles her again. What intervention would you use?

   a. Discuss with Mrs. Barrow alternative ways of handling her dispute with her landlord but disregard her threat because she has a right to self-determination.

   b. Advise Mrs. Barrow that you must inform her landlord of her threat.

   c. Acknowledge Mrs. Barrow's anger and discuss alternative solutions to her problem, but if she repeats her threat, tell her that you must take action to prevent her from carrying through with it.

5. Ms. White has been diagnosed with chronic undifferentiated schizophrenia and during the past ten years has been hospitalized repeatedly for this condition. Last year while in a psychiatric hospital she gave birth to a baby girl. The child was placed in foster care, and now the child-care agency plans to place the child for adoption. Ms. White is now living in a halfway house with other recently discharged psychiatric patients. Currently she exhibits no acute psychotic symptoms, is cooperative about taking psychotropic medications, and has asked for your help in getting her child returned to her. What is the best intervention?

   a. Tell Ms. White that because of the nature of her illness, her child will never be returned to her.

   b. Ask the child-care agency to arrange supervised visits between Ms. White and her child so that her ability to take care of her child can be evaluated.

   c. Advise the foster care agency that in the birth mother's best interests they should return the child as soon as possible to Mrs. White.

6. In the waiting room of your agency you witness a homeless person's being denied service because he cannot provide proof of residence or source of income. What is the best intervention?

   a. Insist that the client be seen, because his needs take precedence over administrative considerations.

   b. Invite the person into your office and refer him to an appropriate agency that does not have residency or income requirements.

Then discuss with colleagues in your agency the possibility of changing intake procedures.

c. Take no action, because such policies are necessary, given the limited resources of the agency.

7. As a medical social worker in a large hospital, you are working with a seventy-year-old man who the doctors say will probably die within six months. He has not been told of the seriousness of his illness but asks you, "Am I dying?" a question that his doctor and his children have evaded. What should be your response?

   a. Deny that he is seriously ill.
   b. Suggest that he discuss his question with his doctor.
   c. Tell him the truth.

8. You are working in a family service agency with Barbara, a fourteen-year-old girl who has been truant from school and often stays out all night. In your first interview with Barbara she tells you that she thinks she is pregnant and that she wants to keep the baby. While she has not yet told her parents, she believes they will be angry and force her to have an abortion. Which intervention is most in accord with professional values?

   a. Advise Barbara that, given the situation, an abortion would be best.
   b. Encourage Barbara to bring in her parents for a family session to discuss the problem and various alternative courses of action.
   c. Because she clearly wants to keep her baby, arrange immediately for Barbara to go to a home for pregnant teenagers.

9. Mr. Randall, a seventy-year-old man with cardiovascular disease, was recently discharged from the hospital after treatment for pneumonia. During the last year he has become increasingly forgetful. In fact, the fire department was summoned to his home last week when he left the gas on by mistake and a fire resulted. Mr. Randall has always been a very independent man and is reluctant to give up his own residence and move into a home for senior citizens. Which intervention best incorporates professional values?

   a. Help Mr. Randall obtain home-care services for eight hours a day because he has the right to remain in his own apartment.
   b. Discuss with Mr. Randall the advantages of residences and take him to visit several so he can choose the one he prefers.
   c. Arrange for Mr. Randall to be admitted to a residence as soon as possible.

10. Mrs. Cooper, one of your clients in a family service agency, reports to you that she has taken an "off-the-books" waitress job to supplement her welfare income. She does not plan to tell the welfare department, because for family reasons she needs the extra income. Which is the best intervention?
    a. Advise Mrs. Cooper that you will tell the welfare department because her behavior is irresponsible.
    b. Discuss with Mrs. Cooper the possible consequences of her actions but realize that the decision is ultimately her own.
    c. Tell Mrs. Cooper that her action is completely appropriate given the meager benefits provided by the welfare department.

Analysis of Responses to Value Exercise

1. Response b is most in keeping with social work values of promoting the dignity and worth of the individual by allowing for self-determination. The social work value of service is also provided by encouraging the client to choose between alternatives. Response a is very directive and does not permit for a client's self-determination. Although this is not the best response in keeping with professional values, a social worker who feels very protective of clients and/or has experienced domestic violence herself may choose this alternative. Response c suggests self-determination without any input from the social worker. It may, however, reflect attention to client's values.

2. Response c maximizes the professional value of dignity and worth of the person by allowing the client to determine if her life is not in danger. This choice is also most sensitive to client values. Responses a and b are most directive, but they minimize self-determination. Societal values, however, may suggest response a or b.

3. Response a is most appropriate for the social work value of protection of life. While response b or c would promote self-determination, professional values suggest that self-determination ends when preservation of life is in question.

4. Response c is the most appropriate as it maximizes the professional value of respect for the individual but recognizes that self-determination must be curtailed when life is threatened. Response a promotes only self-determination and disregards the need to protect the life of

another. Response b does not promote the professional value of respect for the client.

5. Response b is the best intervention as it is in keeping with the professional value of making a thorough assessment. Response a focuses only on the deficits of the client and does not recognize any strengths. Response c promotes the birth mother's self-determination, but does not pursue the appropriate professional role of assessment and evaluation.

6. Response b combines the professional value of service to the client as well as to the employing agency. It recognizes that a social worker can join with other colleagues to change an unjust policy. Response a negates a social worker's responsibility to the agency, while response c denies a social worker's responsibility to clients.

7. Response c is the most supportive of the social work value of truth telling and respect for the client. Although many in medical settings may choose response b, this choice may not promote truth telling. Response a is not in keeping with the social work value of integrity— acting in a trustworthy manner.

8. Response b is most appropriate in terms of social work's values of self-determination, respect for others, and service. Response a does not maximize the adolescent client's right to self-determination and may suggest that the social worker is overly influenced by personal values regarding adolescent parenthood. Response c would negate the social work value in terms of human relationships by preventing an opportunity for a discussion with the family as a whole.

9. Response b recognizes the need to maximize self-determination while, at the same time, protecting others from harm. Response a would promote self-determination, but eight hours a day of supervised care may not be sufficient to prevent a fire that would harm others. Response c negates Mr. Randall's ability to make any choice.

10. Response b is the most respectful of the client, provides service to the client by informing her of possible consequences, and maximizes self-determination. Response a would negate the value of maintaining confidentiality to the client. Response c would promote a social justice theme without advising the client of possible negative consequences of her action.

This questionnaire demonstrates both the complexity of the diverse personal, agency, societal, and professional values that enter into social work and the challenge in choosing an intervention that is most in keeping with professional values.

To provide ethical services to their clients, social workers must begin by exploring their own values as well as those of their clients, their agency, and their profession. Examining values is the first step in the ETHIC model of ethical decision making, which is described more fully in the next chapter.

CHAPTER 4

Social Work Dilemmas and the ETHIC Decision-Making Model

Although social workers share similar professional values, they may differ in how they resolve ethical dilemmas. All social workers agree with the value of the dignity and worth of the individual, but often a question emerges about whose dignity and worth is promoted. For example, in child welfare, promoting the dignity and worth of the parent often conflicts with promoting the well-being of the child, as in the following example.

> Mrs. Brown was arrested for selling drugs, but the charges were dropped because of insufficient evidence. When Jill, a social worker in a child welfare agency, contacts the school the Brown children attend, she learns that the children are often sent to school dirty and without breakfast. To support the well-being of the child, the worker might seek placement of the children in a foster home. However, would this course of action support the dignity and worth of the mother? If an important role for Mrs. Brown is that of mother, what would be the effect of removing her children from her home? A corollary of protecting the dignity and worth of clients is promoting their autonomy and self-determination. If Mrs. Brown's children are removed, what has happened to her self-determination? What if the children, like many others, want to exercise their self-determination by staying with their parent?

The NASW Code of Ethics offers general principles for ethical behavior and does not cover all situations (Reamer, 1995b). The new code lists more specific exceptions to social work values than previous codes. For example, it states that social workers' responsibility to promote self-determination is suspended when in their professional judgment "clients' actions or potential actions pose a serious foreseeable and imminent risk to themselves or others" (NASW, 1996, p. 7). But this provision may lead to ethical dilemmas for the child welfare practitioner working with this family. Are the children at risk? Is the mother taking or selling drugs? Are the dirty clothes and lack of breakfast due to oversleeping one day or are they symptomatic of a more serious problem?

How social workers resolve ethical dilemmas has been a subject of some concern to the profession. Social workers are often guided by two main principles. The first principle, *beneficence* (or positive obligations), speaks to providing good, while the second principle, *nonmaleficence* (or negative obligations), relates to causing no harm (Reamer, 1995b). Both principles affect ethical decision making. Those acting from beneficence would most likely take a proactive stance that might involve placing children in order for them to have a better life. Nonmaleficence would promote causing no harm by intervening the least. Social workers acting from non-maleficence might decide to take no action and wait for further results.

Although social workers may not be aware of it, they frequently rely on two philosophical models—deontological and teleological—in resolving ethical dilemmas (Reamer, 1995b). *Deontological* thinkers believe that social work values such as self-determination and confidentiality are so absolute and so definitive of the profession that they must prevail whatever the circumstances. In the preceding example, a deontologist might support Mrs. Brown's self-determination by permitting her to keep her children and the children's self-determination by allowing them to remain with her if they choose to do so. To take away her children and violate her self-determination might lead to distrust of the profession.

Many social workers, however, use a *teleological* approach that involves examining the consequences of the situation, for example, what would happen if Mrs. Brown's children remain at home with her. Deontologists and teleologists, however, do not always find themselves on opposite sides of an issue. In the preceding example, a deontologist might argue that the overriding principle is self-determination, while another deontologist might insist that preserving life is more important, which would lead to violating self-determination. Similarly, teleologists often do not agree. One teleologist might argue that maintaining self-determination might lead to children's deaths, while another might insist that if self-determination is not supported, the mother and children might never trust social workers again.

Most social workers use a combination of deontological and teleological thinking. One can argue that the values of the profession are deontological in nature but that often social workers use teleological arguments to decide complex ethical dilemmas. Many social workers do not use a philosophical approach at all but base their decisions on practice wisdom (Walden, Wolock, and Demone, 1990) or the Code of Ethics (Congress, 1992a).

A review of the literature shows that several models of ethical decision making have been proposed. Reamer (1995b) proposes a deontological system based on Rawls's theory of justice and Gewirth's rank ordering of conflicting duties. Lewis (1984) has developed a model of ethical decision making that incorporates both deontological and teleological thinking but proposes that the deontological approach should prevail. Lowenberg and Dolgoff (1996) use a hierarchical model in which different values are ranked to help social workers arrive at the best ethical choice. Conrad and Joseph (1996) have developed a process model that uses the Code of Ethics. Social workers, however, frequently make speedy decisions without much deliberation (Wolock, Walden, and Demone, 1990). This may be because there is often little time to make decisions as well as perceived organizational constraints.

The following model, which was developed to help social workers make ethical decisions as quickly and as effectively as possible, includes the consideration of social work values, the Code of Ethics, and the social work context. Relying on an easily remembered acronym, ETHIC, the model is as follows:

E   **Examine relevant personal, societal, agency, client and professional values.**

As discussed in the previous chapter, personal, societal, agency, client, and professional values all influence ethical decision making. The social worker who relies only on professional values is not likely to have a full range of information on which to base a decision. For example, self-determination is a very important value, but what if a client has a strong personal value of family determination? Should the social worker encourage an adolescent to attend a distant college or heed the adolescent's personal value that he or she should stay close to his or her family?

A discrepancy between agency and professional values can also produce dilemmas for the social worker. For example, a social worker may conflict with an agency that has introduced a new computer program that seems to have inadequate safeguards to protect the confidentiality of clients' records.

T   **Think about what ethical standard of the NASW Code of Ethics applies to the situation, as well as about relevant laws and case decisions.**

The ethical standards in the NASW Code of Ethics are divided into six sections:

1.   Social workers' ethical responsibilities to clients
2.   Social workers' ethical responsibilities to colleagues

3. Social workers' ethical responsibilities in practice settings
4. Social workers' ethical responsibilities as professionals
5. Social workers' ethical responsibilities to the profession
6. Social workers' ethical responsibilities to the broader society

If the ethical dilemma involves an issue about appropriate treatment, the social worker might want to examine the section under responsibilities to clients. Topics in this section include conflicts of interest, self-determination, informed consent, confidentiality, access to records, and issues about payment for service and termination of service. The standards can be viewed as deontological (absolute) principles for the profession.

Social workers need to be cognizant of relevant federal, state, and local laws that may relate to an ethical dilemma, because social work ethics often parallels laws. The social worker also needs to be aware of when a law or regulation may support an unethical practice. Historical examples include Jim Crow laws in the South and discriminatory welfare regulations.

H   **Hypothesize about possible consequences of different decisions.** In this step the social worker uses teleological reasoning to resolve ethical dilemmas. If protecting confidentiality is a concern, the social worker should think about different scenarios, one in which confidentiality is maintained and one in which confidentiality is violated. The social worker can list pros and cons about maintaining confidentiality versus breaking confidentiality. Analyzing possible results helps the social worker decide which is the preferred alternative for the specific incident.

I   **Identify who will benefit and who will be harmed in view of social work's commitment to the most vulnerable.** Often social workers must decide between two bad alternatives rather than between one that is clearly right and another that is clearly wrong (Keith-Lucas, 1977). This step may elicit very convincing reasons for or against different courses of action.

Social work's long tradition of concern for the most vulnerable in our society distinguishes it from the other professions (Lewis, 1972). Social workers have a responsibility to identify and nurture strengths of those who were previously described only through their problems (Saleebey, 1997). On a macrolevel, concern for the most vulnerable has been proposed as a vital consideration during downsizing (Reisch and Taylor, 1983). The current code proposes that "social workers should act to expand choice and opportunity for all persons, with special regard for vulnerable, disadvantaged, oppressed, and exploited persons and groups" (NASW, 1996, p. 27). Therefore, this step is very important for social workers in resolving an ethical dilemma.

C   Consult with supervisor and colleagues about the most ethical choice.

Talking to others who can suggest alternatives or present new information is essential when making an ethical decision. A social worker who has a supervisor should use this person as a first resource in ethical decision making. However, because of cutbacks in staffing, experienced and even beginning workers may have minimal supervision. Social workers are therefore encouraged to bring questions about ethical dilemmas to colleagues for informal consultation. Ethical dilemmas can also be presented as part of a case conference, or social workers can help the agency develop an ethics committee. This could be especially useful in a multidiscipline agency in which the social worker and other professionals may not share the same values and ethics. Differences in the values of social workers, physicians (Roberts, 1989), and public school educators (Congress and Lynn, 1994) have been noted. When social workers participate in ethics committees, however, their opinions about ethical dilemmas are often respected by other members (Joseph and Conrad, 1989).

The following example demonstrates how the ETHIC model can be applied.

> Susan, a social worker with a master's degree and three years of experience, has been seeing twenty-seven-year-old Ann Smith and her twenty-eight-year-old husband, Ben, about marital problems. The Smiths were childhood sweethearts, marrying immediately after graduating from high school. They live in a small town with their two daughters—Amy, nine, and Gwen, seven. Much of their marital conflict relates to their financial problems. Ben works at minimum wage for a local landscaping company. He wants to attend a special program in landscaping at a community college but cannot afford to take time from work or to pay the tuition. Because of their insurance coverage they cannot remain in treatment as they had insurance coverage for only six sessions. During their last session Ben tells Susan that, in exchange for continued treatment, he will give her some trees for her new home and help plant them. Should Susan accept Ben's offer?

Following is a discussion of how she arrives at a decision based on ETHIC.

Examine Values

Susan thinks about her own personal values and how they relate to the situation. She has wanted to help people with their problems ever since she was a little girl. She remembers an experience with bartering at college, when she tutored another student in calculus and he repaid her by fixing her car. Susan realizes that she is committed to keeping this couple together. Keenly aware of how countertransference might affect her work with this family, Susan also remembers that she too married her childhood sweetheart.

Married for twenty years, she remembers how difficult the early part of her marriage was because of lack of money. She is very aware of the difficulties children experience when their parents separate, because her parents divorced when she was six, and she was shuffled back and forth between them.

In examining professional values pertinent to this case, Susan notes that both Ann and Ben come from religious families in which divorce is taboo, especially when there are young children. Although she knows that almost 50 percent of marriages end in divorce, Ann also knows that divorce is not that common in the small town where they live.

Considering agency values, Ann notes that the agency has embarked on a new brief-treatment model in which all clients, whether individuals, couples, or families, receive treatment for only six sessions. The agency value is that short-term treatment is preferable, although Ann questions this value for all clients. The Smiths have already attended six sessions, and their insurance has expired.

Knowing that the clinician often does not examine client values before making ethical decisions, Susan begins to assess these. She learns that both spouses believe in preserving marriage. She also learns that Ben and Ann have value conflicts that might be contributing to their current problems. Ben believes that only education will help him advance in his field, while Ann believes that Ben's primary responsibility now is to be the breadwinner and that his education can wait. Initially both Ben and Ann resisted counseling and came only because their family priest strongly recommended it. Both of them still are unclear about the professional role of a therapist and tend to personalize their relationship with Susan. In fact, they invited Susan to their home for a Christmas party, and Ben once volunteered to help her with landscaping.

In examining relevant professional values, Susan acknowledges the importance of service and that she has a responsibility to help people in need. She knows that she should volunteer some portion of her professional time with no expectation of financial return. She recognizes also the social work value that stresses human relationships and her responsibility "to strengthen relationships among people in a purposeful effort to promote, restore, maintain, and enhance the well-being of individuals [and] families" (NASW, 1996, p. 6). Finally, she recognizes the social work value of competence and the need to develop and enhance her professional expertise. To increase her ability to work with couples, Susan took a special postgraduate training program in family and couples therapy and consults regularly with her supervisor about work with couples.

Think about Ethical Standards

Susan turns to the NASW Code of Ethics for help in resolving this ethical dilemma. She pays special attention to the section on responsibility to clients. The code notes the importance of self-determination: "Social workers respect and promote the rights of clients to self-determination and assist clients in their efforts to identify and clarify their goals" (NASW, 1996, p. 5). She knows she must not let her personal value about families staying together override her professional responsibility to help clients identify and clarify their own goals. She knows that the client's right to self-determination is suspended in cases where it could result in "serious, foreseeable, and imminent risk to themselves or others" (NASW, 1996, p. 7). She also looks at the standard on conflict of interest: "Social workers should be alert to and avoid conflicts of interest that interfere with the exercise of professional discretion and impartial judgment" (NASW, 1996, p. 40). Susan is keenly aware of this issue because she and Ann hold disparate views about education. Because she has always believed that education is most important and that women with young children can work outside the home, she knows she must be careful to avoid siding with Ben in the couple's discussion about Ben's return to school.

Susan is very concerned about the possibility of a dual relationship. She knows the new code is very explicit about avoiding dual relationships in which there is a risk of exploitation. She is concerned because they live in a small town and she already knows that her daughter Christine is in Gwen's first-grade class. Last week her daughter's class held a bake sale at the PTA meeting. Susan felt awkward when she ran into Ann, who was also helping at the sale. Susan believes, however, that there is not much risk of exploitation in this dual social relationship.

Another type of dual relationship, however, might be emerging. Susan's primary relationship with the Smiths is that of therapist and clients. She will enter another relationship—that of employer and employee—if she engages Ben to landscape her garden in exchange for therapy sessions. Would she be at risk of exploiting the relationship? How accurately could she measure which landscaping services are equivalent to therapy? What would happen if the trees Ben planted did not do well? If he were not also a client, she could easily complain if the trees died without having to worry about whether her complaints would affect the therapy relationship. Wouldn't she be resentful if she felt she had to keep her anger about her dead trees to herself?

The new Code of Ethics for the first time includes a provision on bartering: "Social workers should avoid accepting goods or services from clients as payment for professional services. Bartering arrangements, particularly for services, create the potential for conflicts of interest, exploitation, and inappropriate boundaries in social workers' relations with clients" (NASW, 1996, p. 14). However, a recent study indicates that one-third of the social workers surveyed believe that bartering for services is inappropriate (Jayartne, Croxton, and Mattison, 1997).

The code's provision on bartering makes Susan very uneasy. Although she lives in a small town, bartering is not an accepted practice. While she is not forcing the client to barter for services, she wonders whether this arrangement would have the informed consent of both parties. She knows that she has the burden of proving that this arrangement is not detrimental to the client or to the professional relationship and she is unsure about the long-term consequences of having Ben do her yard work.

Hypothesize about Different Courses of Action

Susan develops scenarios for three courses of action:

1. Refuse to exchange therapy for landscaping service. If she refuses to barter with the Smiths, they might leave therapy. Their fights might accelerate, which might lead to the breakup of their marriage. Then again, they may have already received enough help and be able to resolve their problems on their own.

2. Accept landscaping services in exchange for therapy sessions. If she allows Ben to work on her yard in exchange for therapy sessions, it may turn out that Ann does not totally approve. One cause of conflict in the marriage is Ben's low salary. If he were doing work for Susan, would not this limit even more his availability for work? Also, she worries about how this arrangement might jeopardize her objectivity. What if while working on her yard, Ben starts to talk about a fight he and Ann had the previous night? Could

Susan set appropriate boundaries and limits if she had more contact with one partner than with another? Also, Susan fears that Ben's landscaping efforts might not work. She has tried unsuccessfully to grow several types of trees in her yard. One reason Ben would be able to help her with her yard is that it is the end of the season. Suppose the trees he planted were past their prime and did not do well. Would she resent giving therapy sessions in exchange for trees that died? Could she continue to provide objective and empathic therapy to the Smiths?

Susan thinks that neither of these two alternatives is desirable. She is very concerned that bartering goes against the new code, but she does not want the Smiths to stop treatment.

3. Extend sessions by means other than bartering. A third alternative might be to cut down on the sessions or reduce the amount she charges for them. She thinks that the Smiths' relationship has improved since they have been coming for sessions. She could explore the possibility of offering a session every other week. That way the Smiths could continue with therapy but not have to pay as much. This arrangement also might be a good way of easing out of therapy altogether.

Identify Who Would Be Helped and Who Would Be Harmed

Susan examines who would be harmed and who would be helped, using the different three scenarios. She fears that she will be engaging in unethical behavior if she goes along with the bartering arrangement. She is also concerned about her professional responsibility to provide service and thinks that this would be compromised if she prematurely terminates therapy. The clients are the most vulnerable, however, and they might be harmed in a bartering relationship.

Consult with Supervisor and Colleagues

Susan decides to consult with her supervisor and present the Smiths at a weekly case conference. Susan's supervisor is supportive of Susan's wish to continue the Smiths' therapy. She indicates that the agency could be flexible about reducing the fee for the Smiths and/or offering biweekly sessions. The supervisor is also concerned that bartering is contrary to the Code of Ethics and that the agency might be liable if a malpractice charge were brought against Susan for violating the Code of Ethics. When Susan discusses her dilemma at the case conference, her co-workers are very empathic about her desire to help others but concur that entering into a bartering arrangement might be unethical.

Conclusion

What is Susan's final decision? Susan decides not to enter the bartering arrangement and discusses with the Smiths why it would not be appropriate. However, she presents the option of attending sessions every other week, a plan that interests them because it seems to promote their independence and indicate that their relationship is improving. Ben and Ann feel assured that Susan is confident that they can resolve conflicts on their own. Resolving the ethical dilemma in this way also helps Susan recognize her clients' strengths and contributes to their empowerment.

CHAPTER 5

Ethical Dilemmas in Mental Health

Although for many years social workers have encountered ethical issues and dilemmas in providing mental health services, the current managed-care environment and technological advances in service delivery present new ethical challenges to the practitioner. The following example illustrates some of these tensions.

> Nancy, a certified social worker, works for Somerset Mental Health Clinic. She has seen Rhoda, a thirty-year-old depressed woman, for three sessions. Rhoda is employed as a secretary for a small company. Under her managed-care program she can be treated for a maximum of four sessions. Rhoda is severely depressed after breaking up with her husband after an eight-year marriage. The impact of her separation was worsened by significant childhood losses, including her father's desertion when she was ten and her mother's sudden death when she was twelve. Rhoda has improved while in therapy, but Nancy is concerned that terminating therapy after only a few sessions will have an adverse effect.
>
> Somerset Mental Health Clinic is proud of having moved into the modern age. When Rhoda first came to the mental health clinic her symptoms were fed into a diagnostic computer program, which offered the diagnosis of dysthymic disorder and a treatment plan consisting of brief cognitive-behavior therapy. All of Nancy's case notes are recorded on computer. Although her computer can receive faxes directly, Nancy received on the office fax machine information about mental health treatment Rhoda was given two years ago.
>
> Somerset Mental Health Clinic has a sophisticated voice mail system. Clients rarely if ever talk to a live person; they are instructed to leave a message and are assured that the therapist will return the call.

The preceding case example illustrates some of the ethical challenges the mental health social worker faces. Nancy knows that Rhoda still needs treatment. But she is also aware of her ethical responsibility to her agency to ensure that they will be reimbursed for her services. Also, she knows that if the agency does not receive payment it may not be able to keep her as an employee or provide treatment for clients like Rhoda.

Social workers' overriding ethical responsibility, however, is to provide service to clients. But what happens when managed-care programs limit the number of allowable sessions? The public in general and social workers in particular have become increasingly concerned about the impact of managed care on services to clients. A recent review of managed-care issues on the Internet yielded 60,000 entries; the overwhelming majority focus on the severe physical and emotional consequences of curtailing or denying services. Social work literature has also recently focused on the threat to clients' well-being posed by managed-care restrictions (Davidson and Davidson, 1996; Munson, 1996; Reamer, 1997).

With the advent of managed care, social workers' role as advocates becomes even more important. The new Code of Ethics stresses that on a microlevel, "social workers should act to expand choice and opportunity for all people," and that on a macrolevel, "social workers should engage in social and political action that seeks to ensure that all people have equal access to the resources, employment, and services they require to meet their basic human needs and to develop fully" (NASW, 1996, p. 27). As an advocate, Nancy can negotiate with the managed-care company to expand the number of sessions it will authorize. Also, social workers are increasingly employed by managed-care companies, which provides them with an inside track when advocating for services. Nancy can become involved in larger efforts to protect clients in managed-care systems. Social workers have advocated for state laws that will protect consumers against the adverse consequences of managed care. Also, the New York City chapter of NASW recently conducted a study of critical incidents to be used in advocating for client services under managed-care programs.

The technology at Somerset makes it easier for Nancy to record her progress notes on the computer. She also does not have to worry as much about leaving her case records open on her desk when she goes to lunch. However, she is concerned that every office, including an open secretarial area, has a computer on which the files of all clients are accessible. The fax machine is located in the general reception area; thus many people have access to incoming faxes. She was out the day the fax about Rhoda's previous treatment arrived, and she is disturbed that it sat in an open box until she returned. Adding to Nancy's concerns, Rhoda tried to get hold of her one day when she was out sick and could not reach any office staff member.

Advanced technology poses threats to confidentiality. The new code stresses that "social workers should take precautions to ensure and maintain the confidentiality of information transmitted to other parties through the use of computers, electronic mail, facsimile machines, telephones, and telephone answering machines, and other electronic or computer technology" (NASW, 1996, p. 12). Social workers like Nancy must continually struggle to maintain confidentiality in a nonconfidential world. They must make decisions about the sensitivity of materials in order to ensure that necessary security is maintained (Rock and Congress, 1997).

Use of DSM-IV

The ethical dilemmas presented by managed care and advanced technology affect many social workers, as a large number of them (40 percent) are involved in providing mental health services (Gibelman and Schervish, 1997). Besides these current issues, there are many continuing ethical conflicts in mental health care, such as the use (and misuse) of the Diagnostic and Statistical Manual (DSM-IV), involuntary hospitalization, the right to treatment, the right to refuse treatment, informed consent, privileged communication, and the duty to warn. These issues focus on two major ethical responsibilities of the social worker: to promote self-determination and to protect confidentiality.

While self-determination has always been an important goal in social work, there are serious questions about how this goal should be achieved. The mental health client may have some impairment in cognitive and/or emotional functioning that leads him or her to seek treatment. The social worker has greater expertise in determining the type of treatment. But as Thompson (1990) indicates, therapists must be clear about their area of expertise and that of clients. Clients are experts in their own feelings, what has happened and is happening to them, what has helped and what has not helped them, and what their interests, values, and goals are, while therapists are experts in observing and interpreting client behavior, ways in which thoughts and actions can become dysfunctional, and ways in which such difficulties can be overcome (Thompson, 1990).

Part of the therapist's expertise is in the area of diagnosis. In order to facilitate the diagnosis and treatment of mental illness and make reimbursement easier, many social workers use DSM-IV in consultation with other mental health professionals. While some social workers have proposed the use of another assessment tool, Person in Environment (PIE) (Karls and Wandrei, 1992), DSM-IV is much more widely used. However, some social workers express concern that DSM-IV stigmatizes clients, and stress that workers in the profession should be aware that a person is not a diagnosis. For example, the social worker should state that a client has a DSM diagnosis of schizophrenic and avoid saying that a client is a schizophrenic. Research on social workers' use of the DSM has shown that social workers tend to use the manual inappropriately by arriving at either a more stringent diagnosis to retain reimbursement or a milder diagnosis to avoid stigmatizing (Kirk and Kutchins, 1992).

Social workers' promotion of clients' self-determination is consistent with the American belief that people should be deprived of liberty only in extreme situations. Deinstitutionalization and the move toward the least restrictive environment, which have characterized mental health treatment for the last forty years, are consistent with social workers' continuing commitment to promoting the autonomy of clients.

But the question can be raised as to the conditions under which a client may legitimately be deprived of freedom. One of the least controversial reasons is the threat of the client's doing harm to him- or herself or to others, as in the case of suicidal or homicidal clients. While states have differing criteria for involuntary hospitalization, most recognize the standard of dangerousness. More rarely the inability to care for oneself is invoked as a reason for commitment to a mental institution (Sands, 1991).

Even as inpatients, clients have the right to refuse treatment. There have been several important cases in which clients' right to refuse to take medications or to submit to other forms of treatment that have adverse effects was upheld (Rennie v. Klein, 1983; Cornos, 1989).

If clients can self-determine not to be treated, can they self-determine to be treated? The right of hospitalized adults and adolescents to be treated has been upheld in several state courts (Alabama, Texas, Washington, D.C.) as well as in federal courts (Sands, 1991). Civil rights such as the right to informed consent, to due process, to vote, and to legal representation have also been confirmed by the courts (Sands, 1991).

An important component of self-determination is informed consent. Three main issues must be considered in a discussion of informed consent: (1) completeness of information, (2) the client's mental competency, and (3) the coerciveness of the situation (Thompson, 1990). Regarding the first issue, how can a client request or refuse a certain type of treatment if he or she does not understand the nature of the treatment? The patient has a right to be informed of the nature of the proposed treatment, its benefits and risks, the prognosis, the length of time involved, and the possible side effects. But how often does this happen, if at all? In a managed-care environment, clients may be informed of the length of treatment, but the nature of the treatment and its advantages and risks may be rarely, if ever, discussed. Courts have usually "defined informed consent according to a 'reasonable person standard,' that is, what a reasonable person would consider significant to know about any proposed treatment, or a 'professional practice standard,' that is, what professionals determine is sufficient for informed consent" (Beauchamp and Childress, 1983, p. 74).

The second issue, competency, renders informed consent problematic if a court rules that a client is incompetent to make a decision. Competency, however, may vary from day to day and even from hour to hour, especially with the cognitively impaired client. The responsibility of the social worker is to try to obtain informed consent by addressing clients when they are most competent and able to understand.

As to the third issue, the presence of coerciveness often negates informed consent. For example, a client who is threatened with never seeing her child again if she does not take medication is certainly not able to exercise informed consent.

Confidentiality and the ETHIC model

While confidentiality is a basic principle of social work, even the most naive social worker knows that one cannot promise unconditional confidentiality. The new Code of Ethics is explicit in stating the limits of confidentiality: social workers should promote confidentiality except when "disclosure is necessary to prevent serious, foreseeable, and imminent harm to a client or other identifiable person" (NASW, 1996. p. 11). Thus, if a client tells a social worker that he is thinking of suicide, the social worker is ethically permitted to break confidentiality in order to prevent serious and irreversible harm to the client. This principle is widely accepted, except by the most radical of thinkers (Szasz, 1974).

The acceptability of breaking confidentiality to prevent harm to others, however, has been widely debated. The Tarasoff case established an important precedent in the issue of mental health professionals' duty to warn by disclosing confidential information. The case involved Prosenjit Poddar, a student at the University of California, who told his counselor that he planned to kill his ex-girlfriend, Tatiana Tarasoff. The counselor notified the campus police, who questioned Poddar and then released him. Several months later Poddar killed Tatiana, and her parents brought suit against the University of California for not warning their daughter of Poddar's threat. The court decided in favor of the University of California, but a higher court overturned this decision. In the words of the majority opinion, "The protective privilege [of confidentiality] ends when the public peril begins" (Tarasoff v. Board of Regents of the University of California, 1976).

States have responded differently to this precedent-setting California decision. Legislatures in seventeen states enacted laws that limit the liability of therapists who have potentially violent clients, while other states now require therapists to breach confidentiality in such situations. (Kagle and Kopels, 1994). While social workers' responsibility to warn potential victims of harm may be limited, it is imperative for them to know and understand the relevant laws in their states.

After familiarizing themselves with state laws about confidentiality, social workers might use the ETHIC model to help them resolve ethical dilemmas in this area:

1. *Examine* relevant personal, social, agency, client, and professional values. The social worker must assess how his or her personal values affect the decision to violate confidentiality. For example, some social workers might feel that a mental health patient who has not taken a shower in a month is potentially violent, while others might feel that while this behavior is eccentric and certainly offensive, it does not portend violence.

   Agency values usually reflect a concern about liability issues. There may be very clear-cut policies that specify how the clinician should deal with clients who threaten violent behavior. Professional values that support respect of the individual and adherence to confidentiality are seen as an important component in this process.

2. *Think* about which ethical standard of the NASW Code of Ethics might apply. The NASW Code of Ethics supports maintaining confidentiality except "when disclosure is necessary to prevent serious, foreseeable, and imminent harm to a client or other identifiable person" (p. 11). Sometimes the clinician may have difficulty assessing when an identifiable person is at risk. Further, it has been shown that even the most knowledgeable mental health practitioner sometimes makes mistakes in assessing how dangerous a client is (Rosenthal, 1993). This may be partly because mental health treatment often encourages clients to express their real feelings, to "get in touch with their anger." Therapists frequently hear such statements as " I am so angry at my husband that I could kill him."

   A social worker's assessment of the seriousness of a threat often involves making a thorough assessment similar to one used to assess suicidal intent. Some useful questions to ask are:

   a. Does the client have the means of carrying out his or her threat? A client with a loaded gun is certainly more of a homicidal risk to his wife than one who has the vague hope that she has a fatal traffic accident.

   b. Does the client have a history of violence, especially toward the victim? While one's first offense may certainly be murder, previous violent episodes increase the possibility of this behavior.

c. Is the client experiencing delusions or hallucinations? Clients with delusions and/or hallucinations involving homicide are at high risk for acting on them.

3. *Hypothesize* about different courses of action and possible consequences. The social worker should consider different scenarios with different endings. For example, if confidentiality is maintained, what is the likelihood that the client will carry out his threats to harm another? Is there a way to protect the intended victim without violating confidentiality? (For example, the client might agree to talk with the therapist before committing a violent act or even agree to be hospitalized.) What might be the personal and professional consequences for the therapist if the client follows through with his or her threat? If the therapist does decide to violate confidentiality, how would the client's trust in the therapist be affected? Would the client leave therapy and commit a violent act anyway? In the end, would the client be pleased that he or she has been prevented from committing violence by being hospitalized? Would the intended victim be thankful about being notified or resent that she or he has been caused perhaps needless worry?

4. *Identify* who will benefit and who will be harmed in view of the social worker's commitment to most vulnerable. Often the intended victim is the most vulnerable. About 93 percent of the victims of domestic violence are women (Zawitz et al., 1993). Because children are also extremely vulnerable, each state mandates that child abuse and neglect be reported. In 1992 there were 1.16 million substantiated reports of child abuse, with over 1,000 fatalities (Ginsberg, 1995).

The new Code of Ethics recognizes that confidentiality can be violated "when laws or other regulations require disclosure without a client's consent." If the intended victim is a child, the social worker is certainly obliged to violate confidentiality; if an adult, the social worker must assess the potential victim's vulnerability. If the intended victim is a member of a vulnerable, frequently oppressed population such as women and/or older people, the social worker must be especially concerned about potential harm.

5. *Consult* with supervisor and colleagues. Can the social worker maintain confidentiality and still share information with others? Social workers cannot promise absolute confidentiality to clients, and it is understood that cases will be discussed with supervisors. Often it is helpful to have another perspective on the duty to warn,

and the supervisor may be able to suggest other courses of action or other ways the social worker can assess the seriousness of the threat. Also, the supervisor is more likely to be aware of the agency's perspective.

Legal Procedures and Social Work Ethics

The social worker must be aware not only of professional ethics, but also of the mental health laws in their state that affect the practice of social work, including confidentiality and the duty to warn. This is especially crucial because of the burgeoning number of malpractice cases in recent years. While in 1970 only one claim was filed with the NASW Insurance Trust, which provides malpractice insurance coverage for social workers, 126 claims were filed in 1990 (Reamer, 1995a).

What social workers fear most is a subpoena. A subpoena may cause the social worker to precipitously send off all records requested. However, subpoenas are very easy to obtain, and the social worker would be well advised to determine exactly what information is being requested and to discuss the subpoena with the client. Also, it is best to consult with the agency attorney before responding to the subpoena (Polowy and Gilbertson, 1997).

Privileged communication is the legal exemption granted to a profession that releases its members from disclosing the confidences of a client (Vandecreek, Knapp, and Herzog, 1988). Originally, the only relationships considered privileged were those between husband and wife, attorney and client, and priest and parishioner. Currently, other relationships may be considered privileged when defined as such by the state legislature. Usually Wigmore's criteria for privileged communication are applied to determine whether communication is privileged (Wigmore, 1961, vol. 8, p. 52). All four criteria must be met:

1. The communication must originate in the belief that it will not be disclosed.
2. The inviolability of the confidence must be essential to achieve the purpose of the relationship.
3. The relationship must be one that society should foster.
4. The expected injury to the relationship through disclosure of the confidential information must be greater than the expected benefit to justice if the witness were forced to testify.

In 1996 a Supreme Court decision recognized as privileged the communication between social worker and client (Greenhouse, 1996).

If the client waives the right to privileged communication, however, the social worker must testify in court, even if the testimony might be damaging to the client.

There are certain circumstances that negate the right to privileged communication. Although the provisions may vary from state to state, some of the most common include:

1. The client is dangerous and threatens to harm another person or her- or himself.
2. There is suspicion of child abuse or neglect.
3. The judge rules that the social worker's testimony is essential to the case.
4. The client plans to commit a crime.
5. The client sues the social worker for malpractice.
6. The client threatens to harm the social worker.

In many states communication cannot be considered privileged if a third party was present. However, some states have extended the designation as privileged to communication heard by other parties, such as during group, marital, and family therapy (Vandecreek, Knapp, and Herzog, 1988). Privileged communication is a legal rather than an ethical concept, but often ethical social work practice is affected by privileged communication. Although federal law now recognizes the communication between client and social worker as privileged, it is important for social workers to become familiar with their own state laws regarding exceptions to privileged communication.

Private Practice

Approximately 20 percent of social workers list private practice as their primary function; another 45 percent list it as secondary (Gibelman and Schervish, 1997). The increase of social workers in private practice has generated controversy in the profession. Some ethical concerns are that the most needy clients will not receive needed treatment and that agency and community practice will be jeopardized (Specht and Courtney, 1994). Another ethical concern is that the private practitioner cannot turn to co-workers for help and support in struggling with ethical problems but must resolve these in isolation. Therefore, because the final step of the ETHIC model—consult with supervisors or colleagues—may not be easily accomplished by the private practitioner, the responsibility falls on him or her to seek out formal supervision with professional social workers or informed consultation with peers when faced with ethical dilemmas. Many of the ethical dilemmas already discussed may be encountered by the private practitioner, but there are particular ethical dilemmas for the private practitioner.

Fees

The agency practitioner often has little input into fees for services; in contrast, the private practitioner has much leeway. The NASW Code of Ethics states that "when setting fees, social workers should ensure that the fees are fair, reasonable, and commensurate with the service performed. Consideration should be given to the client's ability to pay" (NASW, 1996, p. 14). But what exactly is a fair and reasonable fee? Is it the prevailing rate for social workers in the community? Should there be a sliding scale for clients less able to pay? What if the client's financial circumstances change, and he or she can no longer pay? The following example illustrates the latter situation.

> For the past year Tom, the thirty-year-old manager of a large computer store, has been seeing Doreen, a certified social worker, for psychotherapy. Originally, Tom entered therapy because he was depressed after breaking up with his girlfriend. It soon becomes apparent that Tom has other issues to explore, including concerns about his career, and anxiety about whether he will ever be able to form a long-term relationship. Tom recently learned that the computer store where he works has gone bankrupt and will close in two weeks. He really wants to continue in therapy, but he can no longer pay the fee. He suggests that perhaps he could help Doreen fix her computer in exchange for therapy sessions. What should Doreen do?

Tom has proposed entering into a bartering relationship, which the new Code of Ethics specifically prohibits: "Social workers should avoid accepting goods or services from clients as payment for professional services. Bartering arrangements, particularly involving services, create the potential for conflicts of interest, exploitation, and inappropriate boundaries in social workers' relationships with clients" (NASW, 1996, p. 14).

Doreen believes, however, that Tom needs more therapy and that to cut him off at this time would be very damaging. The Code of Ethics reiterates that "social workers should take reasonable steps to avoid abandoning clients who are still in need of services. Social workers should withdraw services precipitously only under unusual circumstances, giving careful consideration to all factors in the situation and taking care to minimize possible adverse effects. Social workers should assist in making appropriate arrangements for continuation of service when necessary." (NASW, 1996, p. 15). Doreen could continue to see Tom pro bono or at a nominal fee, because social work's principle of service states that "social workers are encouraged to volunteer some portion of their professional skills with no expectation of significant financial return (pro bono service)" (NASW, 1996, p. 6).

Another alternative would be to work out an arrangement by which Tom continues seeing Doreen for therapy and pays her when he is once again employed. Another and perhaps less satisfactory alternative would be to arrange to have Tom transferred to a therapist in an agency that charges less. This may be difficult to accomplish because if the first agency's fee is standard for the profession, the client may be expected to pay an equivalent amount at another facility. Also, the social worker must plan such a transfer carefully lest the client feel that he is being dropped without proper preparation. The social worker must remain aware that terminations and transfers are often difficult for clients and may impede their progress.

Competence

The new Code of Ethics states that "social workers should provide services and represent themselves only within the boundaries of their competence, based on their education [and] training" (NASW, 1996, p. 9). However, social workers in private practice often find themselves drawn into treating clients in areas in which they have had little formal training, as the following example illustrates.

Donna, a certified social worker who graduated two years ago, is treating Rachel for depression. It soon emerges that Rachel's depression is related to her family problems. Rachel then brings in her husband and then her teenage daughter. Before Donna realizes it, she is conducting family therapy. She has never taken a single course in this area.

Donna decides that the best way she could have of developing competence as a family therapist is continuing education in this area. She enrolls in a family therapy program to help her develop skills in working with families.

Record Keeping

Social workers in all settings struggle with paperwork, but the interface between social workers in mental health and other agencies and the amount of detail required often make record keeping particularly challenging for the mental health social worker. The Code of Ethics advises social workers to "take reasonable steps to ensure that documentation in records is accurate and reflective of the services provided" (NASW, 1996, p. 19). But what information should be included in a case record? Should the social worker include every detail for the sake of maintaining a full and accurate record? A complete record might contain very personal and somewhat damaging information and confidentiality could not be guaranteed. On the other hand, how helpful is a comment such as "The client reports that she is feeling well and discusses at length her vocational aspirations"? Could not this notation apply to many clients? The social worker often feels torn between the need to be positive, and at the same time comprehensive and accurate (Wilson, 1980a).

The following guidelines can help the social worker keep records about clients.

1. If the agency uses a general format for all records, adopt this format. (One of these is SOAP—subjective comments, objective comments, assessment, and plan.) If the agency does not have a specific outline, develop your own.
2. Individualize your comments.
3. Relate your comments to treatment goals.
4. Omit extraneous and highly personal comments (for example, "The client wore a very unattractive old dress").
5. Emphasize the client's strengths.
6. Separate process notes from case records. They are not identical. Process recordings are verbatim records, while case records are summaries.

Release of Records

Many social workers may not be aware that clients have the right to see their own records. The Code of Ethics specifies that "social workers should provide clients with reasonable access to records concerning them" (NASW, 1996, p. 20). Rarely do clients exercise this right, but when a client does ask to see his or her record, the social worker often becomes very apprehensive. This may be partly because of the worker's usual focus on problems and pathologies rather than on strengths. One colleague said that when questioned by a client about what she wrote about him, she invited him to help her write an entry for that day. She reported that he completed a very accurate case entry and seemed to make much progress that day.

What about a situation in which the social worker fears that a client's access to records will cause harm? The Code of Ethics informs practitioners that they "should provide assistance in interpreting the records and consultation with the clients regarding the records. Social workers should limit client access to social work records, or portions of clients' records, only in exceptional circumstances when there is compelling evidence that such access would cause serious harm to the client" (NASW, 1996, p. 12).

What happens when information about several clients is stored together? The following example illustrates this problem.

Terri has been seeing Marcia for individual therapy and then begins to see her in a group setting. Marcia expresses interest in seeing her record. Terri is concerned about sharing the record because it includes information about other group members.

Terri has a legitimate ethical concern about sharing information with a client when it contains information about another client. The NASW Code of Ethics specifically states that "when providing clients with access to their records, social workers should take steps to protect the confidentiality of other individuals identified or discussed in such records" (NASW, 1996, p. 12).

Sharing Information with Others

Often other individuals and agencies request information about clients. Most social workers are aware that they should not release information about a client to relatives. What must also be held confidential, however, is the fact that the individual is a client of the agency. Very often relatives call an agency and easily learn that a family member is being seen and by whom. Because this information is often conveyed by support staff, it is important that these employees also receive training in the confidentiality of any information regarding clients.

Release of Information to Another Agency

Most social workers are aware of the importance of obtaining a formal release from a client before sending information about that client to another agency. Unfortunately, however, many social workers still ask clients to sign a blanket release form that looks like this:

_____ grants _____
the right to release all information about his or her treatment to

_____.

Instead, the social worker should try to ensure that the client signs a detailed release form that includes the following:

The date
The name of the agency
The name of the agency requesting information
The purpose of sharing the information
The time period of treatment covered by release
The length of time the release is to be in effect
A provision that the information is not to be forwarded to a third party
The signature of a witness

Further, the social worker should try to avoid sending all case notes, but rather should create a summary that includes only information pertinent to the purpose for transferring information.

Often social workers work with clients whose primary language is not English or who have limited intellectual capacity. The social worker has the responsibility of making sure that clients understand releases they sign. The 1996 Code of Ethics states explicitly that "social workers should take steps to ensure clients' comprehension. This may include providing clients with a detailed verbal explanation or arranging for a qualified interpreter and/or translator whenever possible" (NASW, 1996, p. 9).

Finally, social workers may be very diligent about securing releases for written information but less concerned about oral communication. This may be particularly problematic if a caller identifies her- or himself as a doctor or a lawyer. The social worker must also be careful of the way information is conveyed verbally. Often the client is portrayed more negatively in verbal than in written communication. Protecting the client's interests in both oral and written communications is essential to ethical practice.

CHAPTER 6

Ethical Dilemmas in Child Welfare

Almost 30 percent of social workers report that they work with children (Ginsberg, 1995), most in protective services. Personal and societal values strongly influence the area of child welfare. There is some evidence that social workers in child welfare often try to recreate their own family structures in their clients' families (Morrison, 1995). In the first part of this century, the prevailing belief was that abused or neglected children should not remain with their parents, especially if the family was urban and poor. This led to many children being placed with rural families or in congregate residences. Despite Newt Gingrich's brief revival of the idea of orphanages, for the past twenty-five years the prevailing belief has been that raising children with a family, preferably their own or an adoptive one, contributes to their emotional well-being. Fanshel and Shinn's (1978) landmark study on the negative effects of long-term foster care helped launch the current focus on permanency planning.

Permanency planning policy promotes keeping children with their own families or placing them with adoptive families. This focus has led to the development of preventive services to strengthen families and thus avoid the necessity of out-of-home placement. Federal legislation, especially the Adoption Assistance and Child Welfare Act of 1980 (P.L. 96–272), encourages child welfare agencies to try to avoid placement, to arrange placement in the most familiar setting, and to place children in a permanent home within eighteen months (McGowan and Stutz, 1991). This law, which supports prevention of out-of-home placement, seems to have been both financially and socially motivated. While Fanshel and Shinn's research (1978) showed that it was in the best psychological and social interests of children to be raised in families, it is also true that keeping children with their families is much less expensive than financing out-of-home placement. Also, this law contrasts with the Child Abuse Prevention and Treatment Act of 1974, P.L. 93–457, which stresses the protection of vulnerable children by removing them from dangerous situations. This tension between preventive and protective services is apparent today in the delivery of child welfare services and is reflected in the many ethical dilemmas that arise in this area of social work.

Despite these ethical issues and dilemmas, there is little professional literature on ethical decision making in child welfare, with one notable exception (Pine, 1987). While in the past, child welfare workers based decisions on placement on the best interests of the child, now they are instructed to base them on the best interests of the family. Despite this emphasis, often the social worker must decide between the best interests of the child and those of the family.

Each state has a mechanism for reporting and investigating charges of child abuse and neglect, and all states mandate such reporting. Increased social problems, including substance abuse, unemployment, homelessness, and HIV/AIDS, as well as greater public awareness of these issues, has led to more reports of child abuse and neglect. Over half the children in foster care have been placed through protective services because of parental abuse and neglect (McGowan and Stutz, 1991).

The social worker faces difficult ethical dilemmas at different stages of child welfare work: (1) reporting child abuse and neglect, (2) protective services, and (3) adoption.

Reporting Child Abuse and Neglect

Although social workers are usually aware of their mandated role as reporters of child abuse and neglect, they are often conflicted when dealing with these issues. Social workers who work in community settings discover many cases of child abuse in schools, community centers, hospitals, mental health centers, and prevention programs. The social worker may find it easier to report child abuse when there is clear evidence. For example, the social worker in the emergency room who learns that a six-year-old boy with a broken arm has suffered repeated past injuries is not conflicted about calling child welfare protective services. Similarly, a school social worker who visits the family of an eight-year-old child who is frequently absent from school and discovers that his mother has not been home for three days reports the case without question to child welfare. Many incidents of suspected child abuse, however, are not that easily resolved, as this example shows.

Mary, a certified social worker, runs an activity group for latency-age boys in an after-school program. She notices that one child immediately grabs up all the cookies she provides for the children and does not share readily with others. She calls the mother and learns that because of a missed appointment (the letter from the welfare agency was sent to an old address and not forwarded), the family has been cut off welfare. The family has been living on rice, which the mother carefully rations out, until she can straighten out her welfare case.

Is this a question of neglect? Should the family be reported to protective services and the child placed temporarily until the welfare problem is resolved? The social worker makes an assessment that there is no evidence of neglect, but rather this family demonstrates the deleterious effects of poverty and bungled bureaucracy.

Poor families are more likely to be reported for child abuse and neglect because they are more visible. They frequently use public establishments, such as emergency rooms and social service agencies, which brings them into contact with professionals who are especially attuned to child abuse. Also, as the preceding example suggests, often the effects of poverty can be misinterpreted as child neglect. It is important that the social worker not let the economic circumstances of the client affect any decision about child abuse or neglect.

Read the following two cases and decide whether the first or second case would be more likely to be reported as child abuse.

Case Example 1

Susan, a professional social worker, works for a home-care agency that services older adults. One of her responsibilities as a social worker is to visit homes to ascertain the need for continuing home-care services. On her arrival at the home of an elderly couple who live in a very poor section of the city she notices that a young mother with two preschool-age children is just leaving the apartment next door. The children are dirty and shabbily dressed. The mother, who is in her late teens, smells of alcohol.

When Susan enters the apartment of the elderly couple, the woman begins to discuss her concerns about the safety and welfare of her neighbor's children. She reports that at night she hears the children crying and screaming and the mother yelling. The woman does not want to report this young mother for suspected child abuse/neglect because she fears retaliation from the mother's relatives and friends, who frequently visit. The couple indicate that they are glad Susan has come to visit because they are sure she will know how to handle this case of suspected child abuse.

Case Example 2

Susan, a professional social worker, has an apartment in the best section of town. In the four months that she has lived in the building she has noticed a young woman and two preschool-age children who live in the apartment next door. The woman, who always appears well dressed, takes her children to a baby-sitter each morning.

Recently Susan has become concerned about this woman's children. Once when Susan took out her garbage, she noticed that the neighbor's garbage contained nothing but liquor bottles. One morning last week Susan rode down in the elevator with the woman and her children and noted that the woman smelled of alcohol and the children's clothes were dirty. Last night through the walls of the apartment Susan heard both children screaming and crying and the woman yelling very loudly. This morning when Susan saw them in the hall she wondered if a dark mark on the arm of the four-year-old was dirt or a bruise inflicted by the mother.

Ask yourself the following questions about the two case vignettes:

1. What course of action would you take in each case?
2. Would you report either or both mothers for suspected child abuse?
3. If you decided to make a report, what are the reasons?
4. If you decided not to make a report, what are the reasons?

Protective Services: Foster Care, Return to Birth Parents, and Kinship Placements

It has been estimated that a half-million children will be in foster care by the year 2000 (Children's Defense Fund, 1989). If this estimate is accurate, an increasing number of social workers will be faced with difficult decisions about permanency plans for children in foster care.

During the 1990s, the use of kinship placements for children in foster care increased. The current AIDS and substance abuse epidemics have led to many children being raised by their grandmothers. More and more, social workers have developed individual and group treatment to help grandmothers who are raising children (Cohen, 1997). Advocates for kinship placements argue that different ethnic and racial groups have always used such arrangements when birth parents are unable to care for their children and that they help a child maintain family connections. Detractors point out that placing children with relatives often results in a less than ideal environment for the child and frequently means that the parent who has been identified as an abuser continues to care for the child.

A corollary of the belief in kinship placement is the belief that sibling groups should be kept together as much as possible. Again, maintaining the family connection is the main reason behind this policy decision. Placing siblings in the same foster home increases the complexity of ethical child welfare decisions. Often the child welfare worker must make a difficult decision about whether to keep a foster care placement, use a kinship placement, or return the children to the birth mother, as this example illustrates.

All four of Ms. Adams' children (Tom, twelve; Sharon, ten; Mary, five; and Patty, two) were placed eighteen months ago because of their twenty-nine-year-old mother's substance abuse. There was also a suspicion that Sharon had been sexually abused by one of Ms. Adams's crack-using friends, but this report has not been substantiated.

The children were placed in three different foster homes. Tom, who has been diagnosed as learning disabled and has begun to show behavioral problems at school, was placed with foster parents who are very good at relating to children with special problems. However, Tom has not adjusted to this foster home and has run away twice to see his grandmother. Sharon is very quiet, and the social worker has received no complaints from her foster parents. Mary and Patty have been placed in the same home, and reportedly both are adjusting well to their foster home. The foster parents have expressed interest in adopting Patty.

After the placement of the children, Ms. Adams enrolled in a drug treatment program, which she reportedly attends regularly. The social worker wonders, however, if Ms. Adams is beginning to use drugs again. Recently she was picked up by the police because she was close to a drug sale. There has not been enough evidence to substantiate Ms. Adams's involvement, and the charges against her were dropped.

The agency policy is to make a permanent plan for the children at the end of eighteen months. One alternative is to return the children to their mother. Another is to place the children with their fifty-year-old maternal grandmother, who wants to assume responsibility for all of them. She was not considered for a kinship placement when the children were initially placed because she was in the hospital recovering from surgery. Ms. Adams and her mother have had many conflicts over the years, and Ms. Adams feels that her mother cannot adequately care for the children. The grandmother lives in a two-bedroom apartment in a housing project, where she cares for a twenty-four-year-old retarded son. A thirty-year-old son who is addicted to alcohol and heroin visits frequently to "borrow" money from his mother. He was recently diagnosed as HIV positive.

How can this dilemma be resolved using the ETHIC model described in chapter 4?

Examine relevant personal, social, agency, client, and professional values. The worker begins by reviewing her own beliefs and values about birth families. She herself was raised by her grandmother after her own mother had died when she was two. She has fond memories of how caring her grandmother had been, and in fact her grandmother encouraged her to go to social work school. The social worker is aware that what was a positive experience for her might not be for the family with whom she is working. She notes one important difference—that her grandmother did not have any health or other family problems that might have interfered with her care.

The social worker also examines societal and cultural values that relate to this case. She recognizes the prevailing societal belief that families are best at providing children with a sense of security. This value would encourage her to return the children to either the birth mother or their grandmother. Also, the cultural values of the family she is working with support a belief that a relative should care for children.

The agency's values are rooted in permanency planning. The social worker has been given a deadline for making a permanent plan for the children. She is concerned that the deadline seems arbitrary and based as much on the financial need to reduce the number of children in foster care as on a concern for the psychological and social interests of the children. She knows that her agency has recently entered a managed-care contract that dictates that children remain in foster care only a certain length of time and that recently her agency has been having financial problems.

What are her clients' values? The social worker realizes that she is very judgmental of what she sees as the differing values of Ms. Adams and her mother. She is critical of Ms. Adams, believing that she values a good time over the welfare of her children. However, she sees the grandmother as very noble for wanting to care for and keep the family together despite all her problems. The social worker becomes increasingly aware that she really does not know much about her clients' values. Consequently, she has a long discussion with Ms. Adams and is pleasantly surprised to learn how important being a good mother is to her.

Finally, the social worker considers professional values that might help her resolve this ethical dilemma. She knows she has a professional responsibility to provide service to the children, Ms. Adams, her mother, and the foster parents. The social worker also knows that the professional value of social justice might be applicable to this case. She has the responsibility of providing appropriate service to all the clients she has identified. The social worker recognizes that Ms. Adams has the same rights as any other person, despite her poverty and history of substance abuse. She knows that the most recent charges against Ms. Adams were dropped. Thus, she cannot consider Ms. Adams guilty of drug use. The social worker is also aware that professional values stress that she respect the inherent dignity and worth of the person. She should therefore strive not to be judgmental of Ms. Adams, a twenty-nine-year-old unmarried mother of four with a history of substance abuse. She should also avoid judging the grandmother, who has three adult children with special problems.

She sees the social work value to recognize the importance of human relationships as particularly relevant to this situation. The social worker knows that she wants to help strengthen the family. She sees the oldest child's attempts to rejoin his grandmother as a strength rather than a deficit. She identifies a new area to work on—the relationship between Ms. Adams and her mother.

Hypothesize about different courses of action and possible consequences. The social worker believes that she has three possible courses of action:

1. Return the children to Ms. Adams. In the eighteen months the children have been in foster homes, Ms. Adams has complied with the treatment plan by keeping regular appointments at a drug treatment facility. The social worker needs to follow up to find out for sure that Ms. Adams's attendance has been regular, especially during the last month, when there was a suspicion about Ms. Adams's proximity to drug users.

   If the children were to return home, there would be a need for additional services. The social worker is concerned that under the new welfare reform law, the family can stay on public assistance for only two years. Ms. Adams left school at sixteen when she became pregnant with her first child. Prior to that she attended school irregularly and can barely read. The social worker knows that Ms. Adams can only obtain unskilled minimum-wage work. Could she support her family of five, especially with their need for health care? The social worker knows that Ms. Adams might need continued support from the agency, but a recent cutback in funds has brought an end to follow-up services. The social worker fears that the children's return home might be stressful and believes that social work services might be helpful. Tom, a preadolescent, is already displaying behavioral problems in school. The social worker expects that these problems might continue after the children are reunited with their mother.

The wishes of children, especially adolescents, are increasingly being taken into account in making placement decisions (Stein, 1991). The social worker knows that Tom has run away to be with his grandmother. She has yet to explore his relationship with his mother and his feelings about returning to live with her. She must take into consideration that children often may want to return to the familiar environment of home and that birth parents, despite problems, often provide a sense of family that may be lacking in a foster home. Although Sharon did not show any behavior problems, the social worker recognizes that often "quiet" children, like the "lost child" in alcoholic families (Black, 1981), have unacknowledged needs that may become problematic later in life. The social worker resolves to learn more about how Sharon and her younger sisters feel about rejoining their mother.

The social worker is also concerned about the risk that Ms. Adams will begin using drugs again, especially under the strain of raising four children on a limited income. When the children were placed for the first time, they had all been severely neglected. In fact, the precipitating event had been neighbors' reports that they heard a child crying continually. When child welfare workers investigated, they learned that the mother had disappeared two days earlier. Tom and Sharon had not gone to school, and the children had only cereal to eat since their mother's departure. Interviews with Sharon had raised the suspicion that she had been sexually abused, but there was no specific evidence of this. The social worker worries about what might happen if Ms. Adams begins to use drugs again. What new abuse and neglect might occur?

2. Place the children in foster care. If the social worker believes that Ms. Adams is again using drugs, then the best alternative might be to continue the children's placement in foster homes. In recent years the courts have imposed stiff penalties on repeat drug-law

offenders, and those found guilty often receive long prison sentences. In fact, stricter penalties for female drug offenders may be the cause of the increase in the number of children in the foster care system (Hairston, 1996). There is no clear-cut evidence, however, that Ms. Adams is again using drugs, because the police dropped the charge against her.

While placing the children in foster care might remove them from the negative effects of the mother's current or potential drug use, such arrangements might not be ideal. Some children have been abused or even killed in foster care, especially those children with special problems. Also foster care does not provide a permanent plan for child care, although the importance to a child of the psychological parenthood of a foster parent has been noted (Goldstein, Freud, and Solnit, 1973). One focus might be to work toward adoption, but it is unlikely that an adoptive family would want to adopt all four children. One of the current foster families is interested in adopting only the youngest. It might be difficult to find an adoptive home for the oldest child, who has behavioral problems.

3. Arrange a kinship placement for the children. Kinship placements make it possible for children to remain within their extended family networks. Kinship placements formalize a placement method that has been used informally for many years by African-American families in which birth parents need help in raising their children (Boyd-Franklin 1989). Children often prefer to remain in kinship placements, as Tom's running away to his grandmother suggests. Is a return to the birth parents or adoption an appropriate goal for children in kinship placements (Gleeson and Philbin, 1994)? There is also a concern that children in kinship placements often continue to have much unsupervised contact with their birth parents, which may be problematic.

The social worker sees Ms. Adams's mother as a strong, positive parenting resource for the family. She knows that all the children are very fond of her and would probably rather live with her than with anyone else. But she also knows that the grandmother had major surgery last year, from which she has not yet fully recovered. She wonders if the grandmother has the strength to raise four children, especially considering the ongoing care she must give her adult retarded son. Perhaps a home-care worker could help care for the children. But the social worker knows that the agency has cut back services, especially to kinship families. However, she could recommend social services to help this family if the children were returned to the grandmother.

The social worker knows that if this alternative is chosen, she would need to see both Ms. Adams and her mother to help them work on their conflicts, especially insofar as they affect the children. If the grandmother is not able to continue caring for the four children because of her deteriorating health, they could be returned to their mother or placed in a foster home.

Identify who will benefit and who will be harmed in view of social work's commitment to the most vulnerable. Social work usually regards those with limited power as the most vulnerable. In the child welfare field, children are frequently seen as the least powerful, the most vulnerable, and therefore the most in need of social work intervention. A concern for the vulnerability of children led to the adoption of child abuse laws and mandatory reporting of child abuse in all fifty states. A belief of American society in general and of child welfare practice in particular is that a home and family are best for every child. Therefore, the primary goal in child welfare is to develop a permanent plan for each child in placement.

Would the Adams children most benefit from returning to their mother? She may still be abusing drugs. Although Ms. Adams may want the children to be returned to her, there is the possibility that they will be harmed by such a decision. Would the children benefit more from remaining in foster homes? This would create uncertainty about their future, because foster homes are not considered permanent placements, and children often have limited power over the length of time they are placed in foster homes. Already Tom's days in his current foster home might be numbered because of his behavior problems.

An important question is whether one should evaluate the benefits to the whole family as a unit or to individual members. There is the possibility that one of the children may be adopted, which might greatly benefit her but not the others. It can also be argued that adoption will not benefit her if she loses contact with her sibling family. But it might be impossible to find a family that would adopt all four children. Also, one could question the effect of adoption because the children have a connection with their birth mother and their grandmother.

The children might benefit the most by being placed with their grandmother, who would provide both a family connection, and the structure and nurturing so important to children. The grandmother wants the children to live with her, and although there is bound to be stress, she will benefit from this placement. Would Ms. Adams be harmed if the children are placed with her mother? She is against that arrangement, but it can be argued that she would benefit from it because she could have frequent contact with the children.

Consult with supervisor and colleagues about the most ethical choice. Before making the final decision, the social worker discusses the case with her supervisor. She learns about the Ethics Review Committee, which her agency had recently formed to resolve difficult child welfare decisions. Before meeting with this committee the social worker gathers additional information about the family. She learns from the drug reha- bilitation center that Ms. Adams missed several appointments in the last two months, whereas previously she never missed an appointment. Some of the members of the Ethics Review Committee raise the concern that Ms. Adams might not be ready to resume caring for the children. Placing the children with their grandmother seems like a good option. One mem- ber of the committee provides information about a homemaking service that could help the grandmother care for her grandchildren and adult son. Further, the agency has just found out about a new public housing facility with large apartments. The grandmother might be able to move into one of these apartments. With the support of her supervisor and the Ethics Review Committee, the social worker decides to recommend that the children be placed with the grandmother. She plans to offer Ms. Adams continued counseling, with the goal of reintegrating her into the extended family.

Adoption: Rights of Adoptive Parents, Birth Parents, and Adopted Children

The concern for permanency planning for children has led to renewed interest in adoption. The field of adoption has undergone major changes in recent years. First, women's easy access to inexpensive, legal abortion has led to fewer children being placed for adoption. Also, changing societal attitudes toward single parenthood have meant that more women decide to keep their children rather than place them for adoption. While the number of white babies available for adoption has dropped significantly, the number of older children and children with special needs who need adoptive homes has increased because of drug abuse and the HIV/AIDS epidemic. Because older children often have strong connections with their birth fami- lies, open adoptions, which permit continued contact with birth parents, have increased.

Previously, social workers were encouraged to share with the adop- tive family only minimal, and largely positive, information about the birth family. To promote this goal, child welfare agencies had separate adoption and natural-parent departments, and social workers were encouraged to develop "baby stories" that focused only on the strengths of the birth parents and neglected significant physical, mental, and social problems. What was kept in the strictest confidence was the identity of the birth mother, often under the guise that this was her wish.

Over the last thirty years there has been a dramatic change in adoption practices, as more birth parents have sought to reclaim their children and more adoptive children have sought to learn about their backgrounds. Social workers have debated the pros and cons of opening adoption records (Watson, Seader, and Walsh, 1994). Developments in genetics research have added to psychological studies concrete reasons why adoptive children should learn about their birth parents.

While adoption records were once traditionally sealed, social workers in the adoption field now alert prospective couples that their child may want to seek out his or her family of origin, and they as social workers might have to support this. Many of these searches begin in adolescence, when children rebel against their adoptive families and fantasize that their birth parents would have been different. Families are now encouraged to be much more explicit and honest in telling adoptive children about their families of origin. Social workers in adoption services face many ethical dilemmas, as the following example illustrates.

Sarah has worked in the adoption division of a large child welfare agency for twenty-two years. She loves her work and still remembers her first case, when she placed a baby with a couple who had wanted a child for many years. Relatives from both sides of the family were present when she gave the adoptive child to the couple and even she herself thought that the baby resembled the couple. At that time, adoptive parents were given only minimal information about their adoptive child. Parents were encouraged to tell the child that she or he was adopted, and the Smiths had dutifully read stories about adopted children to Jessica when she was a young child. After that Jessica had never discussed being adopted, not even when she was an adolescent, which is when adoptive children often begin looking for their birth parents.

After having had no contact with the adoption agency or her birth family since she was ten days old, Jessica, now married and three months pregnant, contacts Sarah to learn who her birth parents were. She had recently had an amniocentesis and learned that her daughter might be born with a serious birth defect. Although there are some risks involved, it is possible to start prenatal treatment that would minimize this birth defect. Her husband tested positive for a recessive gene linked to this disorder. While she tested negative, it is known that this disease often skips a generation; thus it is important to know the health histories of the maternal grand-parents. Should Jessica be given information that might help her seek out her birth parents?

Applying the ETHIC model of decision making yields the following results:

Examine relevant personal, social, agency, client, and professional values. In adoption work the personal values of the worker often enter professional work. The Smiths had been assured when they adopted Jessica that there would be no more contact with the birth parents. Yet it could be argued that because Jessica is now an adult in her own right, she can make her own decision about seeking her birth parents. Sarah had entered the adoption field because she felt very strongly that every child should grow up in a caring family. She had been particularly impressed by the Smith family and by their close and immediate bond with their adoptive child. Following the policies of the adoption agency where she worked, Sarah had developed a baby story to tell the Smiths. She had perhaps stretched the truth by revealing to them only the positives about Jessica's heritage. The birth mother was a homeless twenty-one-year-old prostitute who had traveled to New York three years earlier on the promise of a job with a rock group. The father could have been one of the twenty men she had slept with the week of Jessica's conception. Sarah's baby story transformed the mother into a young woman who was very committed to her musical career and unable to keep her child because of the demands of her profession. Although Sarah knows that new laws allow adoption records to be opened, she believes that minimal contact with natural parents is probably best for all concerned. However, she realizes that she must not allow her personal values to interfere with her professional work with Jessica and her adoptive parents. Her professional values stress service, respect for the dignity and worth of all persons, and the importance of human relationships. She wonders if there might be a conflict in trying to provide service to all parties.

The values of Jessica, her adoptive parents, and her birth parents might differ. Jessica very much wants to seek out her birth mother. In fact, she confides to Sarah that as an adolescent, she often considered initiating such a search but feared it would hurt her adoptive parents. Her adoptive parents are apprehensive about Jessica seeking her birth mother because they feel threatened that Jessica might develop a close relationship with her. Jessica's birth mother's values are not known, although Sarah realizes that some mothers in similar situations want to forget the experience entirely. On the other hand, she knows some birth mothers who went to great lengths to find children whom they had put up for adoption. Sarah also recognizes that the values of the adoption agency where she works have shifted over the years. When she first began working, the agency separated birth mothers from adoptive families. This separation was symbolized by providing separate workers on separate floors to deal with each party to the adoption procedure. Adoptive families were usually told that the records were sealed and that neither they nor the adoptive child could have access to them.

Three main developments in the last thirty years, however, led to more open adoption records. First, open adoptions are the practice in most European countries, and some states now permit the adoption records to be opened. Second, the number of newborns available for adoption has decreased because of legalized abortion and better family planning. Also, these days single mothers often choose to keep their children rather than put them up for adoption. Legislation to promote permanency planning has led to older children being put up for adoption more often. Older children remember their first home, and open adoption has been viewed as promoting adoptive children's psychological health. Finally, genetic counseling has made knowledge of one's background more important. Knowing one's roots is seen as essential for both emotional and physical health. If one learns about genetic predispositions to certain diseases, preventive treatment or, as in Jessica's case, prenatal treatment can be undertaken early.

With all these changes, agencies that once promised secrecy to adoptive parents now find themselves in the embarrassing position of helping adopted children find their birth parents.

Think about what ethical standard of the NASW Code of Ethics might apply. While the Code of Ethics focuses on generic standards of practice and does not mention adoption at all, it contains provisions that apply to adoption. The concept of confidentiality seems relevant. Are adoption records confidential? Did the worker promise confidentiality to the natural parent twenty-two years ago when Jessica was adopted? Were not the adoptive parents also promised that they would remain unknown to the natural parent? While the code does stress confidentiality (NASW, 1996, pp. 10–12), it also contains the provision that there might be situations "when laws or regulations require disclosure without a client's consent" (NASW, 1996, p. 10). Laws may mandate the disclosure of information in adoption records. The Code of Ethics also addresses the issue that Sarah may have a potential conflict of interest in working with the Smiths, Jessica, and her birth parent. Pursuant to the code, Sarah has the ethical responsibility to "clarify [her] role with the parties involved and take appropriate action to minimize any conflict of interest" (NASW, 1996, p. 10).

Hypothesize about different courses of action and their possible consequences. Sarah can take one of two courses of action. She can inform Jessica that the adoption records are sealed and that she cannot give her any information. To do so, however, would be to go against recent court decisions. The Smiths might be pleased, because they wish to limit contact with the natural parent. Jessica might be angry, however, because she would be unable to acquire information that would help her address the health problems of her unborn child. A second possibility would be for Sarah to tell Jessica what the adoption agency knows about her birth mother. Because this information is twenty-two years old, Jessica may still have difficulty in finding her birth mother. Some birth mothers have never told anyone about their pregnancy and may be angry about being reminded of an event they may have tried to forget. And even if the birth mother or parents are located, they must agree to be tested. But with this genetic knowledge Jessica's child could begin treatment that might prevent a serious birth defect.

Identify who will benefit and who will be harmed. If Jessica learns the identity of her birth mother, she and her unborn child will benefit. For one thing, she will not have to undergo risky treatment that may not be necessary. One could also argue that Jessica and her husband might be spared having a child with special problems. The adoptive grandparents would not have a grandchild with special problems, but they might be concerned that the birth parent might vie with them for the affections of Jessica and their grandchild. Identifying the birth mother may cause her harm if she does not want to be discovered. Hopefully, Jessica would approach her birth mother privately to allow the birth mother to keep her secret if this is her wish.

Consult with supervisor and colleagues. Fortunately, Sarah works in a large agency. She discusses the case with several of her colleagues as well as her supervisor. Last year her agency formed an ethics committee that meets regularly to discuss ethical dilemmas. Sarah presents the case to the multidiscipline team, which includes lawyers, and learns about the latest case decisions in the adoption field. She thinks her decision would be in keeping with the relevant laws in her state.

After using the ETHIC model Sarah selects the following course of action. She tells Jessica what she knows about her birth mother and refers Jessica to an agency that helps adopted children find their birth parents. Sarah also plans to meet with the adoptive parents to tell them of her decision and provide support while Jessica seeks her birth mother. Sarah also plans to stay in touch with Jessica while she searches for her birth mother and through the months of genetic testing and treatment.

In summary, ethical dilemmas arise in child welfare because of conflicts of interest between birth parents, children, foster parents, and adoptive parents. The ETHIC model can help social workers deal with these dilemmas.

CHAPTER 7

Ethical Dilemmas in Health Care

The increasing complexity of ethical issues and dilemmas in the health field during the last two decades has inspired many scholars to focus on ethical issues for the medical social worker (Abramson, 1990a, 1990b; Joseph and Conrad, 1989; Proctor, Morrow-Howell, and Lott, 1993; Reamer, 1985; Ross, 1992). This chapter examines four main aspects of health care that generate ethical dilemmas for the social worker: (1) genetics, neonatal treatment, renal dialysis, and transplants; (2) end-of-life decisions, including those relating to advanced directives and euthanasia; (3) cultural differences; and (4) managed care and social work ethics.

A recent news report on cloning raises concerns about the type of ethical issues social workers, as well as the larger community, will face in the future. While there are laws against cloning in Great Britain and other countries, cloning is not illegal in the United States ("With cloning," 1997). If cloning extends to human beings, who will be cloned? Who decides who will be cloned? What will happen to people who are designated as undesirable for cloning because of intelligence or disability?

While social workers in the twenty-first century will struggle with ethical issues relating to cloning, medical social workers currently face many ethical dilemmas relating to genetic counseling, as the following case example suggests.

Terry, a certified social worker employed in a genetic counseling unit in a large research hospital, has recently been assigned a couple, Bill and Sue Baker, who have a four-year-old daughter. Both have a recessive gene for Huntington's chorea, which is usually passed on to male children. Sue's father had developed the disease while in his mid-forties and died five years ago after twenty years of debilitating illness. Sue is three months pregnant. Through amniocentesis it is learned that Sue's unborn child is male. It is unclear whether he has inherited the gene for this illness. Sue wants to have an abortion, but her husband objects because he wants to have a son.

Terry faces several ethical dilemmas:

1. How can she help the Bakers make use of their knowledge of the disease and of their unborn child?
2. How should she respond to the different positions of each of her clients?

As a social worker Terry knows that it is important to promote the self-determination of her clients, but because her clients have differing views, she does not know whose self-determination to promote. She also wonders about the purpose of genetic counseling if one is not going to use the resulting information.

Ethical dilemmas also arise for social workers in the field of renal dialysis. While renal dialysis can keep more people alive now than ever before, it is expensive as well as physically and emotionally demanding. In some countries dialysis is not available to people over seventy years of age, which reflects an ageist approach that makes social workers uncomfortable. But the renal patient who elects continued treatment often faces severe restrictions on food and water intake. These restrictions may be especially onerous for adolescents, for whom peer relationships are very important. Also, homeless and other poor people may have difficulty following strict rules about food and drink. Should renal dialysis be an option for people who cannot (or will not) follow a strict diet? This question has also been raised concerning AIDS treatment, because if the appropriate protocol for medication is not rigorously followed, the person's health may deteriorate, and he or she might more readily infect other people. What is the responsibility of the social worker if a client resists staying with a prescribed diet or if the client wants to stop renal dialysis completely? Self-determination is clearly prescribed in the Code of Ethics (NASW, 1996), except when "clients' actions or potential actions pose a serious, foreseeable, and imminent risk to themselves" (NASW, 1996, p. 7). A client in need of renal dialysis who does not follow treatment procedures or stops treatment altogether poses a risk to him- or herself. This provision, however, has usually been interpreted as restricting self-determination only when the client threatens to commit suicide. Thus, promoting self-determination is a slippery slope. When should the client be permitted to self-determine, and when should the social worker interfere in his or her self-determination?

While conflicts between autonomy and paternalism often characterize ethical dilemmas faced by the medical social worker, dilemmas regarding distributive justice in health care are also common. From a macroperspective, do all people, whatever their income and status, receive the same type of health care? Differences in infant mortality and life expectancies suggest that the type and quality of health care vary according to income (Hogue and Hargraves, 1993). The NASW Code of Ethics mandates that social workers seek to "ensure access to needed information, services, and resources" (NASW, 1996, p. 5), and this has been construed as a requirement to seek equitable, nondiscriminatory health care for clients (Congress and Lyons, 1992).

Principles of Distributive Justice

When resources are scarce, however, the social worker is often faced with difficult decisions. Four main criteria for distributing scarce resources are often invoked: equality, need, compensation, and contribution (Reamer, 1995b). The supply of organs for transplants is very limited. The number of those in need of heart, liver, and kidney transplants usually far exceeds the number of available organs, so the equal distribution of organs is not possible. How should limited resources like these be distributed? According to a waiting list? Or should a lottery system be used so that each patient has the same chance of receiving an organ?

Often health care decisions are made on the basis of need. Need, however, is difficult to measure. What factors affect the need for a transplant—age, other health problems, life expectancy?

The criterion of compensation often enters into the distribution of scarce resources. Affirmative action programs are based on the principle that because certain groups have been discriminated against in the past, they should receive priority treatment now. If this principle is applied to organ transplants, people and groups who were once discriminated against concerning health care should receive primary consideration.

A final criterion of distributive justice is based on contribution. Fee for service is an example of this principle. Those who can pay for health care receive health care, while those who cannot go without. It has been argued that there is value in paying for services even if the payment is minimal. Aspects of welfare reform that require people to work to receive benefits are an example of this principle. This criterion has also been applied to nonmonetary contribution, enabling people with fame and prestige to go to the top of the list of those awaiting medical treatment. In the summer of 1996 some were concerned when Mickey Mantle did not have to wait at all for a liver transplant, despite several severe health problems that might have rendered other people ineligible. Making decisions about who receives transplants may be repugnant to many social workers, but there is increasing evidence that knowledge and skill in ethical decision making give social workers great influence in this area of health care (Joseph and Conrad, 1989).

Increase in Life Expectancy

Life expectancy is rising. While in 1900 the average American could expect to live only fifty years, now women can expect to live seventy-eight years and men seventy-one (Ginsberg, 1995). Better nutrition, the eradication of many fatal childhood diseases, and modern medical technology have been credited with this increase. People at every stage of life are more likely than their predecessors to survive. While previously one out of every three infants did not survive their first year, now only one of every hundred infants does not survive the first year (Hogue and Hargraves, 1993).

Ethics and Premature Infants

Because of technological improvements in perinatal care, children with birth weights of as little as a pound have been able to live. These premature infants, however, often have underdeveloped lungs and other associated health problems that require long-term, intensive, and expensive treatment, sometimes without the hope that the infant will ever be able to lead a normal life. Perinatal medical social workers are often involved in helping couples make difficult decisions about whether to subject their infant to expensive, painful treatment that often does not turn out well or to let the child die without attempting every possible intervention. Although written primarily for the severely ill adult client, the policy statement from the NASW Delegate Assembly (1993) on end-of-life decisions may help the social worker counseling a family that has a seriously ill newborn. The policy statement stresses that the social worker must be available for the family, be careful not to impose his or her own views, help the family consider different treatments, and support the family in whatever decisions they make.

End-of-Life Decisions

Much attention has been paid to end-of-life decisions of the older client. In the past, people died at a younger age, often because of an infectious disease and often at home. These days death is more likely to occur during old age because of chronic, long-term illness such as cancer or heart disease, except in the case of HIV/AIDS, which most often kills young adults. Technology such as respirators, transfusions, and tubal feedings can keep very sick people alive for a very long time. The cost of this technology is high, and it is estimated that medical expenses during the last month of life equal what an average person spends on health care during his or her entire life up until that time.

Because of increased longevity, escalating health care costs, and advanced technology, there has been renewed discussion of euthanasia and assisted suicide in this country. The word *euthanasia* comes from a Greek word meaning "easy death." The practice of euthanasia originated with the ancients. It is important to clarify what is meant by euthanasia and to distinguish between active and passive euthanasia, and between voluntary and involuntary euthanasia. The following chart illustrates some of these distinctions.

FIGURE 7.1   Euthanasia

	Voluntary	Involuntary
Active	Person hastens death by some means; assisted suicide is an example	Person is unconscious or incompetent because of age (newborn), intelligence (mentally retarded), or emotional condition (psychotic)
Passive	Living will signed by patient; health care proxy; person is removed from life support; DNR order is implemented	Person has not signed living will; family decides on DNR

Passive euthanasia, especially DNR (Do Not Resuscitate) orders, is generally accepted. While individuals are encouraged to make voluntary decisions while they are able, often families make these decisions if the patient is unconscious. While DNR orders are common, decisions about removing life supports such as feeding tubes or respirators are more controversial, especially if the person has not signed a living will or selected a health care proxy.

A living will states what a person does or does not want done to be kept alive, while a health care proxy form names an individual who is empowered to make health-care decisions for a patient unable to do so. States vary in their preference for one of these documents over the other, so it is important for social workers to know which is preferred in their state.

The Patient Self-Determination Act of 1990 spells out the importance of individuals giving advanced directives when they enter hospitals or nursing homes, and health-care facilities have hastened to incorporate a mechanism for completing these forms as part of the admissions process.

While the Netherlands has accepted active euthanasia and assisted suicide for many years, they continue to be controversial in the United States. A 1966 poll showed that two-thirds of Americans surveyed were against active euthanasia, while a similar poll in 1990 showed that two-thirds approved of active euthanasia. Despite Dr. Kervorkian's efforts to make assisted suicide accepted, only Oregon recognizes assisted suicide. In 1997 the Supreme Court ruled that assisted suicide was illegal.

Assisted Suicides

Promoters of assisted suicide argue that it maximizes autonomy, allows clients to die with dignity, and diminishes medical costs and stress on the family. Opponents argue that assisted suicide is against God's laws, that one can never be sure that a condition is terminal, that quality of life is subjective, and that it creates "a slippery slope," meaning that it may evolve into the putting to death of the chronically ill and others. It has also been suggested that depression often impairs the judgment of suicidal people and that assisted suicide may lead to an increased rate of suicide, especially among young people because of peer pressure and the "destigmatization of suicide" (Callahan, 1994, p. 237).

After much debate, social workers at the 1993 Delegate Assembly formulated a policy statement on end-of-life decisions. The policy statement identifies the following issues for social workers to address in counseling clients about end-of-life decisions (NASW, 1993):

1. The legal parameters that affect social work, including limits of confidentiality, state and federal laws that prohibit assisted suicide, and the potential for civil liability.
2. The possible conflict between social workers' values and those of other health care professionals.
3. The increasing pressure to contain costs and ration health care.
4. Terminally ill clients' concern that they may be burdens on their families.
5. Societal limits on individual self-determination and autonomy.
6. The need for safeguards to protect individuals and society in implementing end-of-life practices.

These are not easy issues for social workers, as the following case example indicates.

A seventy-five-year-old widower, Mr. Thomas, and his family have just learned that he has inoperable lung cancer. His prognosis is poor. Until last year Mr. Thomas was in excellent health and always lived very independently. His two adult children show very different reactions. His daughter cannot believe the diagnosis. His son insists that everything be done to keep his father alive as long as possible. He is concerned about finances, though, because he has just lost his job and his father is covered only by Medicaid. Mr. Thomas worries that he will become a burden to his family. He saw a television program about assisted suicide and wants to discuss it with the medical social worker at the hospital.

The social worker can use the following guidelines in working with Mr. Thomas and others facing end-of-life decisions:

1. The social worker should be aware of advance directives such as living wills and health care proxies and be able to discuss these documents with clients. Advance directives enable clients to control end-of-life decisions. A living will specifies a client's choices about medical treatment, while a health care proxy chosen by the client makes decisions on health care if the client is unable to do so. Some states make more use of living wills, while others rely more on health care proxies. Educating clients about the use of health care proxies and living wills is an important task for social workers in health care.

    While some clients and their families may resist discussing these issues, the social worker must be sensitive to where clients stand on them and not force his or her own agenda on the client. Also, family members may have conflicting opinions. In the case of the Thomas family, if Mr. Thomas chooses a health care proxy, he may want to select the child whose beliefs are most compatible with his own. When family differences and conflict arise, an important role for the social worker may be to mediate between family members.

2. Social workers should work to ensure that all clients have equal access to health care. Mr. Thomas's son has raised the concern that health care will not be affordable because he is unemployed and his father is on Medicaid. If Mr. Thomas decides to pursue costly health care, the social worker should try to ensure that he is not denied treatment because of his limited financial resources.

    Some terminally ill clients fear that medical personnel who want to reduce costs will not help them survive if they have signed an advance directive. It is important for social workers to listen to clients' questions and concerns. Clients may believe that an early death is preferable to becoming a burden to their families. Social workers have a responsibility to seek out resources and social supports that would help the family get through such crises.

3. The social worker's role is to make sure clients are informed of possible courses of action and their consequences and then to encourage clients to make their own decisions.

Social workers should not promote any specific point of view but instead be open and available to discuss issues. If because of his or her personal beliefs the social worker is not able to objectively discuss end-of-life decisions with a terminally ill client, he or she has an ethical responsibility to refer the client to a social worker who can fulfill this role.

4. The social worker should act as liaison with other health care professionals and help the client and the family communicate their concerns to other providers. In the case of the Thomas family, the social worker may want to facilitate discussion between the doctor and family members about various treatments. Also, the social worker might explore other medical and social supports, including hospice, home care, and visiting nurse services.

5. It is appropriate for the social worker to discuss with the client such end-of-life decisions as assisted suicide and do-not-resuscitate orders. Although the Supreme Court has ruled assisted suicide illegal, Mr. Thomas may be interested in considering other options. The social worker should be available to discuss them.

6. The social worker must recognize that self-awareness and openness about end-of-life decisions are crucial in working with a dying client and his family.

Feelings of helplessness and hopelessness are common among dying people and their families. Many people—including the client, families, and social workers—may feel uncomfortable in speaking about death and dying. The "secrets" surrounding illness and dying may further isolate people from supportive networks that might be available. Mr. Thomas's daughter's state of denial may make her unavailable to her father. The role of the social worker is to provide support to both the client and his or her family so that these difficult topics might be discussed. End-of-life decisions may affect clients of all ages, especially because of the AIDS epidemic.

Cultural Differences in Health Beliefs

Cultural groups vary in their approach to health, illness, and death. Much of our health system is based on Western European beliefs about these topics. Mental and physical systems are divided into psychiatry and internal medicine. Different medical specializations focus on particular body systems (cardiologist, gastroenterologist), ages (pediatrician, gerontologist), or diseases (oncologist, infectious disease). Disease can be diagnosed by X-rays, blood tests, and MRI, and modern medicine is optimistic that it can be cured through medications, surgery, or radiation.

Immigrants who come to the United States bring with them beliefs about health that may clash with medical procedures that are generally accepted in the United States. For example, some cultures do not make a clear distinction between the physical and the mental. Emotional stress is frequently expressed and described in physical terms. Thus, the Hispanic *dolor de cabeza* (pain in the head) may be considered by some doctors as malingering at worst or a psychosomatic disorder at best.

The American health care system, especially since the advent of managed care, stresses prevention. But prevention is unknown to many people who come from other parts of the world, where medical care is sought only by the sick. Immigrants who do not understand the American health care system may often be criticized, as the following example shows.

Ms. Santos, a Haitian immigrant, brings her two-year-old daughter, Elisa, to the hospital emergency room with a fever of 105 degrees. The child is diagnosed with pneumonia, and the social worker documenting Elisa's health history learns that the child has not been to a doctor since birth. The social worker wonders if she should refer the family to child welfare protective services because of possible neglect. Ms. Santos indicates that she has never brought Elisa to the Well Baby Clinic because the child has never before been sick.

The medical social worker working with an immigrant family may encounter many ethical dilemmas. If such a social worker represents an established medical institution, should she or he insist that the family adopt the Western approach to health care? It should be noted that the practice of Western medicine is continuously changing. Recently there has been a resurgence of interest in a holistic approach to health care, which may include the use of herbal medicine and acupuncture. Many common illnesses are now thought to be caused by viruses, for which the most frequent medical advice is to rest and drink hot beverages. Indeed, most Americans' approach to health care combines prescribed medicines and folk remedies.

The new Code of Ethics stresses that social workers should "have a knowledge base of their clients' cultures and be able to show competence in the provision of services that are sensitive to clients' cultures and to differences between people and cultural groups" (NASW, 1996, p. 9). This is especially important for medical social workers, who frequently interact with clients from diverse cultures.

In a previous article the author suggested the following guidelines to promote ethical practice among medical social workers whose clients have different beliefs about health (Congress and Lyons, 1992):

1. Increase one's sensitivity to culturally diverse beliefs by respecting the uniqueness of each client (Lowy, 1985) and become aware of how one's own biases may affect one's work with culturally diverse clients. Assessment tools such as the ethnic sensitive inventory (Ho, 1991) or the culturagram (Congress, 1994) may help the social worker understand cultural differences.

2. Become acquainted with clients' beliefs about health, disease, and treatment. Social workers must guard against judging clients' beliefs about health and health care. Bilingual and bicultural staff can help the social worker learn about different cultural attitudes toward these issues.

3. Avoid stereotyping and emphasize individual differences in diagnostic assessments. Even people who have been in the United States the same length of time, are the same age, and have the same socioeconomic status may have different and often conflicting beliefs about health care. Individuals may combine the use of the U.S. health care system, their own ethnic healers, prayer, self-help groups, chiropractors, and remedies recommended by their families and friends (McGoldrick, Pearce, and Giordano, 1997).

4. Enable culturally diverse clients to make choices. Poor clients often have only limited access to medical care or none at all. This situation may become worse, because under welfare reform many poor families have lost medical coverage. Furthermore, reform of immigration laws has meant that health benefits are denied to many legal as well as undocumented immigrants. In the face of all these changes, the responsibility of the professional social worker is to help clients receive the health care of their choice.

5. Help other health care professionals understand cultural differences in beliefs about health issues. Interdisciplinary committees (chapter 11) can be a forum for social workers to discuss with other health care professionals the cultural beliefs of their clients. While acquainting other health care team members with the various beliefs, social workers can also encourage integrated approaches to health care that promote the physical and emotional health of clients.

6. Advocate understanding and accepting diverse health beliefs in the health care facility and in the larger community. Social workers have a role as culture mediators within the health care setting (Fandetti and Goldmeier, 1988). With their understanding of cultural differences they can advocate that cultural beliefs be incorporated into treatment plans. On a macrolevel, social workers can also advocate for the development of more sensitive policies

in hospitals and clinics, as well as in the larger political system. As health care becomes increasingly dominated by managed care, social workers have a responsibility to advocate that the treatment accepted by managed-care companies take into consideration cultural differences in health care.

Managed Care

Managed-care systems have greatly altered the delivery of health care in this country. Many aspects of managed care, however, are not new and in fact have long been espoused by social workers. First, managed care's primary emphasis on prevention has always been stressed in social work. For example, social workers have frequently organized groups for adolescents in high schools in an attempt to prevent substance abuse or pregnancy. Managed-care companies often sponsor programs on topics such as good nutrition and exercise to avoid hypertension and diabetes. Second, the focus of managed care on providing the least restrictive environment is also acceptable to social workers, who emphasize the development of clients' own strengths and resources. Social workers in hospitals have frequently been involved in discharge planning, which enables them to help clients find the best and least restrictive environment. Finally, the *raison d'etre* of managed care, to contain the rising cost of medical care, is compatible with the profession of social work. Social workers concur that efficiency (achieving one's goals in the most economical way possible) is an appropriate goal for the delivery of health service, as long as effectiveness (how well a program achieves its goals) is not sacrificed.

Social workers in managed care have been described as "cost-effective coordinators of care, balancing patient and organizational needs" and as direct providers of service inasmuch as they "provide psychosocial assessments, care coordination, and planning, counseling on adjustment to physical and mental illness, and mental health counseling and treatment for patients and their families in medical and psychiatric settings" (NASW, 1995, p. 5).

Social workers, however, are concerned that under managed care needy clients will be denied treatment. There are many disheartening stories about clients being injured or even dying because health care services in a managed-care environment were curtailed. NASW, as well as other professional groups, are attempting to document some of these incidents to use in future advocacy efforts. Some states, including New York, have adopted a consumer protection law for patients in managed-care programs. Social workers have an obligation to continue to advocate for clients to ensure that they are not denied needed health care by their managed-care program. Millions of Americans do not have any health coverage, and social workers have an additional responsibility to advocate for health care for all in need. Poor people covered by Medicaid managed care often seem to be most at risk in a managed-care environment. The New York City chapter of NASW has made the following recommendations for problematic areas in Medicaid managed care:

1. Medicaid managed-care enrollment plans do not permit enough choice. It is vital to inform consumers of their rights to health benefits, to disenroll, and to change providers.
2. Waiting times for appointments with physicians need to be monitored to ensure that there are enough doctors to meet patients' needs within a reasonable time.
3. Homeless families should not be required to enroll in managed-care programs because access to a health facility in a particular location may be limited.
4. Medicaid managed-care consumers must be able to receive necessary emergency hospital care.
5. Special populations such as pregnant women must be allowed to receive prenatal care, and school-aged children must have access to health care in schools.
6. Medicaid managed-care consumers must be able to receive community mental health services.
7. Social work services should be included in managed-care plans.

The ethical response to issues raised by managed care will continue to challenge social workers in the twenty-first century.

CHAPTER 8

Ethical Dilemmas in Group and Family Work

An increasing number of social workers work with groups and families. But social workers are more likely to say that they engage in a variety of activities rather than in only individual, group, or community work (Ginsberg, 1995). In schools of social work, group work is usually studied as part of the overall curriculum rather than separately. A recent unpublished survey of MSW students by the author indicates that the majority had at least one group experience in their field placements.

Similarly, the number of social workers who confine themselves to family therapy is small, but family-oriented social work (Hartman and Laird, 1983) is continually stressed in social work education and practice. Furthermore, the shift in the child welfare field from a child to a family approach has increased social workers' exposure to this area.

The social worker may face many ethical issues and dilemmas in working with groups and families, but the Code of Ethics gives little consideration to these areas. The current code has only three sections that relate to group and/or family work. The first addresses informed consent:

> When social workers provide services to two or more people who have a relationship with each other (for example, couples, family members), social workers should clarify with all parties which individuals will be considered clients and the nature of social workers' professional obligations to the various individuals who are receiving services. (NASW, 1996, p. 10)

The other two relevant sections relate to confidentiality:

> When social workers provide counseling services to families, couples, or groups, social workers should seek agreement among the parties involved concerning each individual's right to confidentiality and obligation to preserve the confidentiality of information shared by others. Social workers should inform participants in family, couples, or group counseling that social workers cannot guarantee that all participants will honor such agreements.

> Social workers should inform clients involved in family, couples, marital, or group counseling of the social worker's employer's and agency's policy concerning the social worker's disclosure of confidential information among the parties involved in the counseling. (NASW, 1996, p. 11)

A review of the literature on group work and ethics also indicates that there has been little attention to group work (Dolgoff and Skolnik, 1992, 1996; Konopka, 1978; Kurland and Salmon, 1992; Skolnik and Attinson, 1978).

A major ethical concern for group workers is confidentiality. Sometimes potential group members may fear joining a group because of the possibility that group members will share personal information with non-group members. When the author once recommended to a depressed client that she join a mutual aid group of Hispanic women in a community mental health clinic, the client refused, saying that she would not want anyone outside the group to "know her business," that is, that her husband was having an affair with a woman who lived down the street.

In the early stages of group therapy, members often question who will find out what is shared in group. While the group leader is bound by professional ethics regarding confidentiality, this is not true of members. Some inexperienced group leaders feel uncomfortable with their inability to promise confidentiality and ignore the issue. However, the social worker is advised to discuss confidentiality early with clients (Cohen and Phillips, 1995) and to inform clients that he or she cannot guarantee that all members will maintain confidentiality (NASW, 1996).

There are times when the group leader may have to violate confidentiality, as the following case example suggests.

In the sixth session of a short-term therapy group for depressed women, a group member, Sandra, tells the group that the night before she had become so angry at her four-year-old son that she could not stop hitting him. Fortunately, her sister arrived and intervened. The social worker, Darlene, had promised members that whatever they said to the group would remain in the room. During this discussion she had also mentioned that there might be times when she would have to violate confidentiality, such as in the case of suspected child abuse, because she was mandated to report such incidents. Thus, breaching confidentiality in this case is not a dilemma for her, because she had already advised the group that she would report incidents of child abuse. Because of her respect for Sandra, however, Darlene asks her to remain after the group had left so that Darlene could discuss a referral to protective services.

Sometimes the social worker, however, faces an ethical challenge to confidentiality that is not easily resolved, as this incident indicates:

Sam, a certified social worker, conducts a group for batterers. One of his clients, Joe, has a history of violence toward his wife. In fact, the last incident, which happened three months ago, resulted in Joe's wife's hospitalization for a concussion and a thirty-day jail sentence for him. Since that incident he has repeatedly stated to the group that he has changed and that he will never hurt his wife again. But in the latest group meeting, Joe says that he is very angry because he has heard that his wife has received a bonus at work which she has not shared with him. Joe promises that when he saw her again, he will tell her a thing or two. When questioned if he will resort to violence, Joe says no, that he does not want to go to jail again. Sam, however, is very uneasy because he feels that Joe has a propensity for violence. At the group's first meeting, the issue of confidentiality was discussed, and Sam had said that he would not violate confidentiality unless there was a clear and present danger to another. To resolve this issue, Sam discusses the case with his supervisor and then calls Joe in for a separate, individual session.

Sometimes group members raise the concern that confidentiality will be violated, while at other times this issue remains hidden until a crisis occurs, as the following example illustrates.

A young social worker, Paula, leads a discussion group for girls at a public high school. From the very beginning Paula has spoken to group members about the importance of confidentiality, but she has always feared that confidentiality will be jeopardized because of the power of adolescent peer relationships. Her fear is realized the day that only two girls, rather than the usual seven, attend the group. Paula explores reasons for her group's diminished attendance. During the last session a sixteen-year-old, Pat, who previously had been very withdrawn, shared that she had had a lesbian relationship the previous summer with a girl she met at camp. Several of the girls stated that although they had never been attracted to women, they felt this relationship was Pat's decision, and they were glad that she had told them about it.

After the meeting one of the girls told her adult cousin, who happened to work with Pat's mother. Pat's mother pulled her out of the group because she feared that the group was encouraging Pat to do "bad things." But why had the other members not returned? At first Paula thinks that the reason is fear of contagion, that the other girls, struggling with their own developing sexual identities, are fearful of lesbian activity. However, Paula speaks to one of the absentees and learns that the real issue is the betrayal of confidentiality. The group members fear that intimate secrets they share with the group will not remain confidential. A crucial issue in adolescent groups involves not sharing information with parents. Paula knows that she told the group at the beginning that any member who violated confidentiality would not be able to return to the group. This issue is much more serious, though, and Paula fears that she will never be able to reconstitute the group because the girls' fragile trust in confidentiality has been broken.

Confidentiality—Task Groups

Social workers see a growing number of clients in task rather than treatment groups, especially with the increased attention that community action, consumer empowerment, and self-help groups have received during the last decade. While treatment groups focus on clients' problems and interactions, task groups focus on formulating group goals and developing an agenda to accomplish them. Confidentiality is rarely if ever discussed in task groups, which can have problematic consequences, as the following example illustrates.

Lisa, a professional social worker, helped organize tenants in an apartment building to improve security and living conditions. Because it is an open-ended task group, she never thought to discuss confidentiality. The tenants decide that the only way to make the landlord be more responsible to them is to organize a rent strike. The fifteen-year-old daughter of a tenant, however, tells a friend (who happens to be the landlord's daughter) about the impending strike, which greatly reduces its effectiveness.

Confidentiality is an issue not only for members of a task group, but also for the social worker, as in the following example.

> John is involved in helping a community organize a special day-long event. One member of the planning committee, Ben, repeatedly comes to meetings intoxicated. John knows that this man is a school bus driver and is concerned about the safety of the children he drives. John, however, is afraid of violating confidentiality if he shares this information with the bus company. Fortunately, another group member who is a member of AA recognizes Ben's alcohol problem and encourages Ben to seek help.

The following guidelines can help social workers struggling with ethical conflicts in task groups (Congress and Lynn, 1997):

1. Reveal personal values and biases that might impact on one's role as group social worker. Ethical guidelines for group counselors suggest the need for them to expose beliefs and values if these might affect the work of the group. Also, these beliefs and values should not be imposed on group members (Toseland and Rivas, 1995). Potential members need to know the values of the group that they are joining. They should feel free not to join the group or to leave the group without peer pressure. Including all of the above-mentioned factors in developing a contract with the group could prevent conflicts of interest.

2. Be explicit in discussing confidentiality issues with task groups. Detrimental consequences of breaches of confidence in task groups suggest that confidentiality is important for task groups and should be explicitly discussed.

3. Develop a norm of confidentiality within groups. Members of task groups are not bound by professional codes of ethics in regard to confidentiality. In order to facilitate the operation of the group, confidentiality, as much as attendance and participation, needs to be developed as a norm.

4. Be explicit in informing members about the benefits and costs of joining the group. Discussing both costs and benefits of group membership promotes honesty and openness and models these behaviors for group members.

5. Facilitate understanding of individual, group, and societal needs. Differences between members should be discussed openly. Hidden agendas of members and leaders alike need to be brought to light in order to facilitate communication and growth within the group.

6. Operationalize values of democracy and self-determination. Fundamental principles of democracy are that all voices shall be heard and all have the right to participate. Leaders of task groups must model participation and promote self-determination, even when members participate in a way that the group leader does not expect.

Privileged Communication in Groups

Privileged communication is a legal concept protecting the right of clients to withhold testimony in a court case. Only the client can waive the right to privileged communication, thus ensuring that private communications between therapist and client will remain confidential. Almost all states recognize privileged communication between social worker and client, and in 1996 it was affirmed by the Supreme Court.

Traditionally, communication has been interpreted as privileged only if a third party is not present. This implies that clients in group, couple, or family therapy could not benefit from the right to privileged communication. Some states, however, have extended this privilege to apply when a third party is present, if the party is crucial to the treatment (Vandecreek, Knapp, and Herzog, 1988). The social worker has the responsibility to learn the laws surrounding privileged communication and third parties in his or her state.

Clients may waive their right to privileged communication. A client who requests that a social worker discuss in court what transpired in group treatment may have waived the right to privileged communication, but other group members have not.

Melinda, a group social worker, has been asked to testify in a court case about her client Sharon's request to have her children returned to her. Sharon has waived the right to privileged communication because she feels that Melinda's testimony about her participation in group will help her case. But Melinda has difficulty discussing Sharon's progress in the group without mentioning the support of another member, Dolores. Dolores has not given Melinda permission to reveal that she is in group therapy. With Sharon's permission, Melinda resolves this issue by explaining her dilemma to the group. All group members, including Dolores, then give Melinda permission to discuss in court their group participation.

Informed Consent

The concept of informed consent began in the medical field with the increased emphasis on patients' right to know their diagnosis and prognosis, the nature of their intended treatment, and its benefits and risks. In social work, informed consent takes place during the contracting period, when the social worker discusses with the client the "purposes of the services, risks related to the services, limits to services because of the requirements of a third-party payer, relevant costs, reasonable alternatives, clients' rights to refuse or withdraw consent, and the time frame covered by the consent" (NASW, 1996, p. 8).

Informed consent is often ignored in therapy, especially group therapy. Many social workers fear that sharing too much about the nature of group therapy may interfere with the treatment process. Furthermore, social workers who have mixed feelings of anger and guilt about managed care may be especially reluctant to tell clients about limits to services because of the requirements of third-party payers. But providing for informed consent should be an important goal for therapists working with all types of groups. There is some evidence that informed consent, especially regarding the goals of treatment, is rarely discussed in children's groups (Shulman, 1992a).

The new Code of Ethics includes a provision about obtaining clients' informed consent before audio- or videotaping clients (NASW, 1996, p. 8). Obtaining informed consent from all group members may be particularly challenging, as the following example shows.

Michelle, an experienced group worker, wants to increase her skills in working with special populations. Recently she started a bereavement group for people who have lost partners or family members to AIDS. Realizing that her own countertransference feelings might interfere with her work, she wants to make a videotape so that she can review her interactions with group members with her supervisor. All but one member of the group agree to the taping. Michelle decides that she cannot ethically tape the group, even if only one member out of the seven objects.

Self-Determination

Self-determination has always been considered one of the most important principles of social work. With the current focus on identifying clients' strengths, self-determination has been increasingly emphasized. As already has been stated, the new Code of Ethics describes self-determination as integral to the inherent dignity and worth of the person. But while the current code stresses the right of clients to self-determination, it states that limits may be placed on self-determination "when clients' actions or potential actions pose a serious, foreseeable, and imminent risk to themselves or others" (NASW, 1996, p. 7). The mutual-aid model in group work especially stresses the importance of clients' self-determination in formulating and working toward goals (Shulman, 1992a). Other authors on the theory of group work have also stressed the importance of self-determination (Kurland and Salmon, 1992; Toseland and Rivas, 1995). Much discussion has focused on the question of what happens when the therapist disagrees with the group. Should the therapist be able to prevail over the group?

Another major question that is less often addressed in the literature is whether self-determination applies equally to all members of a group. For example, groups usually establish a structure and rules to protect against physical acting out. Furthermore, the new code instructs social workers that self-determination cannot be maintained with clients who threaten to harm others.

There are many issues involving self-determination that are not addressed in the code, as this example suggests.

A support group for single parents has been meeting for the last five weeks. During tonight's meeting Joan, a very withdrawn member, finally begins to share her feelings about being deserted by her husband after a ten-year marriage. Several group members, however, are somewhat disparaging of Joan's presentation and try to divert the discussion to other topics. The group worker, Gail, is undecided about how to proceed. Should she allow the group to self-determine in a way that she thinks might not be helpful to Joan? Another ethical challenge occurs the following week when Joan wants to talk about a recent stormy discussion with her ex-husband, and another member focuses on her finding out that her child will have to repeat first grade. Which member has the greater right to self-determine the agenda, especially considering that group work is based on the democratic principle of the equal participation of all?

Group workers' decisions about whose self-determination to promote are even more challenging in task groups. Task groups are usually more open-ended and heterogenous, with the group worker having less control over group membership because members select themselves by reason of a shared problem or location. Sometimes a dilemma arises when a member who self-determines to join a group has a negative effect on the group interaction, as the following case example illustrates.

> Terry, a group social worker, organized a group of parents in a poor community to plan a youth center. As one member, Rhonda, sees it, the main purpose of the youth center should be to provide services such as baby-sitting and welfare advocacy for herself and her family rather than recreational facilities for young people. Because Rhonda is so powerful, she is able to sway the group from its original purpose. Terry has difficulty in countering the self-determination of this one member.

Social Control versus Respect for the Individual

The conflict between social care versus social control is not new. While some have focused on the humanitarian concern of social work to help vulnerable and oppressed populations, others have pointed out that social workers often act as agents of social control. This conflict is certainly evident in group work. While self-determination and autonomy may be acknowledged in therapy groups, leaders of groups made up of mandated clients and/or vulnerable populations often set hidden agendas. For example, the leader of a ceramic group in a day treatment program, an exercise group in a prison, or a music group in a senior center may have social objectives that he or she does not acknowledge and share with clients. This may result in undue pressure on clients, especially in mandated settings, to participate in groups. In these situations, refusing to join a group may result in unforeseen consequences for the decliner. The ethical social worker must continually examine how much the client has the right to self-determine to join and participate in mandated groups.

Family Treatment

Social work education and practice stress a family approach. Social workers are urged to consider the whole family in assessment and treatment. However, many aspects of social work contradict a family approach. Offices are small and often shared, diagnostic assessments and treatment plans are developed for individual clients, short sessions of thirty minutes or less are encouraged, financial reimbursement may cover only one family member, and finally, most managed-care plans do not recognize family treatment.

Nevertheless, a growing number of social workers deal with families or parts of families. Family treatment is certainly consistent with social workers' ecosystemic approach, which holds that individuals affect and are affected by those around them.

Family treatment is perhaps more ethically challenging than any other, mainly because social workers' family values differ so markedly. Almost all social workers have grown up in families. But social workers may have limited awareness of how their families have affected their perceptions. They may try to recreate with clients a family system that they are familiar with or would have wanted for themselves. A study of child welfare workers demonstrated that placement decisions often relate to the family structure of the social worker (Morrison, 1995). The following example illustrates this issue.

> Geraldine, a professional social worker, was recently assigned a young family that has been experiencing much conflict. Twenty-four-year-old Mr. Green has a semiskilled job in a factory; his wife is a clerk at an all-night grocery store. Their four children range in age from six years to six months. The couple married at eighteen when Mrs. Green was six months pregnant. They have been fighting ever since. During family therapy both Mr. and Mrs. Green say that they think the best plan would be to separate.
>
> Geraldine, however, is determined to settle the couple's differences and keep them together. After several months of therapy, there seems to be little change. At first Geraldine thinks that if she knew more she could help the family, so she enrolls in several workshops on family therapy. She then consults with a well-known family therapist, who suggests that her own values might be influencing her work with this family. Geraldine realizes that she is trying to impose her ideal of family on the Greens. Her father deserted her mother when she was six, and Geraldine, the oldest of three children, had witnessed her mother's struggles as a single parent. Geraldine has often thought that her childhood would have been easier if she had had a two-parent home. She finally realizes that she is trying to create with the Greens the family that she wished she had had as a child.

Social workers in family therapy should first examine their own family values. Some questions they should ask themselves are:

1. What was my family like?
2. What do I think an ideal family should be?

3. How does my image of an ideal family and my remembrance of my own family differ from this family?
4. What are the goals and values of the family I am working with?
5. What does this family want for itself?

Culturally Diverse Families

Therapists working with families that are culturally and economically different from them are less likely to have the same values as their clients and more likely to impose inappropriate personal/societal values on them (Congress, 1994). Many social workers have been raised, socialized, and educated in an individualistic approach to families. According to this view, children need the family's support during their early years, but once they reach school age they should become much more independent. But many cultures see families as important, essential sources of support throughout life. Often families espousing this value are accused of promoting enmeshment, contributing to school phobias, or developing parental children.

Conflicts often arise in culturally diverse families when adolescents adopt the American value of independence, while parents try to impose the familial values of their backgrounds. In such cases social workers are most at risk of siding with adolescents against their parents. In addition to being unethical, this behavior may lead to the family abandoning treatment, as this example illustrates.

Joanne, a beginning family therapist, is counseling Mrs. Sanchez and her sixteen-year-old daughter, Maria. Mrs. Sanchez wants Maria to come home immediately after school to help with the housework and the care of her baby brother, while Maria wants to visit and shop with her girlfriends. Joanne sees this family as a perfect opportunity to educate Mrs. Sanchez, who emigrated from the Dominican Republic three years ago, about American customs. She tells Mrs. Sanchez that in the United States, adolescent girls need to strengthen their relationships with their peers and that Maria should be allowed to socialize daily with her friends after school. Joanne never sees the Sanchez family again.

Even the most experienced therapists find it a struggle to balance the needs of the individual against those of the family. What if one partner wants to divorce and the other does not? Who speaks for the family and can best articulate familial needs?

This author faced a challenging ethical dilemma based on conflicting needs when she was counseling a seventeen-year-old boy, Juan, and his mother. The boy had just won a full scholarship to attend a prestigious college a thousand miles from his home. Because of health problems, the mother believed that Juan, her only child, should stay close to home. From an individualistic perspective, one might want to encourage Juan to accept the scholarship and pursue this wonderful educational opportunity. But listening to both family members made it clear that the familial need was for Juan to attend a college closer to home.

Confidentiality Conflicts within Families

While an early family therapist, Nathan Ackerman, stressed that family therapy is most effective when all family members are seen together, social workers now accept that often family members may be counseled individually, either by choice or by necessity. In either case, maintaining confidentiality may challenge the social worker. At the beginning of therapy, family therapists often set guidelines about how confidential information shall be handled (Huber, 1994). Some therapists refuse to talk to individual members between sessions. Others talk to individual members but insist that issues discussed must be brought up in therapy sessions. Still others maintain confidentiality for individual family members when they are being counseled both individually and in the family group.

Because of the increase in single-parent families, differing work schedules of family members, and a family approach within individual client focus settings, social workers are now more likely to counsel only certain family members. What ethical responsibility does the social worker have to family members who do not participate in family therapy? Does the social worker have an obligation to protect the confidentiality of family members who are not in therapy but who provide information?

The new Code of Ethics specifies that social workers should "clarify with all parties which individuals should be considered clients and the nature of social workers' professional obligations to the various individuals who are receiving services" (NASW, 1996, p. 10). The following example demonstrates one type of dilemma that may arise.

Charlene, a school social worker, is counseling John Allen, a seven-year-old boy, who demonstrates acting-out behavior in school. Also, his ten-year-old sister, Doris, has problems in completing her schoolwork. Because both these children began to show problems in school just this year, Charlene suspects that there is a problem at home. When

Charlene talks with the mother, she learns that the children's father left the family suddenly at the beginning of the school year but is still living in the neighborhood.

Charlene begins to counsel John Allen, Doris, and their mother, Ann Marie, as a family group. She tells the family that she would like to contact the father, Michael, but Ann Marie opposes this idea. Suddenly, Michael calls Charlene to set her straight about what the "real" problem is. He tells Charlene that Ann Marie was abusive to him and once threw a pot at him. Michael asks Charlene not to share this information. Charlene notes that both Michael and Ann Marie want secrecy and suspects that the conspiracy of silence contributed to the family breakup.

Charlene had discussed confidentiality with the family members she is counseling and developed the policy that if one of them shared a secret with her individually, then he or she was obliged to share the information at a family session. But Charlene realizes that Michael is not a client and that she had not discussed confidentiality with him in the same way that she had with the other family members. She shares what she learned from Michael at a family session. This leads to Ann Marie's acknowledgment that she had been out of control recently in disciplining the children. Charlene discusses the possibility of referring the case to child protective services, because she had made clear to Ann Marie and the other family members at the beginning of treatment that she was mandated to report suspected child abuse.

CHAPTER 9

Ethical Dilemmas in Aging

The following example illustrates some ethical issues and dilemmas that may arise in working with older persons.

Mrs. Turner, eighty years old, recently moved to the suburbs to live with her fifty-year-old daughter Susan, Susan's husband Tom, and their twenty-year-old daughter Rose. Susan has another daughter, Dawn, who is thirty years old and lives nearby with her two-year-old daughter. Mrs. Turner left her apartment in the city, where she had lived for forty years, because the landlord was vacating the building to build condominiums. Mrs. Turner had thought briefly about going into an adult residence but decided she wanted to live closer to her family. Although Mrs.Turner walks with a cane because of arthritis, overall she is in good health. Tom thinks that his mother-in-law will want to spend her days at home, reading and knitting. "She's had a very full life; now it's time for her to just take it easy, " he says. Susan sees an advertisement in a local paper about a senior citizen center that offers transportation and thinks her mother might enjoy spending time there. Rose reports that there is a college-at-sixty program in the community college that Mrs. Turner might like to try. Dawn hopes that her grandmother will help her with child care, especially because she is eager to return to work.

Tom seems to subscribe to an early theory on aging—the disengagement theory (Cumming and Henry, 1961), which suggests that as people age they become less and less interested in pursuing their usual roles and activities and begin to withdraw from society. An important question is: to what extent is disengagement the older person's choice? Often older people have diminished opportunities to remain active. Mrs. Turner was forced from the apartment she had lived in for many years. Her severe arthritis prevents her from participating in many physical activities. Because of mandatory retirement at age seventy she was forced to leave her job as a store clerk, which she had for many years. In the suburbs, where public transportation is limited, Mrs. Turner, who never learned to drive, is unable to pursue many activities taking place in the community. Is Mrs. Turner disengaged by force or by choice?

What guidance on working with older persons does the Code of Ethics provide ? Older people are mentioned specifically only once in the code in a section that speaks against discrimination: "Social workers should act to prevent and eliminate domination of, exploitation of, and discriminating against any person, group, or class on the basis of . . . age" (NASW, 1996, pp. 22–23).

Our society's orientation toward youth has been well documented. The most cursory glance at popular magazines and television programs reveals that most of the people portrayed are younger than fifty. Not only are older people ignored, but also social workers and others often have negative reactions to older persons, and students of social work frequently do not choose to work with them (Gutheil, 1994).

While older people now make up 12 percent of the population, this proportion will double early in the twenty-first century. The very old (those eighty-five and older) are the fastest-growing segment of the population over sixty-five (U.S. Senate, 1988).

Who are older people and what are their needs? Although there has been an increase in segregated housing for the elderly (senior residences, adult communities), many older people prefer to live with their families. However, the percentage of older people who live with their families has declined dramatically, from 30 percent in 1950 to 15 percent in 1989 (Tepper, 1994). It was usually assumed that culturally diverse elders live with their families, but recent research suggests otherwise (Lockery, 1991). But families with older members often lack social supports as the above example indicates. Older people who live in urban areas can usually remain more active because of public transportation (Cantor and Garland, 1993). While Mrs. Turner may not prefer to sit in a rocking chair and knit all day, living in a suburban community where almost everyone either works or goes to school may force her to disengage.

Mrs. Turner's daughter Susan sees activity as crucial to her mother's well-being. She could encourage her mother to join the senior citizen center that provides transportation. Critiques of activity theory, however, would argue that activity is not always valuable for the older person. The older person may find that making ceramic bowls in a senior arts and craft class is demeaning and boring. The college-at-sixty program may be seen by some as more enriching and worthwhile. But this type of program suggests that older persons have special needs that are not met by a regular college program.

Traditionally, older people have been involved in child care, and this role for older people is increasingly important because most women with children under five now work outside the home. Also, with the current

HIV/AIDS epidemic, more older people are assuming primary care of children (Cohen, 1997).

A new theory on aging—the substitution theory—builds upon the disengagement and activity theories. Tepper suggests that "previous personality, likes and dislikes, physical and mental health, attitudes toward . . . social and work roles, and identities which are especially rewarding are important to consider in working with older persons" (Tepper, 1994, p. 38). The importance of this theory is that it builds on social work values. Very often, well-meaning family members and professionals make decisions for older people that they can make for themselves. In the above example, each family member has a plan for Mrs. Turner, and no family member has specifically asked her what she would like to do.

Ethical social work with older persons begins with the client. All too often social workers adopt a paternalistic attitude toward older persons. Physical infirmity does not mean that clients are not able to make decisions for themselves. Nursing homes have long had the reputation of limiting individual rights. Residents are often denied the right to make daily decisions about what they eat or wear, choices that the average person makes every day. Taking a "values history" often helps workers in nursing homes assess the true preferences of the older person (Collopy and Bial, 1994).

Ethical Dilemmas in Home Care

Most older persons, however, receive home care rather than institutional care. Living in the community rather than in an institution suggests more freedom. But while there may be "emboldened autonomy" in community care, autonomy is often eroded (Collopy, Dubler, and Zuckerman, 1990). Will Mrs. Turner be less able to exercise autonomy living with her family? Susan has already told her mother that the stores are too crowded for her to get around with her cane and that Susan will go be herself to buy a coat for her mother.

While social workers have an ethical responsibility to promote clients self-determination, this value can be especially problematic in working with older people. What if the older person wants to engage in behavior that is potentially dangerous? For example, what if a social worker in a home-care program is asked to buy cigarettes for an older person who has serious circulatory problems (Congress and Chernesky, 1993).

Elder Abuse

Preserving self-determination is particularly challenging in cases of elder abuse. Elder abuse involves physical abuse, psychological abuse, and/or financial abuse (Wolf and Pillemer, 1984). While elder abuse affects 12 percent of the elderly population (U.S. House of Representatives, 1990), only one of every six victims may come to the attention of social service agencies. Social workers may be more aware of child abuse than of elder abuse. The following case example and questions help the social worker compare and contrast elder abuse with child abuse.

Georgina works in a multiservice community-based social service agency. One day when assigned to intake she sees two clients, a twelve-year-old girl and a seventy-five-year-old woman.

The twelve-year-old, Sabrina, came to the agency to sign up for a summer camp program. She seems well adjusted, appropriately dressed, and reports no problems at home or school. The social worker notices a large bruise on her upper arm. When questioned, Sabrina first reports that she fell off her bicycle. Georgina is suspicious, though, because she knows that children often conceal abuse. Finally Sabrina reveals that her mother hit her last night when she did not want to do the dishes. At first she did not want to tell Georgina as she had heard that social workers take children away if their parents hit them. Overall, Sabrina reports that she is very happy at home. She indicates that her mother had only hit her out of stress caused by her father's leaving the family two years ago.

The second client, Mrs. Brown, came to ask about a Meals-on-Wheels program. She seems very competent and able to handle most of her activities very independently. Mrs. Brown tells Georgina that she has lived with her divorced daughter and her three teenaged grandchildren since her husband died five years before. Her daughter works long hours, and the children are usually out with their friends or at their father's home, and it is difficult to prepare her own meals. Georgina notices that Mrs. Brown has a large bruise on her arm which Mrs. Brown attributes to bruising easily and falling against her bed. At first Georgina accepts the explanation, but then notes that Mrs. Brown had looked down and seemed very depressed when talking about her bruise. Finally, Mrs. Brown confides that her daughter struck her. She indicates that she does not want to get her daughter in trouble and that her daughter had struck her only out of stress caused by financial problems and conflict with her ex-husband.

The following questions can be raised:

1. Should Georgina contact the alleged abusers, the daughter of the seventy-five-year-old woman and the mother of the twelve-year-old girl, even though both clients have insisted that she not?
2. Do these cases indicate elder abuse? Child abuse? Should the case involving the twelve-year-old girl be reported to child protective services? Should the case involving the seventy-five-year-old woman be reported?
3. Should the case be reported if the elder abuser were a home care aide or a neighbor?
4. Should social workers be mandated to report elder abuse?

Does the Code of Ethics provide protection from abuse for older persons? The current code calls for maintaining confidentiality unless laws or regulations mandate otherwise. Adult protective service programs supported by state statutes protect impaired adults from abuse and neglect under the *parens patriae* doctrine. Thus the Code of Ethics would allow social workers to intervene in cases where there is serious mental impairment.

What about cases of elder abuse, such as in the above example, in which the client (Mrs. Brown) is endangered but does not have a serious mental impairment? All fifty states have laws mandating social workers to report cases of suspected child abuse and neglect. Why are social workers not mandated to report elder abuse? The main reason is that children are legal dependents, while adults, including older persons, have the right to privacy and self-determination. Thus, unless they are judged incompetent by the courts, older adults have the right to live in whatever circumstances they choose (Brownell, 1994). No matter how abusive the situation is, the government does not have the right to intervene unless the older person requests it. All programs for the elderly abused are voluntary. If Mrs. Brown does not want Georgina to contact her daughter or others, the social worker has to maintain confidentiality. The social worker has a vital role in educating older persons about the nature of elder abuse and about the programs that can offer family support. The American Association of Retired Persons (AARP) can provide important information to elderly victims of abuse and their families (AARP, 1987).

Older people such as Mrs. Brown often minimize the abuse they endure because they do not want outsiders to learn about family stress and conflict. Elder abuse is similar to situations of domestic violence involving younger adults; social workers must afford older persons the same rights to privacy and confidentiality, even if they choose to live in an abusive situation.

Elder abuse is on the increase, with more older persons living longer in the community. Chronic health problems that require more intensive care can result in abuse, as can the stress in families that have limited financial resources. Finally, more adults with chronic mental health problems are now living in the community with older parents, which may place the latter at greater risk for abuse. There is greater need for social workers to educate older persons and their families about the indications of and interventions for elder abuse.

Autonomy—Community Care

Living independently in the community seems to promote the autonomy of older people. The following example, however, illustrates some issues that might arise when an older person living alone has deteriorating health.

Ms. Collins is an eighty-four-year-old African-American woman who lives on Social Security benefits and a small pension. She has always been quite independent and has never needed any outside assistance. Within the last year she has fallen several times and sustained injuries. Since her last fall, she has been confined to a wheelchair and has home aide services for eight hours a day. Ms. Collins has had repeated conflicts with these home-care aides and is continually asking the agency for different workers. A neighbor who helped Ms. Collins with shopping recently moved out of the neighborhood. Ms. Collins was never married and has no children, relatives, or friends who can help her. The home-care agency believes that Ms. Collins is at grave risk if she remains alone at home and recommends that she be placed in an institution. Ms. Collins is mentally alert and does not want to leave the neighborhood where she has lived for the last seventy years. She insists that she can manage on her own. The doctor who treated Ms. Collins after her last injury believes that Ms. Collins's condition will not improve and that without supervision she might experience additional injuries with less probability of recovery. The doctor agrees with the agency that twenty-four-hour home care is necessary and that even that may not be adequate.

Brenda, the social worker who works for the home-care agency faces an ethical dilemma about how to handle Ms. Collins's case. She applies the ETHIC model, with the following results.

Examine relevant personal, social, agency, client, and profes-sional values. In examining her own personal values, Brenda recognizes that she has very mixed feelings about Ms. Collins remaining in the community. Her own grandmother, who lived with her family, sustained a serious hip fracture one day while the family was out shopping. Fortunately, her family returned soon after the accident. Brenda fears that if Ms. Collins injures herself, she will not get help for a long time. Brenda believes that older people with serious health problems are usu-ally better off in institutions, if family members are not available. She realizes that at times she has been very angry at Ms. Collins because she has been so critical of Brenda's many efforts to provide an acceptable home health aide. Brenda recognizes that many people have paternalistic attitudes toward older people. While a younger person with problems getting around can choose to live independently in their own apartment or even in the street, society often believes that they know what is best for the older client. Brenda also examines the values of the agency regarding this client. She knows that the agency is increasingly con-cerned about its liability if Ms. Collins should seriously injure herself while under agency supervision. She also knows that the agency has lim-ited resources when it comes to health-care aides, which makes Ms. Collins's frequent demands for a change in home-care aides more diffi-cult to accommodate. The client has made her values clear—she wants to maintain her independence. Professional values seem to support the client's right to self-determination if such a decision is "socially respon-sible" (NASW, 1996, p. 5).

Think about which ethical standard of the NASW Code of Ethics applies. The Code of Ethics supports clients' right to self-determination. Social workers should limit self-determination only when there is a "seri-ous, foreseeable, and imminent risk to themselves or others." Even though Ms. Collins is at some risk if she remains at home alone, Brenda is not sure how serious the risk is.

Hypothesize about different courses of action and possible conse-quences. Brenda develops different scenarios to analyze this ethical dilemma. In one scenario Ms. Collins is placed immediately in a nursing home. She becomes very depressed, stops eating, and dies within six months. Brenda knows that often older people do not fare well under institu-tional care, especially when they have lived independently for a long while. In another scenario Ms. Collins continues to live in her own home but with more home-care attendants. Ms. Collins is encouraged to participate more actively in the choice and direction of the home-care attendant assigned to her. In a third scenario the home-care agency continues to provide the same level of care. Ms. Collins falls and injures herself shortly after the home-care worker leaves and is found on the floor almost sixteen hours later. Her injuries require a hospital stay and subsequent placement in a nursing home.

Identify who will benefit and who will be harmed in view of social work's commitment to the most vulnerable. The person who will benefit the most will be Ms. Collins, who will be permitted to live out her years according to her wishes. Social workers have a professional commitment to support and advocate for those who are victims of discrimination. Ms. Collins is most at risk for paternalistic actions because she is triply stigmatized as a woman, as an older person, and as an African American (Congress and Johns, 1994).

Consult with supervisor and colleagues about the most ethical choice. Brenda discusses with her colleagues what they would do with this client. Some feel that a nursing home might be the best environment, while others propose that leaving her in her own home would be most helpful to her and most in keeping with social work ethics. One colleague knows about an inexpensive monitoring device that Ms. Collins could use to summon medical help if she needed it. Brenda also speaks to her supervisor, who informs her that the agency wants to do what is best for the client, even if it requires additional staff resources. Brenda learns that the agency has received a special grant to help clients choose home-care workers with whom they are most compatible.

After applying the ETHIC model of ethical decision making, Brenda believes that she is in a better position to arrive at the most ethical decision. She decides to support Ms.Collins's right to self-determine her own life. Ms. Collins remains in her own home, but home-care hours are increased to sixteen hours to provide greater coverage and security during Ms. Collins's waking hours. Ms. Collins is encouraged to participate more actively in choosing health-care workers, which greatly increases her willingness to have home-care workers. For the hours when no one is there, a monitoring device is installed so that she can get help if she needs it.

While the ethical dilemma is resolved for the time being, six months later new developments create a new ethical dilemma. The home health aides begin to report that Ms. Collins seems more confused. For example, after lunch one day she insisted that she had not had her lunch. The situation reached a crisis when the fire department was summoned to Ms. Collins's apartment early one morning because of a stove fire. She had put a pot of water on to boil and forgotten about it.

Brenda knows that she needs to reevaluate her earlier decision, especially in the light of the Code of Ethics. Previously she had assessed that providing self-determination to Ms. Collins did not "pose a serious, foreseeable, and imminent risk," but now she is not so sure. If the fire department had not arrived promptly, Ms. Collins could have been killed in the fire. The other tenants in the apartment building could also have been killed or seriously injured.

Brenda decides that she must take action to protect Ms. Collins and others. She begins to talk with Ms. Collins about different residential opportunities in the community. Consistent with social work values, Brenda seeks the living arrangement that would "enhance [Ms. Collins's] capacity and opportunity to . . . address [her] own needs" (NASW, 1996, p. 6). Brenda looks for the least restrictive environment and finds a small residential center that provides meals and individual rooms that is close to the community where Ms. Collins lives. She takes Ms. Collins to visit this facility and several other residences, thus permitting Ms. Collins to choose the one she prefers.

Culturally Diverse Older People

As American society becomes increasingly culturally diverse, so does the older population. What are some ethical issues and dilemmas that occur with an older culturally diverse population? Although older people may become acculturated less quickly than younger people because they are less likely to be in school or in places of employment, concluding that all older people have the beliefs of their countries of origin is incorrect (Gelfand and Yee, 1991). Stereotyping older people as unacculturated is not respectful of the inherent worth and dignity of older people. It is also both unethical and impractical in developing appropriate services for older people (Congress and Johns, 1994).

The social worker needs to assess the culture of the older person, and the culturagram provides a family assessment tool to help in this process (Congress, 1994). One issue that often emerges, especially when older persons live with their families, is intergenerational conflict. An older person may subscribe to the beliefs of his or her original culture, while younger family members may be more apt to follow the beliefs of the dominant American culture. In the following example, an intergenerational family with differing beliefs was counseled in a family service agency.

Sixty-five-year-old Mrs. Santiago and her fourteen-year-old granddaughter Carmen are having continual conflicts. Two years ago, Mrs. Santiago's daughter Gabriella had died of AIDS, and Mrs. Santiago assumed custody of her granddaughter and two other grandchildren, ages ten and five. Carmen wants to go out after school with her friends, but Mrs. Santiago believes that adolescent girls' primary responsibility is to the family and that Carmen should help after school with her younger siblings. Furthermore, she fears that if Carmen goes out too much, she might become involved with drugs as her mother had.

The social worker's first reaction is to agree with the granddaughter. The social worker, Karen, finds herself starting to tell Mrs. Santiago that in the United States adolescent girls usually socialize with friends after school. Furthermore, the social worker fears that Mrs. Santiago's proclamation that Carmen will end up just like her mother will become a self-fulfilling prophecy.

Karen knows that it is essential to respect the "dignity and worth of the person," including the belief systems of a culturally diverse, older person that differ from her own. She also recognizes the importance of promoting and strengthening the well-being of this family. Through family work, Karen is able to help each member speak freely about their beliefs and to work out a compromise in which Carmen is able to see her friends regularly and also provide some child care for her younger siblings.

Ethical Dilemmas for the Professional Social Worker: Dual Relationships and Impaired Colleagues

Both Janet and Jules are professional social workers employed by Somerset Mental Health and Substance Abuse clinic. Besides having a MSW, Jules is also a CAC; thus many clients with substance abuse as well as mental health problems are referred to him. Jules is in recovery and has been abstinent from alcohol for five years. Last year Jules separated from his wife and Janet knows that he has had reoccurring conflict over visitation and child support issues. She has become increasingly concerned that Jules frequently calls in sick on Mondays and often seems to have a cold.

About two months ago Jules was assigned a young single woman, Doreen, who had abused alcohol since she was a young adolescent. Doreen was sexually and physically abused as a child. Besides her alcohol problems, Doreen has been hospitalized for depression. Jules involved her in Alcoholics Anonymous, and Doreen has not been drinking for six weeks. Jules prides himself on her recovery. He often drives her home from AA meetings, which he also attends and she often calls him at work and on weekends to discuss different problems. Janet is concerned about two issues: (1) Jules's absenteeism may indicate a substance abuse problem, and (2) Jules may be too involved with his client.

Sexual Relationships— Law and Ethics

The Code of Ethics is specific about avoiding either forced or consensual sexual relationships with current, former, or future clients and with relatives or close friends of clients. This prohibition is based upon the concern that sexual activities with the therapist are harmful to the client and make it difficult to maintain appropriate professional boundaries. While most social workers concur that sexual contact with current clients is unethical, there is diverse opinion about the prohibition on sexual contact with former clients. Those who believe that sexual contact with former clients is permissible point out that it is demeaning to clients to believe that once a person is a client he or she is always a client. They argue that from the social work perspective of empowerment, clients are capable of self-determining their choices and can decide when and with whom to pursue a sexual relationship. An ongoing concern, however, is that clients do not exercise self-determination in entering into a sexual relationship with a former therapist. An element of coercion is always operative because of the unchanging disparity in power between client and therapist.

Despite the almost unanimous belief among social workers that sexual contact with clients is unethical (Borys and Pope, 1989), unfortunately there is evidence that social workers do engage in sexual relationships with their clients (Gechtman, 1989; Reamer, 1995a). Sexual contact with clients is not only unethical but also grounds for legal action, because in all states clients may sue for battery or malpractice and seven states consider sexual involvement with clients a felony (Kagle and Giebelhausen, 1994). Some states maintain that terminating therapy to begin a sexual relationship with a client does not end the liability of the practitioner.

Sexual Relationships— Former Clients

Professions differ as to whether they allow sexual relationships with former clients. Psychologists forbid sexual relationships with former clients, while marriage and family therapists specify a statute of limitations of two years. Until 1996 NASW did not have a specific prohibition against sexual relationships with former clients. The current code states that

> social workers should not engage in sexual contact with former clients because of the potential for harm to the clients. If social workers engage in conduct contrary to this prohibition or claim that an exception to this prohibition is warranted . . . it is social workers—not their clients—who assume the full burden of demonstrating that the former client has not been exploited, coerced, or manipulated, intentionally or unintentionally. (NASW, 1996, p. 13)

Some circumstances that might be considered mitigating are the amount of time that has passed since the termination of the therapist-client relationship, the client's competence and mental status, the nature of issues addressed in the therapist-client relationship, the duration of the therapist-client relationship, the circumstances surrounding termination, and the likelihood of harm to the client.

There may be some indications that Jules is headed toward a sexual relationship with his client, but this is unclear at the present time. It should be noted that he is in a high-risk situation. Jules has had serious personal problems in the past year, and there is some evidence that those who have experienced recent separations and loss are more likely to have difficulties maintaining appropriate boundaries (Dziech and Weiner, 1990).

Jules may be developing a social relationship with his client. This may be difficult to avoid, because Jules is in recovery and may be attending some of the same AA meetings as his client. But he seems to have overstepped the boundaries by driving her home from meetings and talking with her on weekends.

Impaired Colleagues

The NASW Code of Ethics' provision about impaired colleagues states:

> Social workers who have direct knowledge of a social work colleague's impairment which is due to personal problems, psychosocial distress, substance abuse, or mental health difficulties, and which interferes with practice effectiveness, should consult with that colleague when feasible and assist the colleague in taking remedial action. (NASW, 1996, p. 17)

The following physical signs and/or behavioral patterns have been linked with substance abuse in the workplace (Congress and Fewell, 1994).

Physical signs
>Drinking at the work site or smell of alcohol on breath
>Red face or bloodshot eyes
>Slurred speech
>Tremulous hands
>Time lag in verbal response
>Poor coordination
>Transient lethargy
>Watery eyes and sniffling
>Rapid speech
>Hyperactivity

Behavioral Patterns
>Erratic work performance or loss of interest in job; this may be inconsistent or alternate between under- and overproductivity.

Rapid changes in mood, especially after a coffee break or lunch

Absenteeism and lateness. Many employees with substance abuse problems may be late for work, leave early, take long lunches, and frequently be absent on Mondays, after long weekends, or because of vague complaints about health.

Instances of poor judgment and forgetfulness

Difficulty in concentration

Increasing suspiciousness

Acting seductively or otherwise inappropriately toward clients or colleagues

Lapses in attention to dress or hygiene

Frequently borrowing money from co-workers

While the presence of only one of the above behaviors may not indicate a substance abuse problem, social workers should be aware that they can be warning signs, especially if they depart from the colleague's prior behavior.

Social workers are often reluctant to speak to a colleague about a suspected problem. Similar to a family secret that all family members know but do not speak about openly, substance abuse by a staff member often becomes an agency secret. The literature on this topic has been scarce, and not until 1993 did a provision about impaired colleagues appear in the Code of Ethics, which may suggest a professional reluctance to address this issue.

Social workers are often very reluctant to approach peers who have a substance abuse problem. The local NASW chapter may suggest ways to talk with a colleague who denies having such a problem.

Janet has a professional responsibility to talk to Jules about his possible substance abuse. Denial is often the first defense of a drug abuser. Thus Jules may deny abusing drugs and use as an excuse that he has been sick every Monday with a variety of ailments ranging from colds or flu to stomach viruses. Earlier codes did not offer any advice about what Janet should do in that case. The new code, however, indicates that if the colleague who has been confronted about an apparent problem with drugs does not take "adequate steps to address the impairment [the social worker] should take action through appropriate channels established by employers, agencies, NASW, licensing and regulatory bodies, and other professional organizations" (NASW, 1996, p. 17). In agencies that have Employee Assistance Programs (EAP), the social worker may want to encourage the colleague to seek help from an EAP counselor. Sometimes NASW chapters have a peer consultation service, which can help a social worker find a way to talk to a colleague with a substance abuse problem. The outcome most in keeping with the social work value of promoting self-determination among colleagues would be that the impaired social worker voluntarily seeks help for his or her substance abuse problem. If this does not happen, however, the professional may have to resort to more coercive methods. All states now have certification and/or licensing requirements. In many states a professional with a substance abuse problem must turn in his or her license while receiving treatment or the license will be revoked.

Jules seems to have ethical problems in two areas—impairment and dual relationships. Substance abuse may have impaired his judgment thus leading him to begin a dual relationship with his client. How should Janet handle her suspicions about Jules's inappropriate dual relationship? The new Code of Ethics contains the provision that "social workers should take adequate measures to discourage, prevent, expose and correct the unethical conduct of colleagues" (NASW, 1996, p. 18). As a first step, social workers are encouraged to discuss their concerns with the colleague if they feel it will be helpful. This is often difficult, but it is important because it promotes self-respect in the individual and gives him or her the chance to correct his or her actions. The new Code of Ethics also informs social workers that if they believe a colleague has acted unethically they "should take action through appropriate channels established by employers, agencies, NASW, licensing and regulatory bodies, and other professional organizations" (NASW, 1996, p. 18). It is often difficult to report a colleague because since early childhood most people have been taught not to "snitch." However, the professional value of protecting vulnerable clients should supersede the personal value of not "telling" on others. The client, Doreen, is very vulnerable, and there is some evidence that the most vulnerable clients with a history of abuse are the most likely to be sexually exploited by their therapists (Edelwich and Brodsky, 1991). The professional responsibility to protect vulnerable clients must override the personal concern about protecting a friend.

Janet first should try to speak to Jules about the problem she sees in his relationship with Doreen. There is always the possibility that (1) Jules is unaware that he has begun to blur the professional boundary between himself and his client, or (2) Jules does not know that the new NASW Code of Ethics has specific prohibitions against dual relationships.

A more negative scenario would result if Jules completely denies any problem by saying, for example: "I'm just trying to help Doreen, and I'm the only person she can trust." In such a case, Janet must decide how she wants to proceed. She might want to gather more evidence (such as by keeping a written record of occurrences of possibly unethical behavior) or discuss her suspicions with a colleague.

Janet can go through two different channels to report unethical behavior. Each local chapter of NASW has a Committee on Inquiry, which adjudicates violations of the Code of Ethics. Janet may want to discuss her concerns with a consultant from the Committee on Inquiry and decide whether there has been a violation of ethics. One caveat, however, is that

Jules must be an NASW member, as the Committee on Inquiry can only adjudicate cases against members. Another avenue would be to contact the state regulatory board. Because sexual contact with clients is a certification or license violation in all fifty states, Janet may want to bring charges to have Jules's certification or license revoked. Sexual involvement with clients can result in either a civil or criminal procedure.

Janet may be uncertain as to whether to report Jules's behavior because she is not absolutely sure that he is sexually involved with his client. This, however, is not a unique situation, because often sexual involvement with a client remains a secret at the time it occurs. Although 98 percent of therapists believe that sexual involvement with clients is unethical (Borys and Pope, 1989), sexual improprieties are the second most frequent malpractice claim against social workers (Reamer, 1995). Sexual contact is more likely to involve a male therapist and a female patient than the reverse. There is little documentation of homosexual and lesbian therapist/patient involvement, but there is some evidence that it does occur. (Congress, 1996; Edelwich and Brodsky, 1991).

Dual Relationships

Are only sexual relationships contrary to the Code of Ethics? Since 1993 the Code of Ethics has contained an explicit prohibition against dual or multiple relationships: "Social workers should not engage in any dual or multiple relationships with clients or former clients in which there is a risk of exploitation or potential harm to the client" (NASW, 1993, p. 10). Dual relationships occur when social workers relate to clients in more than one way. As the primary relationship is a therapeutic one, the presence of a social, business, or sexual relationship would result in a dual relationship.

The literature has long focused on the importance of maintaining appropriate boundaries in relationships with clients (Biestek, 1957; Rhodes, 1992). But while most social workers believe that sexual relationships with current clients are unethical, they are much more divided when it comes to social, occupational, or educational relationships with current clients (Congress, 1996).

Borys and Pope (1989) found that most therapists do not believe that a social or employer relationship with clients is inappropriate. Also, NASW did not have a prohibition against dual relationships until 1993. It has been suggested that dual relationships, even of a nonsexual nature, can lead to role reversal, which is harmful to the client (Kagle and Giebelhausen, 1994). In the preceding example there already may be some indication of role reversal, because Jules, the social worker, may not be maintaining sobriety, while Doreen, the client, is.

Some dual relationships seem very clearly inappropriate, such as a therapist's hiring his client as a babysitter. But while this blurring of personal and professional boundaries seems very apparent, other situations are not as clear, as the following example illustrates.

Tom, a certified social worker, has been seeing Henry, a thirty-nine-year-old divorced father of two, for the last four months. One of Henry's main problems is his troubled relationship with his adolescent son, Peter, who lives across town with his remarried mother. According to the divorce agreement, Peter is to spend weekends with his father. Recently he has stopped wanting to visit, and when he does, he spends the whole time in his room listening to rap music. In addition, Henry has financial problems. The garage that he owns doesn't get as much business now that the main highway had been built outside town. Tom has reduced his fee so that Henry can continue in therapy. Last week Tom's car broke down on the way to his office; thus, he had to cancel Henry's session unexpectedly. Henry told Tom to bring his car in for a checkup. Should Tom accept Henry's offer?

At this time Tom has a therapeutic relationship with Henry. If Tom chooses to bring his car to Henry for repairs, he will also have a business relationship with Henry. On the positive side, Tom knows that Henry is a good mechanic and that he will charge him a fair price for repairs. Henry has not suggested that he will barter his services as payment for therapy sessions, which Tom knows the new Code of Ethics considers unethical (see chapter 4). But Tom is rightfully concerned that employing Henry as his auto mechanic might compromise their therapeutic relationship. Will Henry reduce his charge for repairing Tom's car? What if after the repairs, Tom's car breaks down? Will Tom hold Henry responsible, and would this affect the objectivity of their therapeutic relationship? It might be best for Tom to avoid entering an employer relationship with his client.

This position, however, may reflect an urban bias. In 1993, when the NASW Delegate Assembly voted to include the prohibition against dual relationships, there was much dissent from social workers from rural areas, who indicated that dual relationships were impossible to avoid in smaller communities. For example, social workers' children may attend the same schools as their clients' children. Does this mean that social workers should not participate in PTA for fear of developing dual relationships with their clients?

Social workers can participate in PTA but should be careful in pursuing social relationships. For example, a social worker might participate with her client in a PTA fund raiser but decide not to attend a social function at the client's house after the event. Again, the therapist has the responsibility to find out when there is risk of exploitation and/or potential harm to the patient. Contrary to what is usually thought, a recent study of urban and rural differences indicates that social workers in urban rather than rural areas are more likely to approve of dual relationships with current as well as former clients (Jayartne, Croxton, and Mattison, 1997).

Opinion about whether current clients should enter into a student relationship with their therapist is divided. In training institutes students often see their teachers for therapy, and in fact students seeking therapy are often encouraged to see an analyst from the same institute. But this practice has its pitfalls. What is the primary relationship—therapist/client or teacher/student? If the teacher is also the therapist does he or she have a special relationship with the student/client? How does this relationship affect the other students in the class? Also, what happens when the teacher must evaluate the student? Does this evaluation affect the therapeutic relationship? Will the student/client be harmed if he or she receives a low grade? Because the therapist knows so much about the client, can he or she objectively evaluate the student?

Social workers have conflicting opinions about dual relationships with former clients, especially if the relationships are nonsexual. Kagle and Giebelhausen (1994) believe that nonsexual dual relationships are always dangerous because they may lead to role reversal. They present a case example in which the social worker increasingly began to look to her former client for support and advise about personal problems. This demand for attention was very stressful for the former client and undermined some therapeutic work that had occurred. It can be argued, though, that role reversal of this nature is rare. Borys and Pope (1989) report that less than half of the professionals surveyed would not hire a current client or allow this client to become their student, while only 15 percent believed that it was unethical to become friends with a former client.

Often when a former client invites a social worker to attend an event, the event relates to the achievement of a personal goal that can be attributed to the effectiveness of therapy. Social workers have been invited to the weddings of clients whom they have counseled about relationship problems. On other occasions social workers have been invited to the graduations of clients who have struggled in therapy with issues about continuing in school. The following vignette illustrates this type of dilemma.

Beth, a twenty-five-year-old woman, was having a great deal of difficulty separating from her family. She had lived at home during college, but then began making enough money to move into her own apartment. Although she initially blamed her parents for forcing her to live at home, she finally acknowledges that she had many fears about leaving home. After two years of therapy, Beth feels more confident about herself and puts a deposit on an apartment. She terminates therapy but sends her former therapist an invitation to a housewarming party she is hosting. Should the social worker attend this party?

In this example, the social worker might enter into a social relationship with a client after the termination of a therapeutic relationship. The new code advises social workers to avoid dual relationships of a social nature with former as well as current clients. This would imply that the social worker should not attend the former client's housewarming party to avoid the possibility of developing a social relationship. A key issue is whether there is risk of exploitation or potential harm to the client. Would it harm the former client if the social worker's presence became known to the other guests at the party? What if the former client decides to return to therapy after the party?

Some social workers might argue that it may be therapeutic for a social worker to attend an event as the guest of a client. For example, attending the graduation of a client who has struggled with educational goals or the wedding of a client who has improved his or her interpersonal skills may be a way for the social worker to affirm a client's personal growth and achievement. Also, some believe that because an important goal of social work is to empower, strengthen, and promote independence of clients, a "once-a-client, always-a-client" belief system should not apply, because relationships with clients change over time.

When dual relationships develop with former clients, the professional social worker has the responsibility to continually examine the potential harm and exploitation of the client because of the nontherapeutic relationship. The power differential in therapy relationships increases the possibility of exploitation and potential harm to the client in a social relationship.

Because of the risk of harm, Beth's social worker should be cautious about accepting her invitation to a housewarming. Possibly, the social worker would attend this event and feel pleased to see how well her client has resolved the problems addressed in therapy. But the therapist should think very carefully about all the possible consequences of attending the party.

The party may mark the beginning of a social relationship in which the client may be harmed. Perhaps the client will become too dependent on the social worker. Maybe a role reversal will occur, and the social worker may begin to depend on the former client for advice and guidance. One problem with a social relationship that follows the end of a therapeutic relationship is that the former therapist knows everything about the new friend, while the former client knows virtually nothing about the new friend. This suggests that the relationship begins and may continue on a very unequal basis.

Dual Relationships—Supervisors

According to the new code, dual relationships not only between social workers and their clients, but also between supervisors and supervisees are to be avoided. Of particular concern are sexual relationships that may lead to exploitation and harm of the less powerful, more vulnerable person. The following example illustrates how dilemmas of this type arise.

> Bill, a supervisor in a child welfare agency, has been assigned to work with Beatrice, a new MSW who recently joined the staff. Beatrice confides to Bill that she recently separated from her husband. The focus of the next supervisory sessions were on Beatrice's recent stormy battles with her ex-spouse regarding custody of the children. She reveals that this breakup is particularly traumatic for her because her parents separated when she was the same age as her children are now. Bill confides that he and his wife divorced last year but that he has recovered from the loss. Bill and Beatrice begin to lunch together to discuss Beatrice's problems.

In this example, Bill, although seemingly supportive of Beatrice, should examine very carefully his behavior toward his new supervisee. First, as for their recent supervisory sessions, it seems that he has begun to "therapize" his supervisee, which is clearly inappropriate. To begin a therapy relationship with a supervisee either during agency supervisory sessions or in private practice constitutes a dual relationship in which there is risk of exploitation. Furthermore, unless the supervisee's work performance is detrimentally affected, Bill cannot justify a discussion about Beatrice's personal life as relevant to agency work.

There is certainly a dangerous possibility that a social relationship might be developing. Often when supervisors and/or supervisees are most vulnerable because of a recent loss, there is the greatest possibility of an inappropriate dual relationship. Bill should be very careful about the possibility that he will abuse his power and exploit Beatrice. Although Beatrice at this time does not seem to have any complaints about her supervisor's attention, the question can be raised about what options she has if she does not want to develop a social/sexual relationship with him. According to the revised Code of Ethics, the supervisor, because of greater power, has the primary responsibility to guard against using this power to his or her advantage. Regarding the total organization, how does developing a social relationship with one supervisee affect other staff members? The supervisor must question whether he is on the road to developing a dual relationship in which there is a risk of exploitation. His primary relationship with Beatrice is that of supervisor, not therapist, friend, or sexual partner.

The following guidelines have been developed to help social workers struggling with concerns about dual relationships:

1. Clearly define the nature of dual relationships.
2. Examine carefully the risk of exploitation and harm to the most vulnerable person.
3. Anticipate possible consequences, positive and negative, of proceeding with a dual relationship.
4. Discuss with colleagues and supervisor the advisability of developing a dual relationship.
5. Ascertain which other parts of the code, in addition to the section on dual relationships, might help determine whether a dual relationship is inappropriate.
6. Affirm the responsibility of the professional social worker to avoid even the possibility of exploiting the most vulnerable, whether they are clients, supervisees, or students.

CHAPTER 11

Ethical Dilemmas in Interdisciplinary Collaboration

Social workers increasingly work with other professionals and paraprofessionals in interdisciplinary teams. In educational settings social workers work collaboratively with teachers, guidance counselors, evaluators, and school administrators. In child welfare agencies social workers continually interact with non-MSW social service workers and attorneys. In hospitals and other medical settings social workers are often part of teams that include doctors, nurses, health aides, and administrators. Challenges to ethical practice are more likely to occur in multidiscipline agencies (Congress, 1986), but the social worker may have little direction about how to handle them.

Previous codes did not include any reference to interdisciplinary teams, but the new code devotes a section to the role of social workers in interdisciplinary collaboration. The relevant section states:

> Social workers who are members of an interdisciplinary team should participate in and contribute to decisions that effect the well-being of clients by drawing on the perspectives, values, and experiences of the social work profession. Professional and ethical obligations of the interdisciplinary team as a whole and of its individual members should be clearly established. (NASW, 1996, p. 16)

Social workers have much to contribute to interdisciplinary teams. The presence of social workers on interdisciplinary teams has been seen to be very effective in influencing ethical decision making in health settings (Joseph and Conrad, 1989). The code suggests that it is important for the social worker to delineate the ethical expectations of the profession and also to facilitate the understanding of the ethical perspectives of other professions early in the process of collaboration. Unfortunately, this is rarely done initially but often becomes problematic when a conflict develops.

Social Workers and Educators

The social worker often finds that educational settings are particularly fraught with ethical dilemmas and conflicts, perhaps because other professionals may have different concepts of confidentiality (Congress, 1986). There may be much tension and conflict for school social workers who attempt to maintain confidentiality despite the demands of school personnel (Berman-Rossi and Rossi, 1990; Garrett, 1994). The following example illustrates the type of conflict that can develop.

> Billy, a fourteen-year-old ninth grader, manifests behavioral problems in school. He does not pay attention in class and is continually fighting with other children. This problem began after Christmas vacation; before this he was a model student. Mrs. Sullivan, Billy's teacher, refers Billy to the school social worker, Amy. During individual counseling with Billy, Amy learns that his parents separated over the Christmas holidays. His older brother went to live with his father in another state; Billy still lives with his mother. Billy finds it very difficult to talk about his problems, and he explicitly tells Amy that he does not want anyone to know about his family. He expresses sadness about being separated from his father and older brother. No sooner does Billy leave Amy's office than Mrs. Sullivan comes in to find out what Billy told her. She reminds Amy that she is very concerned about Billy, and because they all work as a team, she knows Amy will share information about Billy.

Amy knows that the Code of Ethics mandates that she maintain confidentiality unless laws or the safety of her client or others are at risk. She also knows that because her client is fourteen, he could be accorded the same rights to confidentiality as an adult (Stein, 1991). Billy specifically asked her not to share information about his family. If Billy were younger, under the *parens patriae* doctrine, she would have the responsibility of acting in his best interests. This might involve sharing information. Unfortunately, the agency had no written policies and procedures about disclosing confidential information to school personnel. Amy is reluctant to share the information. She speaks to her supervisor, who supports her decision.

The following example illustrates what might happen when information is shared.

> Susan, a fourth grader, is very quiet and withdrawn in class and does not socialize with the other children. She never participates in discussions, and her school work is below grade level. The school social worker is acquainted with Susan and her family and learns that Susan's mother is

terminally ill with AIDS and frequently needs to be hospitalized. Although Susan does not know her mother's specific diagnosis, she knows her mother is seriously ill. Often she stays home from school to help her mother with household chores or to visit her in the hospital. The school social worker shares this information with Susan's classroom teacher, thinking that it would lead to the teacher being more supportive and understanding of Susan's poor performance in school. One day when Susan is out, the teacher instructs the other students to try to include Susan in all activities because she is sad over her mother's illness. Fortunately, the teacher stops short of sharing that Susan's mother has AIDS, which most state laws consider highly confidential information. When the school social worker learns that the teacher shared information about Susan's mother with the other children, she expresses concern to the teacher that she did not keep this information confidential. The teacher retorts that a greater good might result because Susan might have more peer support to help her get through this stressful period of her life.

The school social worker and the teacher seem to have different ideas about confidentiality, with the social worker having the most restrictive definition. Differing views of confidentiality often lead to tensions between professionals in school settings.

The increasing number of immigrant children in the schools is creating ethical challenges for school social workers. It is estimated that by the middle of the twenty-first century, half the population of the United States will be from non-Western European backgrounds (Congress, 1994). Most of this population will be made up of children. Developing an educational system that works in a multicultural environment will be one of educators' biggest challenges in the new millennium (Allen-Meares, 1992). Although the educational system is changing, much of its curriculum and policies are still rooted in the Western European tradition (Congress and Lynn, 1994).

The profession of social work is firmly committed to promoting cultural diversity and working against oppression and injustice based on ethnicity or race. Although educators also have a commitment to the diverse needs of their students, the social workers' central focus on supporting diversity may lead to conflicts in the school setting. The following case example illustrates a potential conflict.

Karen, a second-year social work student, leads a discussion group for immigrant children. One day a ten-year-old Dominican boy, Juan, is in tears. Karen learns that his teacher told him that he did not complete his homework assignment correctly. The class had been asked to bring in a newspaper article about the upcoming presidential election. Juan brought in an article in Spanish. Karen is very angry at the teacher, whom she feels was not culturally sensitive. She knows that Juan's family does not speak English. Bringing in an article from a paper that is available to Juan and his family is perfectly appropriate for him.

How should the social worker handle this incident? Karen faces two issues: (1) What should she say to Juan and the other group members? and (2) Should she report this incident to the teacher or other school personnel? She knows that it is not ethical to demean her colleague publicly, as the new code states that "social workers should avoid unwarranted negative criticism of colleagues in communication with clients or other professionals" (NASW, 1996, p. 15). She encourages Juan to discuss his feelings and other group members to share similar feelings of being hurt by culturally insensitive behaviors of others. From a strengths and empowerment perspective, many group members emerge from the session feeling stronger that they knew two cultures and languages. As Juan says, he could translate this article from Spanish to English, a skill that many do not have.

While Karen feels that her group intervention has been successful, she is less certain about how to intervene on a macrolevel. The new code recognizes that there may be disagreements in interdisciplinary collaboration. "Social workers for whom a team decision raises ethical concerns should attempt to resolve the disagreement through appropriate channels. If the disagreement cannot be resolved, social workers should pursue other avenues to address their concerns consistent with client well-being" (NASW, 1996, p. 16).

Karen is very uncomfortable about taking any action against the teacher because she feels that she has limited power as a social work student in a host agency. As a first step, Karen discusses the incident with her supervisor, who supports the way she handled the incident in the group. They discuss ways to handle this and other incidents that show cultural insensitivity. Karen decides not to confront the teacher directly but rather to give a presentation on cultural sensitivity at the monthly school staff meeting. In this meeting she stresses the importance of being sensitive to the language and customs of students from other cultures. Also, Karen introduces the issue of educating school personnel about cultural sensitivity at a NASW meeting of school social workers.

Social Workers and Attorneys

Social workers in the field of child welfare frequently interact with attorneys. Public and private agencies may retain attorneys to represent the agency in hearings involving termination of parental rights. Furthermore, the child, birth parents, and adoptive parents are represented by attorneys in court proceedings. Social workers usually conduct psychosocial studies and make recommendations to the attorneys about the best interests of the child. Conflict between attorneys and social workers are usually in four main areas: (1) differences in recording information, (2) task delineations, (3) the definition of *client*, and (4) confidentiality (Stein, 1991). Social workers may rely primarily on inferential recording, for example, "Ms. R. was not motivated to follow a case plan," while attorneys, on the other hand, want specific descriptive facts, such as what the parent did or did not do. Because lawyers and social workers often do not confer about the case until immediately before the court date, sometimes it is impossible for the social worker to reconstruct specific facts, which leads to conflict between the lawyers and social workers and leaves the latter feeling inadequate. This situation points to the need for social workers in child welfare to be especially careful to maintain good factual records to improve their communication with attorneys before court appearances. Also it should be noted that a good inferential assessment should be based on facts. For example, the social worker should not report that a client is unmotivated unless there are specific facts that substantiate this conclusion.

In child welfare settings where there is contact between attorneys and social workers, there has to be clear delineation about tasks in order to prevent disagreement between charges in a petition and future recommendations. (Russel, 1988). Problems may emerge when these professionals stray from their areas of competence; for example, when judges and lawyers make psychosocial assessments and social workers assume the lawyer's role by withholding evidence for fear that it will be misconstrued (Goldstein, Freud, Solnit, and Goldstein, 1986). In order to act ethically, the social worker must understand the role of each party in a legal proceeding.

The greatest conflict between social worker and attorney, however, emerges when it is not clearly specified who the client is. The lawyer can represent only one party, such as the birth parent, the agency, the child, or the adoptive agency. In court this leads lawyers to assume an adversarial role in presenting only evidence that helps the party they are representing and suppressing evidence that does not. Social workers, however, adopt more of a mediation role; that is, they try to reconcile conflicting positions. While the NASW Code of Ethics states that social workers should promote the best interests of their clients, the definition of client is left unclear. A social worker in a child welfare agency may find herself trying to balance the conflicting demands of an agency that is pushing to have children returned to their birth parents, a birth mother who seems uncertain about resuming care of her children, and a child who wants to remain with his foster parents.

Differences in ideas of confidentiality often produce conflicts between attorneys and social workers. All fifty states mandate social workers but not attorneys to report child abuse. This often produces ethical challenges for the social worker, especially when he or she works for a legal agency, as this example suggests.

Susan, a social worker with the legal aid service that is representing eight-year-old Tony's birth mother in a pending termination-of-parental-rights hearing, notes that when the mother comes to the agency with Ben, a five-year-old who is still in her care, Ben has bruises on his arms, which the mother attributes to a fall from his bike. Susan wants to report this suspected abuse to the child abuse central registry but is told not to by the attorney because such a report might damage the mother's court case. Susan is very concerned because she is a mandated child abuse reporter and wants to promote the best interests of her many clients, including Tony and Ben, while the lawyer seems to be concerned only with Mrs. Smith's interests.

Susan can talk with the attorneys at the legal agency to increase their understanding of a familial approach to child welfare. If Ben is abused, Tony may also become abused, which ultimately may have negative consequences for the lawyer's primary client. Before accepting employment in a legal agency it is important for the social worker to learn about the agency's policies in situations regarding child abuse. If legal ethics seem to override social work ethics, the social worker can make an informed decision about whether she wants to work at that agency.

Social workers may also find that birth parents are their primary clients, as this example indicates.

Carmen, a bilingual social worker in a mental health clinic, has been seeing Cecilia, a thirty-four-year-old Mexican woman, for individual therapy. When Cecilia was hospitalized last year for chronic undifferentiated schizophrenia, her five-year-old child, Juan, was placed in foster care.

Carmen receives a call from the attorney with the public child welfare agency that placed Cecilia's child. The attorney wants to know the following:

1. What is Cecilia's immigration status?
2. What relatives and friends does she have in the city?
3. What behavior led up to Cecilia's hospitalization?
   Was she abusive to her son?
4. Does Cecilia come regularly for treatment?
5. What has been discussed during these treatment
   sessions?
6. Does Cecilia have delusions about her child?
7. What antipsychotic medication is Cecilia taking?
8. How long will Cecilia remain in treatment?
9. Does Carmen think that Juan will be at risk if he is
   returned to Cecilia's care?

The attorney indicates that she will be subpoenaing the records for the pending termination-of-parental-rights case.

First, Carmen should be very careful about what information she shares. If the other party in interdisciplinary collaboration has *Dr.* before his or her name or an *Esq.* after it, the social worker may feel intimidated and share more information than he or she should. Information about a client should never be shared unless the client has signed a release-of-information form that includes the name of the client, to whom the information is to be released, the nature of the information to be released, and the time limit for the release of information (Wilson, 1978). Even assuming that there is an acceptable release on file, Carmen should be careful about releasing information over the phone because the caller's identity cannot be verified. A better strategy is to take the caller's number and call back to verify his or her identity.

Should Carmen answer every question the attorney has asked? Cecilia's immigration status is highly confidential information, especially because there is currently renewed emphasis on deporting illegal immigrants. Carmen's professional responsibility is to her client. Assuming there are no laws to the contrary, she is not required to report her client's immigration status to any public agency. Carmen should be concerned about what use the attorney may make of this information, especially because it does not seem related to the issue at hand.

Some of the questions the attorney asked are informational—"What antipsychotic medication is Cecilia taking?"—while others involve assessment—"Does Cecilia have delusions about her child?"—or prediction—"Does Carmen think that Juan will be at risk if he is returned to his mother?" Assuming that Carmen has a release in Cecilia's folder, she can feel safest about answering informational questions. If Carmen answers assessment questions, she must be sure that they are based on facts. Also, according to the strengths perspective and client advocacy model it is often best to frame responses in a positive way—for example, "Cecilia was seen three times for individual therapy" rather than "Cecilia missed most of her therapy appointments, coming only three times." Prediction questions are the most difficult to answer, and it is best to avoid answering them if possible. Even the most skilled practitioners have difficulty predicting future violence (Rosenthal, 1993). Social workers would do well to avoid making damaging generalizations, as one social worker did early in her career. In a telephone conversation, this social worker described a client as "the craziest client I've ever seen." Four years later her statement was quoted at a termination-of-parental-rights hearing.

A social worker who receives a request for information from a professional in another agency should discuss this with the client. This affords the client the greatest respect for his or her autonomy and honors the Code of Ethics provision that "social workers should inform clients, to the extent possible, about the disclosure of confidential information and the potential consequences, when feasible before the disclosure is made. This applies whether social workers disclose confidential information on the basis of a legal requirement or client consent" (NASW, 1996, p. 10).

In the preceding example, a conflict of interest exists between Carmen and the attorney of the child welfare agency. Carmen's primary client is Cecilia, while the attorney's client is the child welfare agency. Carmen must maintain confidentiality for her client except when laws or regulations dictate otherwise. Carmen is a mandated child abuse reporter, and if she learns that Cecilia is abusing Juan during a weekend visit, she is required to report it, even though it may challenge the trusting relationship that she and her client have developed.

How should Carmen handle the subpoena? Social workers often become anxious when they receive a subpoena and fear that they must release all confidential information. The NASW General Counsel offers the following suggestions to social workers who receive a subpoena:

1. The social worker should read the subpoena carefully, including the date for response, the action required, and the court and attorney issuing it.
2. The social worker should give the client a copy of the subpoena and ask for the client's written consent to release the information it requests. If the client does not want to have the information released, the information can be kept confidential, now that communication with social workers is considered privileged (Greenhouse, 1996).
3. If the information is privileged or the subpoena is procedurally incorrect, the social worker can file a written objection, request a protective order, or file a motion to rescind or change the subpoena.

4. The social worker should consult with the agency attorney about the best way to handle the subpoena (Polowy and Gilbertson, 1997).

Social Workers and Health Care Professionals

Hospitals and other medical facilities have traditionally provided opportunities for social workers to participate in interdisciplinary consultation with other professionals. With the current focus on managed care and reduced hospital stays, these opportunities may increase. Social workers are respected for their input into ethical decision making within health care settings (Joseph and Conrad, 1989). Technological advances in the health field that affect the terminally ill and elderly as well as severely impaired newborns have created ethical dilemmas for social workers and others in the health field (Abramson, 1990).

Social workers in the health field often interact with doctors whose professional values may conflict with theirs. Roberts (1989) lists the following conflicting professional values: (1) length of life versus quality of life; (2) paternalism versus autonomy in setting goals; (3) hard data versus soft data; (4) differing degrees of receptiveness to patients with emotional problems; and (5) authoritarian versus participatory model on interdisciplinary teams. Social workers focus more on the psychosocial aspects of a patient's life, while physicians are more concerned with saving a life, regardless of the quality of life of the patient and his or her family. When these different goals conflict, the social worker can support the patient and his or her family when support is not forthcoming from the physician. The social worker can also be more attentive to the physician's sense of failure in not being able to save all patients (Roberts, 1989). Knowing that patients often become noncompliant if they do not participate in setting their own goals, the social worker is much more likely to encourage the patient's input in setting treatment goals, while the physician, assuming that all patients want to improve their health and live as long as possible, unilaterally presents a treatment plan to realize these goals. Social workers are more likely to give credence to soft data (the report from the client), while doctors rely more heavily on hard data (lab tests, X-rays, and so on). Social workers may be more empathic and supportive of patients who have emotional problems. Finally, physicians on interdisciplinary teams are more likely to assume an authoritarian role rather than to follow the participatory model that social workers favor. The following suggestions can help social workers in their interactions with doctors in health settings (Roberts, 1989):

1. Become familiar with the daily activities of doctors. Participating in grand rounds often provides an opportunity for social workers to

learn more about the difficult decisions that doctors have to make and the time pressures under which they work.

2. Be specific in describing clients' needs and psychosocial problems. This approach is respected by doctors, who are more receptive to "hard data." For example, instead of saying "The client discussed psychosocial issues related to his illness" it is better to say "The client was concerned about whether his illness would limit his playing golf, which is his main recreational activity."

3. Familiarize doctors and other health professionals with the professional values and ethics that are the basis of social work.

4. Gain credibility on interdisciplinary committees by displaying a willingness to work with challenging patients and to contribute to doctors' understanding of psychosocial issues.

Hospitals and other health facilities often have ethical committees to resolve ethical dilemmas. In hospitals, ethics committees are usually composed of doctors, social workers, nurses, clergy, administrators, attorneys, and community representatives. Functions of such committees include providing education, making policies, offering consultation to other staff, and reviewing cases. The diverse membership of ethics committees may increase the likelihood of conflicts, but consensus does not always have to be obtained for the group to be successful (Reamer, 1987). Social workers' skills in fostering collaboration and participation often help bring disparate members together. Also, social workers' advocacy of clients' needs and rights makes them essential for "ethical" ethics committees. While most ethics committee are advisory, many in hospitals expect that ethics committees will generate binding decisions.

Social workers who sit on ethics committees need to be clear about their responsibilities to protect clients' autonomy and confidentiality, as this example indicates.

Jennifer, a social worker at a long-term-care health facility, is a member of an ethics committee that consists of the staff doctor, nurse clinician, licensed practical nurse, facility administrator, and recreational counselor. The committee was first established to discuss continuing life support for severely ill clients. The committee also deals with situations such as Anna's. Anna has severe diabetes and circulatory problems. Her blood sugar fluctuates wildly, and Jennifer notices that every time Anna's sister visits, Anna's blood sugar becomes elevated. When Jennider discusses this with Anna, Anna finally tells Jennifer (after being promised confidentiality) that her sister usually brings her candy. Anna knows that candy is bad for her, but she wants to see her sister and also looks forward to eating the candy. Should Jennifer tell the ethics committee what Anna has told her?

Social workers, even when members of ethics committees, must be true to their professional value and ethical system, which supports clients' right to assume primary responsibility for decisions that affect their lives. As Reamer has pointed out, "Ethics committee members must ensure that their activities do not lead to gratuitous meddling in clients' lives" (Reamer, 1987, p. 190).

Power differentials in ethics committees can also become problematic for the social worker. A beginning social worker, Carol, sits with her supervisor on an ethics committee in a nursing home. Carol hesitates to share information or question other committee members for fear of getting a negative evaluation. For example, she once commented that her client had seemed very lethargic for the last month, and she wondered if he should have a medical consultation. This made the team doctor very defensive because he had not seen the patient recently, despite prescribing a powerful new drug. Her supervisor was very critical of her after the meeting and told her that she had been wrong to challenge the doctor's authority.

Another ethical challenge for the social worker who is a member of an interdisciplinary team may arise when the ethics committee is an extension of the agency administration. Alicia, a social worker on the ethics committee of a mental hospital, becomes upset when she learns that the main agenda for the ethics committee seems to be discharging patients as soon as possible. When she tries to explain that a certain client has no family or social supports to live independently, she is told that he has exceeded his thirty-day limit and must be discharged as soon as possible.

How should a social worker on an interdisciplinary team respond if her or his ethical responsibility to clients seems compromised? These guidelines have been developed to help social workers function more effectively as members of interdisciplinary teams:

1. Clarify the function of the interdisciplinary team and the roles of its members.
2. Educate other professionals about the role of social workers in professional practice.
3. Demonstrate to other members of the committee what social workers can do in terms of both client contact and committee participation.
4. Stress the social work values of autonomy and confidentiality in discussions about clients and their families.
5. Build alliances with other committee members in handling areas of conflict.

6. Advocate within the ethics committee for the rights and interests of clients.
7. Advocate with social work professionals in similar fields for the needs and rights of clients.

An interdisciplinary model supports social work's focus on inclusion and mediation. Social workers can play an important role in developing and sustaining their worthwhile participation in this important area.

CHAPTER 12

Ethical Dilemmas Relating to HIV and AIDS

Since AIDS was first identified as a disease in the early 1980s, the number of its victims has dramatically increased, especially in large urban areas. Over 500,000 individuals with AIDS have been reported to the Centers for Disease Control, and 343,000 have died (CDC, June 1996). With new medications AIDS victims are living longer than ever before but may require extensive, costly treatment (Richardson, 1997).

While early cases of AIDS in the United States were confined almost exclusively to the male homosexual population, currently the fastest growing group of AIDS sufferers is women of color (Kaplan & Krell-Long, 1993). It is estimated that there are 100,000 children in New York City who have been orphaned because of AIDS (Romano and Zayas, 1997). To its credit, the profession of social work was one of the first to respond to the AIDS epidemic; in 1984 NASW issued a policy statement that stressed preserving the confidentiality of those afflicted with AIDS (NASW, 1984).

The Americans with Disabilities Act (1990) supported protecting persons with disabilities against discrimination in employment, public accommodations, transportation, and public services. The courts have interpreted this act to apply to people with HIV/AIDS (Hermann, 1991).

The HIV/AIDS epidemic confronts the professional social worker with many ethical issues and challenges. The NASW Code of Ethics does not specifically mention AIDS, in keeping with its practice of using generic language to preclude a discussion of any specific illness. But many provisions of the new Code of Ethics can be applied in working with people with HIV/AIDS. This chapter will focus on five main issues with regard to HIV/AIDS, present relevant case examples, and discuss how social workers might apply the code and a model of ethical decision making in dealing with AIDS-related problems. These five issues are: responsibility to vulnerable, oppressed populations; mandatory testing; rights to confidentiality; service delivery; and supervision and administration.

Oppressed Populations

Because of its association with blood, sex, and death, AIDS has been a stigmatized disease. It has been compared with the smallpox plagues of the nineteenth century and the Black Death of medieval times (Sontag, 1990). Even social workers who know better fear contagion. A professional social worker in a mental health clinic expressed that working with a depressed young man recently diagnosed as HIV-positive made her extremely anxious because he cried frequently and she feared catching the disease by coming in contact with his used tissues. Thus, increased knowledge about AIDS is important for professional social workers as well as students.

While in other countries AIDS victims were usually heterosexuals, in the United States HIV/AIDS first surfaced among the homosexual male population. In fact, until 1984 HIV/AIDS was called the gay disease. It has been argued that because the disease began among gay men, a frequently oppressed and stigmatized population, public health officials and researchers were slow to recognize that HIV/AIDS was an epidemic (Shilts, 1987). It has even been noted that the *New York Times* did not publish a front-page story on the AIDS epidemic until the first heterosexual case was identified (Shilts, 1987).

Homophobia is found not only in the general public; even social work students are more homophobic than one might expect (Berkman and Zinberg, 1997). The Code of Ethics clearly states that social workers should try to eliminate discrimination based on sexual orientation (NASW, 1996). In keeping with this goal, the 1996 NASW Delegate Assembly voted to change its representation for election to national offices to ensure that those with differing sexual orientation would be included and also voted for a resolution to support same-sex marriage.

Intravenous drug users have also been greatly affected by the AIDS epidemic. This is another vulnerable population which social workers often describe as "resistant," "manipulative," and not "receptive to help." It is essential that social workers examine how their personal reactions to clients' problems affect their work. The medical and psychosocial needs of people with HIV/AIDS may be neglected if these clients also have a substance-abuse problem.

Like the "unworthy" poor who were the subjects of the English Poor Law, homosexuals and substance abusers are often considered the "unworthy" victims of HIV/AIDS and are blamed for having brought this disease upon themselves. Hemophiliacs and babies who are born HIV-positive, on the other hand, are considered the "worthy" (innocent) victims. The newest group of "unworthy" AIDS victims are women of color (Kaplan and Krell-Long, 1993). Often this population is triply stigmatized—first because they are women, then because of their race, and finally because of their illness. There is evidence that the life expectancy of women with HIV/AIDS may be shorter than that of men, possibly because HIV/AIDS in women is not diagnosed early enough for effective treatment and/or because poor women of color often have so many other immediate problems (Kaplan and Krell-Long, 1993). For example, a twenty-five-year-old Puerto Rican mother of two children who after frequent urinary infections learned that she was HIV-positive reported that she was more worried about how she was going to pay the rent next month. Afflicted women are often blamed for having brought the illness upon themselves because of marriage or involvement with partners who are HIV positive.

In order to effectively work with people with HIV/AIDS, social workers must examine their own values regarding sexual orientation, gender, and racial and ethnic differences. The NASW Code of Ethics specifically prohibits discrimination based on any of these qualities, as well as disability (NASW, 1996).

Testing for HIV

Much controversy surrounds the area of testing for HIV antibodies. The debate has focused on the issues of universal versus selective testing and mandatory versus voluntary testing. Very few have recommended universal testing (Rhame and Maki, 1989). Arguments against universal testing stress that besides being costly it would be cost-ineffective, that it might lead to discrimination against those found to be HIV positive, and that tests for AIDS sometimes produce false positive results. Also, if universal testing were mandatory, the traditional civil liberties of privacy and autonomy would be severely compromised. Universal testing for a health-related problem never has been mandated, nor is there a guaranteed treatment for the disease. The argument that individuals who know their HIV status will change their behavior has not been proven (Field, 1990).

While most social scientists and physicians view selective testing as preferable to universal testing, there has been considerable debate about (1) which groups should be tested and (2) whether the testing should be voluntary or mandatory. Some have recommended that those in high-risk groups voluntarily seek testing so that they can begin treatment earlier and reduce high-risk behavior (Childress, 1991). A risk/benefit analysis can be applied to this issue. While there are benefits of being treated early and of changing sexual behavior, the social risks (discrimination, stigma) and psychological risks (heightened anxiety, depression, suicide) must also be considered (Childress, 1991). Also, merely testing for the presence of HIV is not sufficient because some may need counseling both before and after being tested.

Because AIDS is viewed as a public health problem, many point to the past use of mandatory testing for public health problems such as syphilis. There are many instances of mandatory testing for HIV/AIDS. For example, all blood donors are screened, as are all members of the armed forces, all immigrants, and all prisoners (Childress, 1991). Also, many hospital patients have "routine" testing for HIV antibodies. Two states—Illinois and Louisiana—once required that applicants for marriage licenses be tested for HIV, but abandoned the practice because it was not cost effective. In Illinois it cost $312,000 to identify 8 out of 70,846 applicants for marriage licenses as HIV-positive (Turnock and Kelly, 1989).

Perhaps the most controversial issue in mandatory testing has been the question of whether to test pregnant women and/or newborns. Those in favor of such mandatory testing argue that early detection permits the use of life-prolonging medication for both mothers and children. Those opposed to mandatory testing raise concerns that those identified as HIV positive may face discrimination and stigmatization. In 1995 the New York State legislature voted to mandate HIV testing for all newborns and to tell the mother the results so that treatment could be provided during infancy (Dao, 1995).

As the number of AIDS deaths has declined because of early detection and new medications, there has been renewed interest in the mandatory testing and reporting of those infected with HIV (Richardson, 1997). Several years ago many thought that the current New York law on mandatory testing for newborns would never pass because of the strength of AIDS, gay, and feminist groups in that state. Recently a new bill—the HIV Prevention Act—that would force states to inform anyone who has been exposed to HIV and permit doctors to test for HIV before performing surgery has been endorsed by the American Medical Association and introduced to Congress.

Confidentiality and HIV/AIDS

Since the early 1980s when HIV/AIDS was first identified as a very serious but greatly stigmatized health problem, there has been much stress on maintaining the confidentiality of people with HIV/AIDS. While physicians have focused on public health issues, such as the benefits of early detection and the duty to warn, social workers continue to stress the need to maintain confidentiality in working with people with AIDS. Confidentiality has been seen as essential to establishing and maintaining a helping relationship (Abramson, 1990b).

With the spread of AIDS to the heterosexual population and more specifically to those with no known risk behavior, the preservation of confidentiality in all circumstances surrounding AIDS has been questioned. Disturbing from a social justice perspective is that the privacy rights of gay middle-class victims are more respected than those of the most recent population showing a high rate of AIDS infection—poor women and children of color (Richardson, 1997).

The new Code of Ethics promises confidentiality except when "disclosure is necessary to prevent serious, foreseeable, and imminent harm to a client or other identifiable person" (NASW, 1996, p.10). This principle relates to the Tarasoff decision, in which the California court of appeals established that a social worker has a duty to warn a potential victim of a client by stating that "the protective privilege ends when the public peril begins" (Tarasoff v. Board of Regents, 1976; 336). Some argue that the Tarasoff decision is not applicable to the AIDS situation, because often potential victims cannot be identified. Also, violating a client's trust may cause the client to discontinue treatment and/or abandon safe-sex practices. Others argue that an HIV-positive individual places an uninformed sexual partner at risk, and thus his or her situation is relevant to the Tarasoff decision. The courts as well as ethicists seem to be divided about the correct course of action, but a model of ethical decision making can help the clinician clarify the issues involved and begin to resolve the ethical dilemma regarding his or her duty to warn others about clients who are HIV positive.

What follows is a case example in which a clinician uses the ETHIC model to gain greater understanding about this dilemma.

Marlene, an experienced MSW, is seeing the Smith family for marital therapy. Their conflicts have increased steadily over their four-year marriage. One of their main stressors is financial (Tom has not found steady employment, but occasionally works at short-term construction jobs, while Joan works full time as a cashier at a local grocery store). Another stressor involves their futile attempts to start a family. Both come from large families and want many children, but after four years, they are still childless. Joan's only pregnancy ended in a miscarriage after three months. Another area of concern is that Tom frequently comes home late from construction jobs after stopping off at a local bar to have a few beers with his friends.

One afternoon Marlene receives a frantic call from Tom. Recently he had applied for a maintenance job at a local hospital and been hired. He has just completed routine medical tests needed for employment, and his test for HIV antibodies has come back positive. He thinks there must be a mistake and is going to have the test repeated. He is calling Marlene because he needs to talk to someone. Tom feels that he cannot tell his wife because she might leave him. If the test result is correct, she is sure to blame him for his illness

because last year he disappeared during a three-day drinking
binge and does not remember anything that happened during
that time. Tom repeatedly asks Marlene not to tell his wife.
He reminds Marlene that he was promised confidentiality
when he first began treatment.

In an attempt to resolve this ethical dilemma, Marlene applies the
ETHIC model:

*Examine relevant personal, social, agency, client and professional
values.* Marlene looks very carefully at her own countertransference reactions to people with AIDS, as many social workers have negative attitudes
toward people with AIDS (Ryan and Rowe, 1988). Marlene realizes that
although her professional education taught her otherwise, she feels that people afflicted with AIDS almost always have brought it upon themselves. She
thinks about homosexuals who are very sexually active and about IV drug
users who continue to exchange needles despite the risks. She remembers
the "black sheep" in her family—her second cousin, who had abused drugs
since early adolescence and died last year of AIDS. She wonders if she
blames Tom for not getting help with his alcohol problem earlier, which
would have averted his three-day binge and infection with HIV.

As she thinks about her treatment of this couple, Marlene wonders
if she was always more supportive of Joan as the partner who seemed to be
trying harder to make the marriage work. She also thinks that her identifica-
tion with and greater support of the wife in a marital couple might be related
to her interest in feminist issues.

Marlene is aware of negative social values regarding people with
AIDS. She acknowledges that her own personal values have been shaped in
part by society's tendency to blame the victim. People with AIDS are often
thought to be responsible for their illness because of their behavior as members of stigmatized populations—homosexuals and IV drug abusers. Tom
would be considered an "unworthy" AIDS victim because he "brought the
illness on himself," while Joan, if she were to contract the disease, would be
viewed as a "worthy" AIDS victim because she caught the disease unknow-
ingly as the wife of an infected person.

What are the agency's values about AIDS and about confidentiality?
Marlene knows that the mental health agency where she works does not have
any written policies about AIDS, despite a growing number of clients who are
HIV positive. She wonders if her agency's silence about AIDS is a way of
denying its existence. Her agency does have policies about confidentiality.
Most of these policies, however, focus on individual clients, despite the growing number of clients being treated in marital, family, or group modalities.

What are the client's values? Marlene realizes that as a marital
therapist she must understand the values of both her clients. She knows now

that Tom seems to place a high value on confidentiality, and perhaps a lesser value on keeping the relationship together. Marlene is less clear on Joan's values about confidentiality, probably because the subject has never come up. She does know that Joan is very committed to maintaining the marriage, regardless of the couple's problems.

Finally, Marlene examines professional values. She knows that the social work profession believes that people with HIV/AIDS are often stigmatized. Maintaining confidentiality is seen as important to preventing discrimination. But as a professional, Marlene feels her responsibility to both clients. Concerned with ethical issues in regard to working with a couple, she had discussed at the beginning of the couple's therapy that information should be shared with both people, and that she would not keep "secrets" with one member. But she had not anticipated that the secret would concern AIDS, about which there was a strong demand to maintain confidentiality.

Think about which ethical standard of the NASW Code of Ethics applies as well as about relevant laws and case decisions. Marlene looks carefully at the new Code of Ethics to try to determine the best course of action. She reads about the client's "right to privacy [and protecting] the confidentiality of all information obtained in the course of professional service, except for compelling professional reasons" (NASW, 1996, p. 2). She wonders if protecting Joan and a possible child is a "compelling professional reason" for which "disclosure is necessary to prevent serious, foreseeable, and imminent harm to a client or other identifiable person" (NASW, 1996, p. 2). The state she lives in supports strict confidentiality about HIV status. Marlene knows that there have been some attempts to apply the duty-to-warn principle of the Tarasoff decision to HIV/AIDS cases, and that the results have been mixed.

Hypothesize about different courses of action and possible consequences. Marlene thinks through various courses of action. If she maintains confidentiality, Tom will be pleased. He will continue to attend therapy sessions to work with Joan on their marriage. Furthermore, she could support Tom and help him address psychological or physical consequences of his HIV/AIDS diagnosis. Marlene could encourage him to tell his wife about his health status at a later time.

On the other hand, not sharing information about Tom's HIV status with Joan might have serious consequences. Right now Joan might not be HIV positive, but every day Marlene delays telling her increases her risk of also becoming infected, especially because the couple are trying to have children. If Joan learns after the fact that Marlene knew that she might catch AIDS but did not tell her, she could sue Marlene for exposing her to a "clear and imminent danger." Also, by maintaining Tom's confidentiality, Marlene would seem to be affirming that Tom's right to confidentiality is more important that Joan's right to well-being. She would appear to be siding with one partner by colluding with him to keep a secret.

What would be the consequences of violating confidentiality? In the best possible scenario, Joan would be kept from becoming HIV positive and would be very supportive of Tom. Tom may secretly thank Marlene for telling Joan the secret he could not share. More negative consequences would be that Tom would leave treatment, break up with Joan, or have more drinking binges which might increase his chances of infecting others. Also, he could file a complaint with the NASW Committee on Inquiry, the State Licensing Board, and/or the state court system charging Marlene with violating confidentiality.

Identify who will benefit and who will be harmed in view of social work's commitment to the most vulnerable. If Marlene maintains confidentiality, it would seem that Tom would benefit because his HIV status would remain secret. It can be argued, however, that this secret could not be kept for long. Joan would seem to be harmed because she is unaware of her exposure to AIDS; furthermore, her hoped-for child would be at risk.

If Marlene decides to tell Joan about Tom's HIV status, it would appear that Joan would benefit because she could avoid exposure to the virus and also avoid giving birth to an HIV-infected child. Tom may be harmed because his trust in the therapeutic relationship may be diminished.

The 1996 Code of Ethics emphasizes social workers' responsibility to vulnerable people, and social work literature has repeatedly stressed that the rights of the most vulnerable should prevail (Lewis, 1972; Reisch and Taylor, 1983). One might argue that in the above case, Joan is the more vulnerable and thus that the benefit to her should carry greater weight than the benefit to Tom.

Tom and Joan's differing rights are in conflict. While the principle of confidentiality (Tom's right) is certainly a basic principle of social work, the principle of preserving life (Joan's right) seems more important. When conflicting benefits are in question, considering a hierarchy of rights, such as the one presented by Lowenberg and Dolgoff (1996), may be helpful.

Consult with supervisor and colleagues about the most ethical choice. At lunch Marlene discusses the dilemma with two of her colleagues and receives conflicting advice. One social worker believes that Marlene definitely should call up Joan, because she (Marlene) has the power to keep another person from becoming infected with AIDS. Also Joan is her client, too. What is her responsibility when it comes to protecting Joan? Marlene's other colleague is concerned that Tom, or for that matter Joan, might never trust Marlene again. Doesn't Marlene realize why the social work profession stresses that knowledge of HIV/AIDS infection must be treated with the utmost confidentiality? By violating confidentiality, would Marlene increase the possibility that Tom as well as Joan would be stigmatized and discriminated against?

Unlike many graduates with two years of experience, Marlene still has a supervisor whom she sees regularly. Her supervisor suggests that

Marlene think about her discussions about confidentiality with her clients. Marlene remembers that at the beginning of therapy she discussed confidentiality extensively with both Tom and Joan. Ironically, at that time Tom had expressed the concern that Joan would be repeatedly calling Marlene with complaints about him and that Joan would not air the complaints in the joint sessions. They had then agreed that whatever either of them discussed individually with Marlene would have to be brought up in the general session and that Marlene would support and facilitate this process.

Marlene then relates the information about Tom's HIV status to this earlier discussion about confidentiality. She finally encourages Tom to tell Joan about his HIV status in a joint session, where she would support the couple. Ironically, what seemed to be a major stressor, i.e., Tom's diagnosis, brings the couple closer together, because Tom and Joan decide to work together on coping with this new problem.

The preceding discussion shows how the ETHIC model can be applied to an ethical dilemma involving AIDS and confidentiality. It also demonstrates the importance of establishing guidelines regarding confidentiality at the beginning of treatment.

One might ask if the situation would have been different if Joan had not been a client. Would Marlene be obliged to inform a nonclient of a partner's HIV status? What about nonclient multiple partners? The duty-to-warn principle has not been applied to situations in which there are multiple nonspecific victims (Reamer, 1991).

Service Delivery

Some ethical issues and dilemmas in social work revolve around service delivery on both macro- and microlevels to people with HIV/AIDS and their families. Funding for AIDS treatment continues to be a major issue, especially now that health costs have increased so dramatically and people with AIDS are living longer but with chronic illnesses that require medical attention. Many private insurance companies do not cover members who test positive for the AIDS virus. Without a federal program of universal health care, many working people do not have health coverage. People who are HIV positive may not be able to buy medications to keep the disease in check. Under the new Welfare Reform law if an individual who is HIV positive is too ill to work, he or she may have difficulties establishing the need for welfare and medical benefits. Providers of medicaid managed care, however, have recognized people with HIV/AIDS as a special-needs group, which bodes well for the provision of needed medical and social service.

Funding for prevention and care for the chronically ill is needed. Some programs, such as educational programs in high schools that aim at preventing AIDS, have been severely affected by financial cutbacks. Acute care has received the most attention, but there will be increasing need for care for the chronically ill as more people live longer with AIDS.

More responsibility for welfare and social services has been delegated to the states. This may result in disparate levels of care and benefits for people with AIDS. One might predict that the more liberal states and/or those with the most AIDS victims will provide the best care, while more conservative states with smaller AIDS populations will provide only limited care.

The whole area of AIDS research presents many dilemmas regarding service delivery. In order to test new medications, it is often necessary to use a control group. This means that decisions must be made to create groups of HIV-positive individuals who are not given the benefit of new medications that may prolong their lives. Denying a specific group access to needed treatment that can save their lives has been considered unethical (Richardson, 1997).

A clear responsibility of social workers is to try to assure that all those suffering from AIDS get adequate care, regardless of ability to pay. But social workers have increasing demands on their time. How are they going to assure the delivery of equitable service to people with AIDS? With case loads increasing dramatically because of downsizing and cutbacks, social workers often must make hard decisions. Some social workers adapt a social triage system, that is, the AIDS victim who is the most savable gets the greatest attention. For example, if a social worker must choose between seeing a person with AIDS who is able to maintain his own apartment and is still working and one who is homeless and shows signs of dementia, who will the social worker service first?

Administration and Supervision

The AIDs epidemic presents increasing challenges for the social work administrator/supervisor. The supervisor must advise workers as to which clients need immediate attention. Yet many clients who do not have AIDS have serious social, psychological, and medical problems. Because clients with AIDS are very needy and have been greatly stigmatized, should they receive immediate attention or the most attention? Administrators must often make these difficult decisions in directing workers whose clients have AIDS.

An increasing problem for social work administrators is the employee who is HIV positive. First, what does the administrator do with the information that an employee is HIV positive, especially given the confidential nature of AIDS? If the administrator chooses to say nothing, rumors may develop that harm the employee in particular and the work environment in general. But strict laws on confidentiality prohibit the sharing of information about HIV/AIDS status.

Another concern for the administrator may be the allocation of work assignments. An employee with AIDS may have frequent health-related absences. But the administrator is charged with the responsibility of making sure that work is completed. Also, how can the administrator justify giving a lighter work load to the person with HIV, especially when cutbacks in personnel mean that many employees are working harder than ever before? The social work administrator, however, must be very sympathetic to the personal issues of the worker with AIDS and remain aware of the effect of discrimination on people with AIDS and of their legal and social rights to continue working as long as possible.

The administrator's responsibility toward the worker with AIDS as well as in managing performance expectations and staff reactions regarding the worker has been the subject of heated debate (Anonymous, Mack, and Emery, 1992). Much of the conflict rests on whether the administrator (identified as Anonymous) should focus first on the needs of the individual worker or on the organizational needs that Mack and Emery suggest. When it became absolutely necessary, the clinically focused administrator accommodated the employee's declining health by assigning shorter hours and ultimately reassigning tasks. The administratively focused administrator stressed taking action as soon as the worker's performance changed and planning for alternatives, taking into account the client's legal rights and the organization's need for productivity. Most administrators were clinicians before they became administrators; they therefore may find it difficult to keep an organizational rather than individual perspective when they are dealing with an employee with AIDS. Education is essential to help staff work through phobias and workplace rumors about AIDS, but it may be difficult to reduce deep-rooted fears about AIDS in the workplace.

The new code stresses the important role of advocacy, "with special regard for vulnerable, disadvantaged, oppressed, and exploited people and groups" (NASW, 1996, p. 27). As people with AIDS are certainly a vulnerable population, the social work administrator should advocate for the needs of the person with AIDS, both in the workplace and in the larger community.

CHAPTER 13

Ethical Dilemmas in Supervising and Managing

Despite increased interest in ethics in general, the literature on ethics in supervision and administration is scanty. Only 6 percent of the articles in *Social Work Research and Abstracts* over the last ten years focus on ethics and administration. Lewis raises the question "Is ethical management possible, or is this combination of terms an oxymoron?" (Lewis, 1988, p. 271). Whether the Code of Ethics should apply to managers has been debated, with the author taking the affirmative position (Congress and Gummer, 1996).

Ethics for Administrators

In an early publication on ethics for administrators Levy (1983, p. 277) proposed that "the ethical framework within which it is incumbent upon every social worker to operate" pertains to the chief administrator as much as to the direct-service practitioner. Others have reiterated the important role of the ethical administrator (Cooper, 1990; Joseph, 1983; Lewis, 1988; O'Neill, 1992).

Just as social work educators serve as role models for students (Congress, 1992b; Lewis, 1987), the agency administrator sets the tone for ethical practice throughout the agency. The new Code of Ethics is much more explicit than any previous code in requiring ethical practice of social work administrators as well as supervisors and field instructors. The 1996 Code of Ethics has several provisions that specifically apply to administrators. Administrators are now advised to become advocates both "within and outside of their agencies for adequate resources to meet clients needs" (NASW, 1996, p. 31). The 1996 Code of Ethics spells out the following provision: "Social workers should advocate for resource allocation procedures that are open and fair. When not all clients' needs can be met, an allocation procedure should be developed that is nondiscriminatory and based on appropriate and consistently applied principles" (NASW, 1996, pp. 20–21). Administrators often use principles of distributive justice in deciding how to allocate scarce resources.

Principles of Distributive Justice

Reamer (1995b) cites four main principles of distributive justice that social workers often use to make hard decisions about managing limited resources. The principle of equality implies that everyone will receive an equal amount. But can this principle always be applied in practice? For example, should all people receive housing subsidies, the millionaire as well as the homeless person? Another argument against using the equality principle in all situations is that sometimes resources cannot be divided. For example, there may be only one bed available in a nursing home and four clients who want it. It is not possible to give each client a fourth of a bed.

A second principle of distributive justice, and one that social workers frequently favor, is based on need. Scarce resources can be distributed according to the greatest need. This principle might help in deciding to give a housing subsidy to a homeless person or a bed in a nursing home to the sickest client. But deciding among competing needs is not always easy. There might be a hundred homeless families in need of a housing subsidy but only enough money for ten families. An administrator in a nursing home might have only one bed but several clients with severe but competing needs. Two clients might have terminal illnesses and no families to help. Another client might need nursing home service for only a short while and thus be able to free up the bed for another client.

Need is often determined according to a social triage model. The concept of triage stems from World War II, when difficult decisions as to who would be given medical treatment were made on the battlefield. Soldiers whose condition was the least critical were often the first to receive treatment. Considering social workers' commitment to helping the most vulnerable, the model of social triage may seem abhorrent, but it is often practiced by social service agencies deciding which clients to service or individual practitioners determining which clients to treat.

A third principle of distributive justice, that of compensation based on past and current oppression, has always been important in social work. Affirmative action policies stem from this principle. The 1996 NASW Delegate Assembly reaffirmed this principle in selecting leaders for the professional association, and social workers with a concern for the most vulnerable often apply it in their work. Sometimes, however, it is difficult to determine who is the most vulnerable and which client groups should benefit from compensation.

A final principle of distributive justice, that of contribution, implies that goods or services will be distributed according to what the person has contributed. Social workers concerned about social justice might initially question this principle. But decisions about social services are often made according to this criteria. Poor clients do not receive the same services as middle-class clients. Should an ethical social worker use contribution as a criterion for distributing services? There are some who argue that clients should contribute something for service, even if only a minimal amount. Most sliding scales do not begin at zero. The principle of contribution may be inherent in welfare reform legislation, which proposes that welfare recipients can only receive benefits for a limited amount of time and that each person must participate in workfare in order to receive benefits.

Sometimes contribution is measured by status or power rather than money. For example, in an agency with a waiting list, a relative of a member of the Board of Directors might move to the top of the list Some social workers argue that this granting of special privilege is contrary to the social work value of equal access and opportunity for all, while others maintain that it is necessary if agencies are to continue to provide treatment despite cutbacks in funding for social services.

Administrators struggle with difficult decisions relating to downsizing caused by escalating costs and reduced funding for social service programs. Over a decade ago Reisch and Taylor (1983) made the following suggestions for cutback management that are consistent with social work values and ethical principles:

1. The programs that primarily benefit those less well off should be maintained, while social workers should continue to strive to restore services to all who need them. Preserving programs for the most needy is consistent with the Code of Ethics, which stresses social workers' duty to advocate "with and on behalf of vulnerable and oppressed individuals and groups of people" (NASW, 1996, p. 5). However, it may be difficult to decide who is the most needy. For example, an administrator in a multiservice center encountered a difficult dilemma in deciding whether to maintain a day care center for preschool children or a recreational program for mentally retarded adults.

2. Agencies have an obligation to provide services based upon need rather than on a calculation of cost/benefit. Unfortunately, more and more agencies, including nonprofit agencies, provide services based on cost-benefit analysis rather than on client needs. Social workers must advocate to make client need at least part of the equation when cutbacks in human service agencies are being decided.

3. A unitary mode of service delivery should be developed, because a two-tier model often leads to inferior services for the poorest and most vulnerable segment of society. When poor people are forced into Medicaid managed care, middle- and high-income people may still have private options for fee-for-service medical care. This two-tier system often leads to poor people having less choice and less quality in care.

4. Administrators have the responsibility to avoid cutting services to the politically powerless, who are least able to resist and/or cope with the loss of services. Often social workers work with the most vulnerable, disadvantaged, oppressed, and exploited people and groups, who have very limited resources, if any.

5. Administrators need to be politically active in order to gain support for programs that will benefit the most needy. The new code stresses that social workers "should engage in social and political action that seeks to ensure that all people have equal access to the resources, employment, services, and opportunities" (NASW, 1996, p. 27).

Although providing service to the most vulnerable is an important principle of distributive justice, it is not always easy to determine who is the most vulnerable, as the following case example illustrates.

> Andrea is the director of a small family counseling agency that employs five professional social workers, two paraprofessionals, and two support staff members. The agency is funded through a small state grant for preventive service and a private foundation. Andrea has just learned that government funding for her agency will be greatly reduced next year. She must decide which programs to eliminate. She has already cut community education programs about violence and hot lines that victims of violence could call for more information or help. Should she now cut the child abuse program which is held in schools? Or her newest program, which focuses on family violence across the life cycle and provides services for victims of elder abuse and grandparents raising children? Are children the most needy clients of her agency? Should programs that benefit only adults, such as elder-abuse programs, be eliminated? One can easily see the difficulties in deciding which clients are the most vulnerable.

Andrea has a responsibility to her supervisees as well as to her clients. The 1996 Code of Ethics states that "social workers who are administrators should take reasonable steps to ensure that adequate agency or organizational resources are available to provide adequate staff supervision" (NASW, 1996, p. 21). But Andrea knows that if she continues to use Jane, a senior staff person, to supervise the other workers, Jane will have less time to see clients. The agency has always offered field placement to two social work students, but Andrea wonders if she can take students this year because of their need for supervision.

Andrea's most difficult decision, however, involves the need to reduce staff. Should she lay off Carol, a new graduate who completed a field placement with them last year? Carol had been an outstanding student and demonstrated excellent social work skills. She knows that the job market for social workers is limited and wonders if Carol, her newest employee, could easily find another job. Or should she encourage Sandra, who has been with the agency for thirty years, to take early retirement? On the other hand, she could lay off Stella, a social worker who has been absent a great deal lately because of her husband's serious illness. But Andrea knows that Stella needs the job now more than ever because she is the sole support of her family. Fortunately, it turns out that Andrea is able to deal with staff cutbacks through attrition. One of her social workers, Cindy, informs Andrea that she is resigning at the end of the month to join her boyfriend in California. While reducing staff by attrition is certainly the most ethical way to deal with cutbacks, this may not always be possible.

Andrea also has to struggle with work assignments. Each worker is now given four additional cases, and vacation times are reduced to two weeks. Andrea has always believed that continuing education is important for social workers, but now she thinks she might have to limit the five conference days she allows each year. The 1996 Code of Ethics explicitly states that "social work administrators . . . should . . . provide or arrange for continuing education and staff development" (NASW, 1996, p. 32), but Andrea knows that with limited staff it is difficult to spare a social worker for even a one-day conference.

Social Work Supervisors

Social work supervisors have a responsibility to their workers as well as to management. But first and foremost supervisors are social workers and as such are bound by the Code of Ethics. The 1996 code is very explicit in its demands on supervisors of line workers as well as of social work students.

Social work supervisors often encounter ethical dilemmas in carrying out their work. Ethical dilemmas can involve macro-issues such as the supervisor's responsibility to the administration and the distribution of workloads or micro-issues such as his or her relationships with supervisees. The middle manager is often squeezed between the demands of administration and those of line workers. Now that agencies are facing serious cutbacks, this stress is greater than ever. While supervisors have always had to make difficult decisions in maintaining quality client service with limited staff resources, decreases in staff, greater unionization, and more accountability make the supervisor's role more challenging than ever.

A main administrative task of supervisors is to allocate tasks to supervisees in a fair and equitable manner. Supervisors often use the following principles of distributive justice in making difficult decisions about the use of scarce employees:

1. *Equality.* This principle implies that all workers with the same job title and salary have the same responsibilities and should have equal work assignments.
2. *Clients' needs.* The Code of Ethics states that "social workers' primary responsibility is to promote the well-being of clients" (NASW, 1996, p. 7). This implies that work assignments should be based on an assessment of clients' needs.
3. *Workers' needs.* Workers have different needs that must enter into decisions about work assignments. In the case of disabilities, the Americans with Disabilities Act (1990) provides for accommodations in the workplace to help employees carry out assigned tasks. Workers, however, may need work assignments to be temporarily reduced because of physical and emotional limitations. The Code of Ethics addresses the issue of serious impairment resulting from substance abuse or mental health problems. But even when impairment is minor or short-term, supervisors often can adjust the employee's workload.
4. *Worker power.* While workers do not often think of themselves as powerful, this is not the case. Supervisors may not make assignments to new workers, if they feel that this will entail lengthy, supervisory time that they do not have. Also, supervisors may be reluctant to give extra assignments to workers who are perceived as adversarial.

The following example illustrates some of these issues.

Joan, a supervisor in the Bayview Family Counseling Agency, has five supervisees. Each supervisee has a caseload of thirty clients and their families. The five supervisees are:

1. Abby, an inexperienced worker, performs at a marginal level and needs much supervision.
2. Brian has been with the agency for five years. He is very competent and often assumes new tasks. Recently Joan heard a rumor that he is looking for another job.
3. Carol, who has been with the agency for fifteen years, does the bare minimum of work and is frequently late. Last year Joan unsuccessfully initiated a union grievance because of Carol's lateness.

4. Darryl has worked for the agency for the last two years. He was a good worker until six months ago, when he became ill. Since then he has been out frequently, and Joan believes that he may have to go on medical disability.
5. Evelyn, employed for the last year, is very energetic and enthusiastic. Although she eagerly takes on any new assignment, sometimes she does not follow through.

Joan has recently learned from the director that her unit must take on twenty new clients referred from the governmental agency that funds Bayview. As a middle manager, Joan knows that she cannot refuse to accept the new cases, especially because they are referrals from a funding source. How should she allocate these additional cases?

Should Joan divide the clients equally among her five workers following the principle of equality, giving each employee four cases? Or should she make individual assessments based on client need or employee capacity? Joan knows that if she relies on the principle of client need, she will assign the new clients to the workers who she feels will work with them best. She has the greatest confidence in Brian. But she feels that if she burdens him with more work, he is more apt to leave the agency. Joan knows that Darryl needs special medical care, so she is reluctant to assign him new cases. If she assigns more cases to Abby, she will have to spend more time supervising her and Joan is already overextended. Evelyn will also need close supervision if she is given additional assignments.

Before assigning these cases, Joan reviews each one and makes an additional assessment about the level of service needed. Four are very challenging, six require minor interventions, and the other ten are of moderate complexity. If you were the supervisor, how would you assign these cases?

Relationship with Supervisees

The new code specifically focuses on social work supervisors and their relationship with supervisees. Social work supervisors are advised to supervise only within their areas of knowledge and competence. Are experienced social work supervisors always competent to supervise staff and students in emerging areas of social work practice? Supervisors may need continuing education, which has become a requirement for maintaining certification in many states.

An important aspect of ethical conduct for supervisors requires avoiding dual relationships and setting clear, appropriate boundaries. The new Code of Ethics extends these ethical principles explicitly to supervisors of direct staff workers as well as to field instructors.

The following example illustrates the ethical (or not so ethical) practice of a social work field instructor.

Lisa graduated from social work school about twenty years ago. Right after graduation she went to work in Haven Family Counseling Agency, and for the last fifteen years she has been supervising beginning social workers and students. Schooled in the psychoanalytic method, Lisa believes that this model is the most effective in working with clients. Although her agency now uses primarily a brief-treatment model, she has never had any continuing education on this model.

This year she has had increasing difficulty with one of her students. Lisa questions whether this student, Maureen, will make a good social worker. Their conflict began on the first day of field placement, when Maureen told her clients that she was a student. Lisa does not believe that clients should be told about student status, because it might make them leave treatment or conclude that they are getting inferior treatment. Maureen tries a new cognitive behavioral method with one of her clients, which Lisa predicts will not be successful. Lisa responds very negatively to Maureen when she presents this case at a staff conference and submits a very negative evaluation in which she reiterates that Maureen's approach to the client indicates her immaturity and naivete in attempting to "reinvent the wheel." She tells Maureen that the latter is the worst student she has ever had and wonders why Maureen is not as receptive to supervision as other students.

Lisa believes that Maureen's "personal issues" are interfering with her work with clients. In supervisory sessions Lisa begins to spend more time talking about Maureen's past and present life than about Maureen's clients. Lisa learns that Maureen had a very violent childhood and that she is currently breaking up with an abusive boyfriend. Lisa tells Maureen that she could see her for individual therapy at a reduced rate because Maureen is a student with limited funds.

Is Lisa engaging in ethical practice as a supervisor? She expresses concern for clients and for her supervisee, but much of her behavior seems contrary to the 1996 Code of Ethics. A positive addition to the new code are provisions that directly apply to social work supervisors. But although previous codes may not have been as explicit, social work literature for some time has focused on the ethical behavior of social work supervisors (Cohen, 1987; Congress, 1992a; Levy, 1973). In a classic article Levy (1973) depicted the fundamental value orientation of social work supervisors as including confidentiality, self-determination, and respect for the individual. Cohen (1987) discussed these principles of ethical supervision as they apply to practice dilemmas. Congress (1992a) found that social work supervisors are knowledgeable about the Code of Ethics and apply it readily in resolving ethical dilemmas.

In the previous case example, Lisa, like most social work supervisors, learned on the job and never received formal training in supervision. However, Lisa's lack of continuing education is somewhat unusual among social workers, most of whom attend conferences and take courses to acquire newly emerging knowledge and skills. The new Code of Ethics requires supervisors to provide instruction based on the most current information and knowledge available in the profession. Not only has Lisa not satisfied this requirement, but also there are signs that she is disdainful of new methods in social work, a position that is harmful to supervisees as well as to clients. On the positive side, Lisa is meeting the Code of Ethics requirement that social work supervisors "provide instruction only within their areas of knowledge and competence." Lisa feels that she knows the psychoanalytic model, and she is trying to teach her student about it.

Lisa, however, does not seem to be cognizant of the new code provision that states: "Social workers who function as educators or field instructors for students should take reasonable steps to ensure that clients are routinely informed when services are being provided by students" (NASW, 1996, p. 29). The pros and cons of maintaining secrecy about student status have been discussed in the literature (Feiner and Couch, 1985). The new code makes explicit the supervisor's responsibility to convey this information to clients. Lisa uses the argument that clients will leave treatment if they know that a student is treating them. However, this is only an assumption, and often a discussion about student status enables the clients to reveal feelings about therapy and the therapist that may previously have been hidden.

The importance of evaluating supervisees in a fair and respectful way has repeatedly been stressed in social work literature (Kadushin, 1992; Shulman, 1992b; Wilson, 1978). The 1996 code reiterates this position. It is doubtful whether Lisa relates to Maureen "in a manner that is fair and respectful" (NASW, 1996, p. 29), which the new code requires of supervisors in their dealing with both employees and students. By openly criticizing

Maureen at a staff meeting, and by comparing her unfavorably with other students, Lisa does not seem to be affording Maureen proper respect. While it is appropriate for supervisors to make constructive criticisms, Lisa seems to rely mainly on negative feedback.

Lisa's most alarming ethical violation, however, involves dual relationships. The 1996 code states explicitly that "supervisors should not engage in any dual or multiple relationships with supervisees in which there is a risk of exploitation of or potential harm to the supervisee [or] to the student" (NASW, 1996, p. 29). Social workers are further charged with setting clear and appropriate boundaries. Lisa has suggested that Maureen become her private client. The dangers of "therapizing" the student is perceived as a problem area for supervisors (Congress, 1997) and demonstrates a failure to maintain appropriate boundaries. This situation is even worse because Lisa is trying to initiate a dual relationship, that of therapist with Maureen. Lisa and Maureen already have a supervisor/supervisee relationship. To take Maureen into Lisa's private practice would harm the student. Because of their ongoing conflict, Maureen may not want to enter into a therapeutic relationship with Lisa. But what would happen if Maureen refuses to enter into this relationship? If Maureen chooses not to begin therapy with Lisa, will the former's progress in school be threatened? Is she at risk of receiving an evaluation that is even worse than the earlier one? Social work supervision should embody elements of self-determination and informed consent (Congress, 1997). Both would be jeopardized if Maureen begins therapy with Lisa. Because Lisa has the greater power, she must be the one to avoid engaging Maureen in a dual relationship.

Implications

Students and beginning workers often learn ethics by observing the ethical behavior of their supervisors (Congress, 1992b; Lewis, 1987). Supervisors have an important responsibility not only to acquaint their supervisees with the Code of Ethics but also to model appropriate behavior for their supervisees. Social workers who are ethically supervised as students are more likely to engage in ethical practice with their clients.

CHAPTER 14

The Future of Social Work Ethics

What will be the state of social work ethics in the twenty-first century? A profession uses a code to define its values and ethical standards to its members as well as to the public. The 1996 NASW Code of Ethics is the most comprehensive so far and delineates for the first time social work values as well as ethical standards. In contrast to previous codes, the current code is appropriate for social workers at different levels and in many different fields of practice. It also discusses timely topics such as cultural diversity and sexual harassment.

A professional code is never a finished product. One can predict that in the new millennium the Code of Ethics may be revised because of changes in the environment. Globalization, privatization, managed care, and hypertechnology will certainly influence social workers' Code of Ethics in the twenty-first century.

Because the Code of Ethics only became effective in January 1997, the committees of inquiry associated with each NASW state chapter have not received much feedback on it. The code states that "some of the standards . . . are enforceable guidelines for professional conduct, and some are aspirational" (NASW, 1996, p. 7). To help social workers function effectively in an increasingly litigious environment, revisions of the code might differentiate enforceable guidelines from aspirational standards.

It has been argued that the code's lack of historical or case references, interpretive guides, or formal or informal opinions make it difficult to apply (Jayartne, Croxton, and Mattison, 1997). However, to be useful to social workers involved in many different fields, a code of ethics must be general. Thus, too much case specificity would not be helpful. The code provides only limited help in resolving ethical dilemmas, in that it "does not specify what values, principles, and standards are most important and ought to outweigh others in instances when they conflict" (NASW, 1996, p. 3). NASW does publish pamphlets on professional standards in different practice areas. These pamphlets could be expanded to include specific examples and information that would help resolve ethical dilemmas. Also, future revisions of the code could include a hierarchy of ethical values and standards to help social workers struggling with ethical conflicts.

Who will we be (Gibelman and Schervish, 1997), what will the profession look like (Raffoul and McNeece, 1996), and how will ethics be integrated into social work practice are key questions for social workers as we approach the twenty-first century. Some scholars in the field predict the "death of social work" because of "bold new hypertechnologies [that] will make interventive skills obsolete," "the collapse of the grand narratives [of Marxism and psychoanalysis]," and "radical dislocations in the social structure," including an increasingly international focus and reduction of public sector social services (Krueger, 1997, p. 19). This author, however, believes that social workers will be needed more than ever in the next century to direct the new technologies for the benefit of the most needy. The "grand narratives" of Marx and Freud were somewhat limited and perhaps did not adequately reflect the profession's concern for social justice, especially for the most vulnerable in an increasingly diverse society. Thus the "collapse of [these] narratives" certainly suits the social work profession at the beginning of the new millennium. Finally, expanded employment opportunities in the international arena and the private sector potentially extend social workers' area of operation beyond a narrowly defined nonprofit American market. Our value base will help define and strengthen our role in the new society. Social workers now practice in a new world of globalization and privatization, and our professional responsibility will be to incorporate our value system into ethical practice in a changed environment.

Who will be the social workers in the years to come? Gibelman and Schervish (1997) note the increase of women social workers and how this relates to status and income level in the profession. The Code of Ethics addresses gender discrimination and stresses that social workers should strive to promote nondiscrimination both in micro- and macro-practice in social work and in the larger community.

American society is becoming increasingly diverse. For the first time, the code includes a section on cultural competence, advising social workers to incorporate cultural sensitivity and competence in agency and educational practice. The labor force in social work demonstrates increasing diversity. NASW leadership uses an affirmative-action model to ensure diversity in its ranks, and individual chapters, such as New York City, have developed special cultural and racial interest groups. However, there is more work to be done in involving diverse members in professional associations (Gibelman and Schervish, 1997). Diversity in our membership is essential to promoting an ethnically sensitive Code of Ethics.

The average age of a student entering graduate social work education has declined (Lennon, 1995); thus social workers are younger as they begin their careers. What impact will a younger population of social workers have on the profession and on ethical practice? The notion of confidentiality is very different for social workers who have been raised on computers. While, as a student, I learned not to leave case records open on my desk when I went to lunch, students now learn to use passwords and firewalls to protect confidential information. It is not that ethics is dead, as Kreuger (1997) implies, but rather that ethical practice must be discussed and maintained in different ways.

It is not who we are and will be but rather what we will be doing that has the most serious consequences for ethical practice. The increase of social workers in the mental health field has been noted (Gibelman and Schervish, 1997). Although DSM-IV diagnoses are increasingly required by managed-care companies, social workers must be ever diligent to avoid stigmatizing clients. Social workers need to be encouraged to apply all axes of DSM-IV, especially those that relate to social work assessments—Axis 4 on psychosocial problems and Axis 5 on the client's overall functioning. Social workers in the mental health field can promote "the least restrictive environment" for clients. This policy is certainly in keeping with the Code of Ethics, which promotes maximizing clients' motivation, resources, and opportunities. Furthermore, the least restrictive environment is also the least expensive, which coincides with the cost-containment concerns of managed-care providers.

Social workers are moving away from public and nonprofit agencies into private agencies or private practice. Nonprofit agencies are being replaced by profit-motivated agencies. Social workers are ethically bound to promote social justice (NASW, 1996). There is a concern that private agencies are more motivated by financial costs and benefits than by human costs and benefits. Social workers have a responsibility to bring their perspective on client service into the agency that employs them. As more managed-care companies begin to employ social workers, social workers will be able to work from the inside to incorporate their values into the delivery of services.

The move to private practice is of concern, as social workers may be "abandon[ing] its mission to help the poor and the oppressed and to build communality" (Specht and Courtney, 1994, p. 4). The Code of Ethics encourages social workers "to volunteer some portion of their professional skills with no expectation of significant financial return (pro bono service)" (NASW, 1996, p. 5). Social workers in private practice must expand their practice to include some pro bono work, especially because more and more people have little or no mental health insurance coverage. Social workers in private practice are often thought to be unconcerned about social justice (Specht and Courtney, 1994). But a recent study indicated that social workers rarely made termination decisions based on the client's financial status (Jayartne, Croxton, and Mattison, 1997), which seems to demonstrate a concern for social justice.

An increase in empirically based practice is predicted for the twenty-first century (Raffoul and McNeece, 1996). As long as research is based on social work values, an empirical perspective is not incompatible with ethical practice. The literature on social work ethics reflects this trend by its increasing efforts to objectively measure social work values and ethical practice (Walden, Wolock, and Demone, 1992; Dolgoff and Skolnik, 1996; Jayartne, Croxton, and Mattison, 1997). This focus on empiricism in the field of ethics bodes well for ethical practice in the future.

The environment in which social workers practice is rapidly changing. Managed care in both public and private sectors has led to limits on the length of treatment, a greater focus on measurable outcomes, and less privacy for the client. Ethical social workers are concerned about curtailment of and limits to services to clients. NASW is compiling a critical-incident study based on client, social worker, and agency reports of denial or curtailment of services. This report will be used to advocate politically for client needs on federal, state, and local levels.

While paying more attention to measurable outcomes is not unethical, social work values must always be part of any treatment plan. For example, even if aversive behavioral therapy demonstrates positive outcomes in treating a client's phobia, because it shows lack of respect for the individual it is unacceptable as a treatment. A final ethical concern with managed care relates to confidentiality. While in the past, communication between therapist and client was kept confidential, in the new managed-care environment others routinely review sensitive client material (Corcoran and Winslade, 1990). It is estimated that at least seventeen people review the treatment report of a client covered by managed care (Munson, 1996).

Social workers must remain diligent in ensuring confidentiality to clients in a managed-care environment. It is not sufficient to have clients sign lengthy waivers describing the limits of confidentiality. Social workers must partner with managed-care companies and clients to protect client confidentiality, especially in sensitive areas. Furthermore, social workers need to rethink what type of information must be shared with managed-care companies and submit reports accordingly.

Technology in general challenges ethical social workers' view of client interactions. With voice mail, fax machines, computers, e-mail, and the Internet, information that was once private is now public. Clients should be informed about limits to confidentiality caused by new technology, and agencies must develop systems to protect sensitive information. Social workers must assess the level of confidentiality needed for the type of information and transmit the information in the least risky way (Rock and Congress, 1997).

A final concern for the ethical social worker in the late 1990s is the widening gap between rich and poor. Welfare reform, workfare, curtailment of benefits to immigrants, and limited job opportunities have led to a growing population without financial, social, and educational supports. More than any previous code the new Code of Ethics stresses the social worker's duty "to expand choice and opportunity for all people, with special regard for vulnerable, disadvantaged, oppressed and exploited people and groups" (NASW, 1996, p. 27). These challenging times demand that social workers attend to the goal of promoting ethical social work in the twenty-first century.

The NASW Code of Ethics

Ethical Principles

The following broad ethical principles are based on social work's core values of service, social justice, dignity and worth of the person, importance of human relationships, integrity, and competence. These principles set forth ideals to which all social workers should aspire.

Value: *Service*
Ethical Principle: *Social workers' primary goal is to help people in need and to address social problems.*

Social workers elevate service to others above self-interest. Social workers draw on their knowledge, values, and skills to help people in need and to address social problems. Social workers are encouraged to volunteer some portion of their professional skills with no expectation of significant financial return (pro bono service).

Value: *Social Justice*
Ethical Principle: *Social workers challenge social injustice.*

Social workers pursue social change, particularly with and on behalf of vulnerable and oppressed individuals and groups of people. Social workers' social change efforts are focused primarily on issues of poverty, unemployment, discrimination, and other forms of social injustice. These activities seek to promote sensitivity to and knowledge about oppression and cultural and ethnic diversity. Social workers strive to ensure access to needed information, services, and resources; equality of opportunity; and meaningful participation in decision making for all people.

Value: *Dignity and Worth of the Person*
Ethical Principle: *Social workers respect the inherent dignity and worth of the person.*

Social workers treat each person in a caring and respectful fashion, mindful of individual differences and cultural and ethnic diversity. Social workers promote clients' socially responsible self-determination. Social workers seek to enhance clients' capacity and opportunity to change and to address their own needs. Social workers are cognizant of their dual responsibility to clients and to the broader society. They seek to resolve conflicts between clients' interests and the broader society's interests in a socially responsible manner consistent with the values, ethical principles, and ethical standards of the profession.

Value: *Importance of Human Relationships*
Ethical Principle: *Social workers recognize the central importance of human relationships.*

Social workers understand that relationships between and among people are an important vehicle for change. Social workers engage people as partners in the helping process. Social workers seek to strengthen relationships among people in a purposeful effort to promote, restore, maintain, and enhance the well-being of individuals, families, social groups, organizations, and communities.

Value: *Integrity*
Ethical Principle: *Social workers behave in a trustworthy manner.*

Social workers are continually aware of the profession's mission, values, ethical principles, and ethical standards and practice in a manner consistent with them. Social workers act honestly and responsibly and promote ethical practices on the part of the organizations with which they are affiliated.

Value: *Competence*
Ethical Principle: *Social workers practice within their areas of competence and develop and enhance their professional expertise.*

Social workers continually strive to increase their professional knowledge and skills and to apply them in practice. Social workers should aspire to contribute to the knowledge base of the profession.

Ethical Standards

The following ethical standards are relevant to the professional activities of all social workers. These standards concern (1) social workers' ethical responsibilities to clients, (2) social workers' ethical responsibilities to colleagues, (3) social workers' ethical responsibilities in practice settings, (4) social workers' ethical responsibilities as professionals, (5) social workers' ethical responsibilities to the social work profession, and

(6) social workers' ethical responsibilities to the broader society.

Some of the standards that follow are enforceable guidelines for professional conduct, and some are aspirational. The extent to which each standard is enforceable is a matter of professional judgment to be exercised by those responsible for reviewing alleged violations of ethical standards.

1. SOCIAL WORKERS' ETHICAL RESPONSIBILITIES TO CLIENTS

1.01 Commitment to Clients

Social workers' primary responsibility is to promote the well-being of clients. In general, clients' interests are primary. However, social workers' responsibility to the larger society or specific legal obligations may on limited occasions supersede the loyalty owed clients, and clients should be so advised. (Examples include when a social worker is required by law to report that a client has abused a child or has threatened to harm self or others.)

1.02 Self-Determination

Social workers respect and promote the right of clients to self-determination and assist clients in their efforts to identify and clarify their goals. Social workers may limit clients' right to self-determination when, in the social workers' professional judgment, clients' actions or potential actions pose a serious, foreseeable, and imminent risk to themselves or others.

1.03 Informed Consent

(a) Social workers should provide services to clients only in the context of a professional relationship based, when appropriate, on valid informed consent. Social workers should use clear and understandable language to inform clients of the purpose of the services, risks related to the services, limits to services because of the requirements of a third-party payer, relevant costs, reasonable alternatives, clients' right to refuse or withdraw consent, and the time frame covered by the consent. Social workers should provide clients with an opportunity to ask questions.

(b In instances when clients are not literate or have difficulty understanding the primary language used in the practice setting, social workers should take steps to ensure clients' comprehension. This may include providing clients with a detailed verbal explanation or arranging for a qualified interpreter or translator whenever possible.

(c) In instances when clients lack the capacity to provide informed consent, social workers should protect clients' interests by seeking permission from an appropriate third party, informing clients consistent with the clients' level of understanding. In such instances social workers should seek to ensure that the third party acts in a manner consistent with clients' wishes and interests. Social workers should take reasonable steps to enhance such clients' ability to give informed consent.

(d) In instances when clients are receiving services involuntarily, social workers should provide information about the nature and extent of services and about the extent of clients' right to refuse service.

(e) Social workers who provide services via electronic media (such as computer, telephone, radio, and television) should inform recipients of the limitations and risks associated with such services.

(f) Social workers should obtain clients' informed consent before audiotaping or videotaping clients or permitting observation of services to clients by a third party.

1.04   Competence
(a) Social workers should provide services and represent themselves as competent only within the boundaries of their education, training, license, certification, consultation received, supervised experience, or other relevant professional experience.

(b) Social workers should provide services in substantive areas or use intervention techniques or approaches that are new to them only after engaging in appropriate study, training, consultation, and supervision from people who are competent in those interventions or techniques.

(c) When generally recognized standards do not exist with respect to an emerging area of practice, social workers should exercise careful judgment and take responsible steps (including appropriate education, research, training, consultation, and supervision) to ensure the competence of their work and to protect clients from harm.

1.05   Cultural Competence and Social Diversity
(a) Social workers should understand culture and its function in human behavior and society, recognizing the strengths that exist in all cultures.

(b) Social workers should have a knowledge base of their clients' cultures and be able to demonstrate competence in the provision of services that are sensitive to clients' cultures and tc differences among people and cultural groups.

(c) Social workers should obtain education about and seek to understand the nature of social diversity and oppression with respect to race, ethnicity, national origin, color, sex, sexual orientation, age, marital status, political belief, religion, and mental or physical disability.

1.06   Conflicts of Interest

(a) Social workers should be alert to and avoid conflicts of interest that interfere with the exercise of professional discretion and impartial judgment. Social workers should inform clients when a real or potential conflict of interest arises and take reasonable steps to resolve the issue in a manner that makes the clients' interests primary and protects clients' interests to the greatest extent possible. In some cases, protecting clients' interests may require termination of the professional relationship with proper referral of the client.

(b) Social workers should not take unfair advantage of any professional relationship or exploit others to further their personal, religious, political, or business interests.

(c) Social workers should not engage in dual or multiple relationships with clients or former clients in which there is a risk of exploitation or potential harm to the client. In instances when dual or multiple relationships are unavoidable, social workers should take steps to protect clients and are responsible for setting clear, appropriate, and culturally sensitive boundaries. (Dual or multiple relationships occur when social workers relate to clients in more than one relationship, whether professional, social, or business. Dual or multiple relationships can occur simultaneously or consecutively.)

(d) When social workers provide services to two or more people who have a relationship with each other (for example, couples, family members), social workers should clarify with all parties which individuals will be considered clients and the nature of social workers' professional obligations to the various individuals who are receiving services. Social workers who anticipate a conflict of interest among the individuals receiving services or who anticipate having to perform in potentially conflicting roles (for example, when a social worker is asked to testify in a child custody dispute or divorce proceedings involving clients) should clarify their role with the parties involved and take appropriate action to minimize any conflict of interest.

1.07   Privacy and Confidentiality
(a) Social workers should respect clients' right to privacy. Social workers should not solicit private information from clients unless it is essential to providing services or conducting social work evaluation or research. Once private information is shared, standards of confidentiality apply.

(b) Social workers may disclose confidential information when appropriate with valid consent from a client or a person legally authorized to consent on behalf of a client.

(c) Social workers should protect the confidentiality of all information obtained in the course of professional service, except for compelling professional reasons. The general expectation that social workers will keep information confidential does not apply when disclosure is necessary to prevent serious, foreseeable, and imminent harm to a client or other identifiable person or when laws or regulations require disclosure without a client's consent. In all instances, social workers should disclose the least amount of confidential information necessary to achieve the desired purpose; only information that is directly relevant to the purpose for which the disclosure is made should be revealed.

(d) Social workers should inform clients, to the extent possible, about the disclosure of confidential information and the potential consequences, when feasible before the disclosure is made. This applies whether social workers disclose confidential information on the basis of a legal requirement or client consent.

(e) Social workers should discuss with clients and other interested parties the nature of confidentiality and limitations of clients' right to confidentiality. Social workers should review with clients circumstances where confidential information may be requested and where disclosure of confidential information may be legally required. This discussion should occur as soon as possible in the social worker–client relationship and as needed throughout the course of the relationship.

(f) When social workers provide counseling services to families, couples, or groups, social workers should seek agreement among the parties involved concerning each individual's right to confidentiality and obligation to preserve the confidentiality of information shared by others. Social workers should inform participants in family, couples, or group counseling that social workers cannot guarantee that all participants will honor such agreements.

(g) Social workers should inform clients involved in family, couples, marital, or group counseling of the social worker's, employer's, and agency's policy concerning the social worker's disclosure of confidential information among the parties involved in the counseling.

(h) Social workers should not disclose confidential information to third-party payers unless clients have authorized such disclosure.

(i) Social workers should not discuss confidential information in any setting unless privacy can be ensured. Social workers should not discuss confidential information in public or semipublic areas such as hallways, waiting rooms, elevators, and restaurants.

(j) Social workers should protect the confidentiality of clients during legal proceedings to the extent permitted by law. When a court of law or other legally authorized body orders social workers to disclose confidential or privileged information without a client's consent and such disclosure could cause harm to the client, social workers should request that the court withdraw the order or limit the order as narrowly as possible or maintain the records under seal, unavailable for public inspection.

(k) Social workers should protect the confidentiality of clients when responding to requests from members of the media.

(l) Social workers should protect the confidentiality of clients' written and electronic records and other sensitive information. Social workers should take reasonable steps to ensure that clients' records are stored in a secure location and that clients' records are not available to others who are not authorized to have access.

(m) Social workers should take precautions to ensure and maintain the confidentiality of information transmitted to other parties through the use of computers, electronic mail, facsimile machines, telephones and telephone answering machines, and other electronic or computer technology. Disclosure of identifying information should be avoided whenever possible.

(n) Social workers should transfer or dispose of clients' records in a manner that protects clients' confidentiality and is consistent with state statutes governing records and social work licensure.

(o) Social workers should take reasonable precautions to protect client confidentiality in the event of the social worker's termination of practice, incapacitation, or death.

(p) Social workers should not disclose identifying information when discussing clients for teaching or training purposes unless the client has consented to disclosure of confidential information.

(q) Social workers should not disclose identifying information when discussing clients with consultants unless the client has consented to disclosure of confidential information or there is a compelling need for such disclosure.

(r) Social workers should protect the confidentiality of deceased clients consistent with the preceding standards.

1.08   Access to Records
(a) Social workers should provide clients with reasonable access to records concerning the clients. Social workers who are concerned that clients' access to their records could cause serious misunderstanding or harm to the client should provide assistance in interpreting the records and consultation with the client regarding the records. Social workers should limit clients' access to their records, or portions of their records, only in exceptional circumstances when there is compelling evidence that such access would cause serious harm to the client. Both clients' requests and the rationale for withholding some or all of the record should be documented in clients' files.

(b) When providing clients with access to their records, social workers should take steps to protect the confidentiality of other individuals identified or discussed in such records.

1.09   Sexual Relationships
(a) Social workers should under no circumstances engage in sexual activities or sexual contact with current clients, whether such contact is consensual or forced.

(b) Social workers should not engage in sexual activities or sexual contact with clients' relatives or other individuals with whom clients maintain a close personal relationship when there is a risk of exploitation or potential harm to the client. Sexual activity or sexual contact with clients' relatives or other individuals with whom clients maintain a personal relationship has the potential to be harmful to the client and may make it difficult for the social worker and client to maintain appropriate professional boundaries. Social workers—not their clients, their clients' relatives, or other individuals with whom the client maintains a personal relationship—assume the full burden for setting clear, appropriate, and culturally sensitive boundaries.

(c) Social workers should not engage in sexual activities or sexual contact with former clients because of the potential for harm to the client. If social workers engage in conduct contrary to this prohibition or claim that an exception to this prohibition is warranted because of extraordinary circumstances, it is social workers—not their clients—who assume the full burden of demonstrating that the former client has not been exploited, coerced, or manipulated, intentionally or unintentionally.

(d) Social workers should not provide clinical services to individuals with whom they have had a prior sexual relationship. Providing clinical services to a former sexual partner has the potential to be harmful to the individual and is likely to make it difficult for the social worker and individual to maintain appropriate professional boundaries.

1.10   Physical Contact
Social workers should not engage in physical contact with clients when there is a possibility of psychological harm to the client as a result of the contact (such as cradling or caressing clients). Social workers who engage in appropriate physical contact with clients are responsible for setting clear, appropriate, and culturally sensitive boundaries that govern such physical contact.

1.11   Sexual Harassment
Social workers should not sexually harass clients. Sexual harassment includes sexual advances, sexual solicitation, requests for sexual favors, and other verbal or physical conduct of a sexual nature.

1.12 **Derogatory Language**
Social workers should not use derogatory language in their written or verbal communications to or about clients. Social workers should use accurate and respectful language in all communications to and about clients.

1.13 **Payment for Services**
(a) When setting fees, social workers should ensure that the fees are fair, reasonable, and commensurate with the services performed. Consideration should be given to clients' ability to pay.

(b) Social workers should avoid accepting goods or services from clients as payment for professional services. Bartering arrangements, particularly involving services, create the potential for conflicts of interest, exploitation, and inappropriate boundaries in social workers' relationships with clients. Social workers should explore and may participate in bartering only in very limited circumstances when it can be demonstrated that such arrangements are an accepted practice among professionals in the local community, considered to be essential for the provision of services, negotiated without coercion, and entered into at the client's initiative and with the client's informed consent. Social workers who accept goods or services from clients as payment for professional services assume the full burden of demonstrating that this arrangement will not be detrimental to the client or the professional relationship.

(c) Social workers should not solicit a private fee or other remuneration for providing services to clients who are entitled to such available services through the social workers' employer or agency.

1.14 **Clients Who Lack Decision-Making Capacity**
When social workers act on behalf of clients who lack the capacity to make informed decisions, social workers should take reasonable steps to safeguard the interests and rights of those clients.

1.15 **Interruption of Services**
Social workers should make reasonable efforts to ensure continuity of services in the event that services are interrupted by factors such as unavailability, relocation, illness, disability, or death.

1.16 **Termination of Services**
(a) Social workers should terminate services to clients and professional relationships with them when such services and relationships are no longer required or no longer serve the clients' needs or interests.

(b) Social workers should take reasonable steps to avoid abandoning clients who are still in need of services. Social workers should withdraw services precipitously only under unusual circumstances, giving careful consideration to all factors in the situation and taking care to minimize possible adverse effects. Social workers should assist in making appropriate arrangements for continuation of services when necessary.

(c) Social workers in fee-for-service settings may terminate services to clients who are not paying an overdue balance if the financial contractual arrangements have been made clear to the client, if the client does not pose an imminent danger to self or others, and if the clinical and other consequences of the current nonpayment have been addressed and discussed with the client.

(d) Social workers should not terminate services to pursue a social, financial, or sexual relationship with a client.

(e) Social workers who anticipate the termination or interruption of services to clients should notify clients promptly and seek the transfer, referral, or continuation of services in relation to the clients' needs and preferences.

(f) Social workers who are leaving an employment setting should inform clients of appropriate options for the continuation of services and of the benefits and risks of the options.

2. SOCIAL WORKERS' ETHICAL RESPONSIBILITIES TO COLLEAGUES

2.01 Respect
(a) Social workers should treat colleagues with respect and should represent accurately and fairly the qualifications, views, and obligations of colleagues.

(b) Social workers should avoid unwarranted negative criticism of colleagues in communications with clients or with other professionals. Unwarranted negative criticism may include demeaning comments that refer to colleagues' level of competence or to individuals' attributes such as race, ethnicity, national origin, color, sex, sexual orientation, age, marital status, political belief, religion, and mental or physical disability.

(c) Social workers should cooperate with social work colleagues and with colleagues of other professions when such cooperation serves the well-being of clients.

2.02   Confidentiality
Social workers should respect confidential information shared by colleagues in the course of their professional relationships and transactions. Social workers should ensure that such colleagues understand social workers' obligation to respect confidentiality and any exceptions related to it.

2.03   Interdisciplinary Collaboration
(a) Social workers who are members of an interdisciplinary team should participate in and contribute to decisions that affect the well-being of clients by drawing on the perspectives, values, and experiences of the social work profession. Professional and ethical obligations of the interdisciplinary team as a whole and of its individual members should be clearly established.

(b) Social workers for whom a team decision raises ethical concerns should attempt to resolve the disagreement through appropriate channels. If the disagreement cannot be resolved, social workers should pursue other avenues to address their concerns consistent with client well-being.

2.04   Disputes Involving Colleagues
(a) Social workers should not take advantage of a dispute between a colleague and an employer to obtain a position or otherwise advance the social workers' own interests.

(b) Social workers should not exploit clients in disputes with colleagues or engage clients in any inappropriate discussion of conflicts between social workers and their colleagues.

2.05   Consultation
(a) Social workers should seek the advice and counsel of colleagues whenever such consultation is in the best interests of clients.

(b) Social workers should keep themselves informed about colleagues' areas of expertise and competencies. Social workers should seek consultation only from colleagues who have demonstrated knowledge, expertise, and competence related to the subject of the consultation.

(c) When consulting with colleagues about clients, social workers should disclose the least amount of information necessary to achieve the purposes of the consultation.

2.06   Referral for Services
(a) Social workers should refer clients to other professionals when the other professionals' specialized knowledge or expertise is needed to serve clients fully or when social workers believe that they are not being effective or making reasonable progress with clients and that additional service is required.

(b) Social workers who refer clients to other professionals should take appropriate steps to facilitate an orderly transfer of responsibility. Social workers who refer clients to other professionals should disclose, with clients' consent, all pertinent information to the new service providers.

(c) Social workers are prohibited from giving or receiving payment for a referral when no professional service is provided by the referring social worker.

2.07   Sexual Relationships
(a) Social workers who function as supervisors or educators should not engage in sexual activities or contact with supervisees, students, trainees, or other colleagues over whom they exercise professional authority.

(b) Social workers should avoid engaging in sexual relationships with colleagues when there is potential for a conflict of interest. Social workers who become involved in, or anticipate becoming involved in, a sexual relationship with a colleague have a duty to transfer professional responsibilities, when necessary, to avoid a conflict of interest.

2.08   Sexual Harassment
Social workers should not sexually harass supervisees, students, trainees, or colleagues. Sexual harassment includes sexual advances, sexual solicitation, requests for sexual favors, and other verbal or physical conduct of a sexual nature.

2.09   Impairment of Colleagues
(a) Social workers who have direct knowledge of a social work colleague's impairment that is due to personal problems, psychosocial distress, substance abuse, or mental health difficulties and that

interferes with practice effectiveness should consult with that colleague when feasible and assist the colleague in taking remedial action.

(b) Social workers who believe that a social work colleague's impairment interferes with practice effectiveness and that the colleague has not taken adequate steps to address the impairment should take action through appropriate channels established by employers, agencies, NASW, licensing and regulatory bodies, and other professional organizations.

2.10   Incompetence of Colleagues

(a) Social workers who have direct knowledge of a social work colleague's incompetence should consult with that colleague when feasible and assist the colleague in taking remedial action.

(b) Social workers who believe that a social work colleague is incompetent and has not taken adequate steps to address the incompetence should take action through appropriate channels established by employers, agencies, NASW, licensing and regulatory bodies, and other professional organizations.

2.11   Unethical Conduct of Colleagues

(a) Social workers should take adequate measures to discourage, prevent, expose, and correct the unethical conduct of colleagues.

(b) Social workers should be knowledgeable about established policies and procedures for handling concerns about colleagues' unethical behavior. Social workers should be familiar with national, state, and local procedures for handling ethics complaints. These include policies and procedures created by NASW, licensing and regulatory bodies, employers, agencies, and other professional organizations.

(c) Social workers who believe that a colleague has acted unethically should seek resolution by discussing their concerns with the colleague when feasible and when such discussion is likely to be productive.

(d) When necessary, social workers who believe that a colleague has acted unethically should take action through appropriate formal channels (such as contacting a state licensing board or regulatory body, an NASW committee on inquiry, or other professional ethics committees).

(e) Social workers should defend and assist colleagues who are unjustly charged with unethical conduct.

3. SOCIAL WORKERS' ETHICAL RESPONSIBILITIES IN PRACTICE SETTINGS

3.01 Supervision and Consultation

(a) Social workers who provide supervision or consultation should have the necessary knowledge and skill to supervise or consult appropriately and should do so only within their areas of knowledge and competence.

(b) Social workers who provide supervision or consultation are responsible for setting clear, appropriate, and culturally sensitive boundaries.

(c) Social workers should not engage in any dual or multiple relationships with supervisees in which there is a risk of exploitation of or potential harm to the supervisee.

(d) Social workers who provide supervision should evaluate supervisees' performance in a manner that is fair and respectful.

3.02 Education and Training

(a) Social workers who function as educators, field instructors for students, or trainers should provide instruction only within their areas of knowledge and competence and should provide instruction based on the most current information and knowledge available in the profession.

(b) Social workers who function as educators or field instructors for students should evaluate students' performance in a manner that is fair and respectful.

(c) Social workers who function as educators or field instructors for students should take reasonable steps to ensure that clients are routinely informed when services are being provided by students.

(d) Social workers who function as educators or field instructors for students should not engage in any dual or multiple relationships with students in which there is a risk of exploitation or potential harm to the student. Social work educators and field instructors are responsible for setting clear, appropriate, and culturally sensitive boundaries.

3.03   Performance Evaluation

Social workers who have responsibility for evaluating the performance of others should fulfill such responsibility in a fair and considerate manner and on the basis of clearly stated criteria.

3.04   Client Records

(a) Social workers should take reasonable steps to ensure that documentation in records is accurate and reflects the services provided.

(b) Social workers should include sufficient and timely documentation in records to facilitate the delivery of services and to ensure continuity of services provided to clients in the future.

(c) Social workers' documentation should protect clients' privacy to the extent that is possible and appropriate and should include only information that is directly relevant to the delivery of services.

(d) Social workers should store records following the termination of services to ensure reasonable future access. Records should be maintained for the number of years required by state statutes or relevant contracts.

3.05   Billing

Social workers should establish and maintain billing practices that accurately reflect the nature and extent of services provided and that identify who provided the service in the practice setting.

3.06   Client Transfer

(a) When an individual who is receiving services from another agency or colleague contacts a social worker for services, the social worker should carefully consider the client's needs before agreeing to provide services. To minimize possible confusion and conflict, social workers should discuss with potential clients the nature of the clients' current relationship with other service providers and the implications, including possible benefits or risks, of entering into a relationship with a new service provider.

(b) If a new client has been served by another agency or colleague, social workers should discuss with the client whether consultation with the previous service provider is in the client's best interest.

3.07   Administration

(a) Social work administrators should advocate within and outside their agencies for adequate resources to meet clients' needs.

(b) Social workers should advocate for resource allocation procedures that are open and fair. When not all clients' needs can be met, an allocation procedure should be developed that is nondiscriminatory and based on appropriate and consistently applied principles.

(c) Social workers who are administrators should take reasonable steps to ensure that adequate agency or organizational resources are available to provide appropriate staff supervision.

(d) Social work administrators should take reasonable steps to ensure that the working environment for which they are responsible is consistent with and encourages compliance with the NASW Code of Ethics. Social work administrators should take reasonable steps to eliminate any conditions in their organizations that violate, interfere with, or discourage compliance with the Code.

3.08   Continuing Education and Staff Development
Social work administrators and supervisors should take reasonable steps to provide or arrange for continuing education and staff development for all staff for whom they are responsible. Continuing education and staff development should address current knowledge and emerging developments related to social work practice and ethics.

3.09   Commitments to Employers
(a) Social workers generally should adhere to commitments made to employers and employing organizations.

(b) Social workers should work to improve employing agencies' policies and procedures and the efficiency and effectiveness of their services.

(c) Social workers should take reasonable steps to ensure that employers are aware of social workers' ethical obligations as set forth in the NASW Code of Ethics and of the implications of those obligations for social work practice.

(d) Social workers should not allow an employing organization's policies, procedures, regulations, or administrative orders to interfere with their ethical practice of social work. Social workers should take reasonable steps to ensure that their employing organizations' practices are consistent with the NASW Code of Ethics.

(e) Social workers should act to prevent and eliminate discrimination in the employing organization's work assignments and in its employment policies and practices.

(f) Social workers should accept employment or arrange student field placements only in organizations that exercise fair personnel practices.

(g) Social workers should be diligent stewards of the resources of their employing organizations, wisely conserving funds where appropriate and never misappropriating funds or using them for unintended purposes.

3.10 Labor–Management Disputes
(a) Social workers may engage in organized action, including the formation of and participation in labor unions, to improve services to clients and working conditions.

(b) The actions of social workers who are involved in labor–management disputes, job actions, or labor strikes should be guided by the profession's values, ethical principles, and ethical standards. Reasonable differences of opinion exist among social workers concerning their primary obligation as professionals during an actual or threatened labor strike or job action. Social workers should carefully examine relevant issues and their possible impact on clients before deciding on a course of action.

4.   SOCIAL WORKERS' ETHICAL RESPONSIBILITIES AS PROFESSIONALS

4.01 Competence
(a) Social workers should accept responsibility or employment only on the basis of existing competence or the intention to acquire the necessary competence.

(b) Social workers should strive to become and remain proficient in professional practice and the performance of professional functions. Social workers should critically examine and keep current with emerging knowledge relevant to social work. Social workers should routinely review the professional literature and participate in continuing education relevant to social work practice and social work ethics.

(c) Social workers should base practice on recognized knowledge, including empirically based knowledge, relevant to social work and social work ethics.

4.02   Discrimination
Social workers should not practice, condone, facilitate, or collaborate with any form of discrimination on the basis of race, ethnicity, national origin, color, sex, sexual orientation, age, marital status, political belief, religion, or mental or physical disability.

4.03   Private Conduct
Social workers should not permit their private conduct to interfere with their ability to fulfill their professional responsibilities.

4.04   Dishonesty, Fraud, and Deception
Social workers should not participate in, condone, or be associated with dishonesty, fraud, or deception.

4.05   Impairment
(a) Social workers should not allow their own personal problems, psychosocial distress, legal problems, substance abuse, or mental health difficulties to interfere with their professional judgment and performance or to jeopardize the best interests of people for whom they have a professional responsibility.

(b) Social workers whose personal problems, psychosocial distress, legal problems, substance abuse, or mental health difficulties interfere with their professional judgment and performance should immediately seek consultation and take appropriate remedial action by seeking professional help, making adjustments in workload, terminating practice, or taking any other steps necessary to protect clients and others.

4.06   Misrepresentation
(a) Social workers should make clear distinctions between statements made and actions engaged in as a private individual and as a representative of the social work profession, a professional social work organization, or the social worker's employing agency.

(b) Social workers who speak on behalf of professional social work organizations should accurately represent the official and authorized positions of the organizations.

(c) Social workers should ensure that their representations to clients, agencies, and the public of professional qualifications, credentials, education, competence, affiliations, services provided, or results to be achieved are accurate. Social workers should claim only those relevant professional credentials they actually possess and take steps to correct any inaccuracies or misrepresentations of their credentials by others.

4.07 Solicitations
(a) Social workers should not engage in uninvited solicitation of potential clients who, because of their circumstances, are vulnerable to undue influence, manipulation, or coercion.

(b) Social workers should not engage in solicitation of testimonial endorsements (including solicitation of consent to use a client's prior statement as a testimonial endorsement) from current clients or from other people who, because of their particular circumstances, are vulnerable to undue influence.

4.08 Acknowledging Credit
(a) Social workers should take responsibility and credit, including authorship credit, only for work they have actually performed and to which they have contributed.

(b) Social workers should honestly acknowledge the work of and the contributions made by others.

5. SOCIAL WORKERS' ETHICAL RESPONSIBILITIES TO THE SOCIAL WORK PROFESSION

5.01 Integrity of the Profession
(a) Social workers should work toward the maintenance and promotion of high standards of practice.

(b) Social workers should uphold and advance the values, ethics, knowledge, and mission of the profession. Social workers should protect, enhance, and improve the integrity of the profession through appropriate study and research, active discussion, and responsible criticism of the profession.

(c) Social workers should contribute time and professional expertise to activities that promote respect for the value, integrity, and competence of the social work profession. These activities may include teaching, research, consultation, service, legislative testimony, presentations in the community, and participation in their professional organizations.

(d) Social workers should contribute to the knowledge base of social work and share with colleagues their knowledge related to practice, research, and ethics. Social workers should seek to contribute to the profession's literature and to share their knowledge at professional meetings and conferences.

(e) Social workers should act to prevent the unauthorized and unqualified practice of social work.

5.02   Evaluation and Research

(a) Social workers should monitor and evaluate policies, the implementation of programs, and practice interventions.

(b) Social workers should promote and facilitate evaluation and research to contribute to the development of knowledge.

(c) Social workers should critically examine and keep current with emerging knowledge relevant to social work and fully use evaluation and research evidence in their professional practice.

(d) Social workers engaged in evaluation or research should carefully consider possible consequences and should follow guidelines developed for the protection of evaluation and research participants. Appropriate institutional review boards should be consulted.

(e) Social workers engaged in evaluation or research should obtain voluntary and written informed consent from participants, when appropriate, without any implied or actual deprivation or penalty for refusal to participate; without undue inducement to participate; and with due regard for participants' well-being, privacy, and dignity. Informed consent should include information about the nature, extent, and duration of the participation requested and disclosure of the risks and benefits of participation in the research.

(f) When evaluation or research participants are incapable of giving informed consent, social workers should provide an appropriate explanation to the participants, obtain the participants' assent to the extent they are able, and obtain written consent from an appropriate proxy.

(g) Social workers should never design or conduct evaluation or research that does not use consent procedures, such as certain forms of naturalistic observation and archival research, unless rigorous and responsible review of the research has found it to be justified because of its prospective scientific, educational, or applied value and unless equally effective alternative procedures that do not involve waiver of consent are not feasible.

(h) Social workers should inform participants of their right to withdraw from evaluation and research at any time without penalty.

(i) Social workers should take appropriate steps to ensure that participants in evaluation and research have access to appropriate supportive services.

(j) Social workers engaged in evaluation or research should protect participants from unwarranted physical or mental distress, harm, danger, or deprivation.

(k) Social workers engaged in the evaluation of services should discuss collected information only for professional purposes and only with people professionally concerned with this information.

(l) Social workers engaged in evaluation or research should ensure the anonymity or confidentiality of participants and of the data obtained from them. Social workers should inform participants of any limits of confidentiality, the measures that will be taken to ensure confidentiality, and when any records containing research data will be destroyed.

(m) Social workers who report evaluation and research results should protect participants' confidentiality by omitting identifying information unless proper consent has been obtained authorizing disclosure.

(n) Social workers should report evaluation and research findings accurately. They should not fabricate or falsify results and should take steps to correct any errors later found in published data using standard publication methods.

(o) Social workers engaged in evaluation or research should be alert to and avoid conflicts of interest and dual relationships with participants, should inform participants when a real or potential conflict of interest arises, and should take steps to resolve the issue in a manner that makes participants' interests primary.

(p) Social workers should educate themselves, their students, and their colleagues about responsible research practices.

6.   **SOCIAL WORKERS' ETHICAL RESPONSIBILITIES TO THE BROADER SOCIETY**

6.01   **Social Welfare**
Social workers should promote the general welfare of society, from local to global levels, and the development of people, their communities, and their environments. Social workers should advocate for living conditions conducive to the fulfillment of basic human needs and should promote social, economic, political, and cultural values and institutions that are compatible with the realization of social justice.

6.02   **Public Participation**
Social workers should facilitate informed participation by the public in shaping social policies and institutions.

6.03   **Public Emergencies**
Social workers should provide appropriate professional services in public emergencies to the greatest extent possible.

6.04   **Social and Political Action**
(a) Social workers should engage in social and political action that seeks to ensure that all people have equal access to the resources, employment, services, and opportunities they require to meet their basic human needs and to develop fully. Social workers should be aware of the impact of the political arena on practice and should advocate for changes in policy and legislation to improve social conditions in order to meet basic human needs and promote social justice.

(b) Social workers should act to expand choice and opportunity for all people, with special regard for vulnerable, disadvantaged, oppressed, and exploited people and groups.

(c) Social workers should promote conditions that encourage respect for cultural and social diversity within the United States and globally. Social workers should promote policies and practices that demonstrate respect for difference, support the expansion of cultural knowledge and resources, advocate for programs and institutions that demonstrate cultural competence, and promote policies that safeguard the rights of and confirm equity and social justice for all people.

(d) Social workers should act to prevent and eliminate domination of, exploitation of, and discrimination against any person, group, or class on the basis of race, ethnicity, national origin, color, sex, sexual orientation, age, marital status, political belief, religion, or mental or physical disability.

Abramson, M. (1990a). Ethics and technological advances: Contributions of social work practice. *Social Work in Health Care, 15*(2), 5–17.

Abramson, M. (1990b). Keeping secrets: Social workers and AIDS. *Social Work, 35*(2), 169–173.

Allen-Meares, P. (1992). Prevention and cross-cultural perspective: Preparing school social workers for the 21st century. *Social Work in Education, 14*, 3–5.

American Association of Retired Persons. (1987). *Maltreatment of the elderly: Toward prevention.* Criminal Justice Services Program Development (Pamphlet).

American Association of State Social Work Boards. (1996). Social work laws and board regulations: A state comparison study.

Anonymous, Mack, J, & Emery, A. (1992). Staff reactions to AIDS in the workplace. *Families in Society, 73*(11), 559–567.

Beauchamp, T. & Childress, J. (1983). *Principles of biomedical ethics* (2nd Ed.). New York: Oxford.

Berkman, C. & Zinberg, G. (1997). Homophobia and heterosexism in social workers. *Social Work, 42*(4), 319–332.

Berman–Rossi, T. & Rossi, P. (1990). Confidentiality and informed consent in school social work. *Social Work in Education, 12*(3), 195–207.

Biestek, F. (1957). *The casework relationship.* Chicago: Loyola University Press.

Black, C. (1981). *It will never happen to me.* Denver: MAC

Borys, D. & Pope, K. (1989). Dual relationships between therapist and client: A national study of psychologists, psychiatrists, and social workers. *Professional Psychology: Research and Practice, 20*(5), 283–293.

Boyd–Franklin, N. (1989). *Black families in therapy: A multisystems approach.* New York: Guilford Press.

Brown, L. (1991). *Groups for growth and change.* New York: Longman.

Brownell, P. (1994). Elder abuse: Policy and practice. In I. Gutheil (Ed.), *Working with older people: Challenges and opportunities* (pp. 85–108). New York: Fordham University Press.

Callahan, J. (1994). The ethics of assisted suicide. *Health and Social Work, 19*(4), 237–252.

Cantor, M. & Garland, B. (1993). *Growing older in New York City in the 1990's: A study of changing life styles, quality of life and quality of care.* New York: Center for Policy in Aging of New York Community Trust.

Centers for Disease Control and Prevention. (1996). *HIV/AIDS Surveillance Report.* Hyattsville, MD: U.S. Public Health Service, National Center for Health Statistics.

Children's Defense Fund. (1989). *A vision for America's future.* Washington, DC:CDF.

Childress, J. (1991). Mandatory HIV screening and testing. In. F. Reamer (Ed.), *AIDS and ethics* (pp. 50–76). New York: Columbia University Press.

Cohen, B. (1987). The ethics of social work supervision revisited. *Social Work, 32*(3), 194–196.

Cohen, C. (1997). The impact of culture in social work practice with groups: The grandmothers as mothers again case study. In E. Congress (Ed.), *Multicultural perspectives in working with families* (pp. 311–331). New York: Springer.

Cohen, C. & Phillips, M. (October, 1995). *Talking about not talking: The paradox of confidentiality in groups.* Paper presented at the Annual Symposium of the American Association of Social Work with Groups, San Diego, CA.

Collopy, B. & Bial, M. (1994). Social work and bioethics: Ethical issues in long term care practice. In I. Gutheil (Ed.), *Work with older people* (pp. 109–138). New York: Fordham University Press.

Collopy, B., Dubler, N., & Zuckerman, C. (1990). The ethics of home care: Autonomy and accommodation. *Hastings Center Report, 20*(2), 1–16.

Congress, E. (1986). Ethical decision making among social work supervisors. Ph. D. diss., City University of New York, New York.

Congress, E. (1992a). Ethical decision making of social work supervisors. *The Clinical Supervisor, 10*(1), 157–169.

Congress, E. (1992b). Ethical teaching of multicultural students: Reconsideration of social work values for educators. *Journal of Multicultural Social Work, 2*(2), 11–23.

Congress, E. (1993). Teaching ethical decision making to a diverse community of students: Bringing practice into the classroom. *Journal of Teaching in Social Work, 7*(2), 23–36.

Congress, E. (1994). The use of the culturagram to assess and empower culturally diverse families. *Families in Society, 75*, 531–540.

Congress, E. (1996). Dual relationships in academia: Dilemmas for social work educators. *Journal of Social Work Education, 32*(3), 329–338.

Congress, E. (1997). Value dilemmas of faculty advising: Significant issues in a Code of Ethics for faculty advisors. *Journal of Teaching in Social Work, 14*(2), 89–110.

Congress, E. & Chernesky, R. (1993). Representative payee programs for the elderly: Administrative, clinical, and ethical issues. *Journal of Gerontological Social Work, 21*(1/2), 77–93.

Congress, E. & Fewell, C. (1994). Recognizing substance abuse in a colleague: What can I do? What should I do? *Currents* (Feb.March).

Congress, E. & Gummer, B. (1996). Is the Code of Ethics as applicable to agency administrators as it is to direct service providers? In E. Gambril and R. Pruger, *Controversial issues in social work ethics, values, and obligations* (pp.137–150). Boston: Allyn and Bacon.

Congress, E. & Johns, M. (1994). Cultural differences in aging. In I. Gutheil (Ed.), *Working with older people: Challenges and opportunities.* New York: Fordham University Press.

Congress, E. & Lynn, M. (1994). Group work programs in public schools: Ethical dilemmas and cultural diversity. *Social Work in Education, 16*(2), 107–114.

Congress, E. & Lynn, M. (1995). Using group work skills to promote cultural sensitivity among social work students. In R. Kurland & Salmon, R., *Using group work skills to promote cultural sensitivity among social work students* (pp. 73–87). New York: Haworth Press.

Congress, E. & Lynn, M. (1997). Group work practice in the community: Navigating the slippery slope of ethical dilemmas. *Social Work with Groups, 20*(3), 61–74.

Congress, E. & Lyons, B. (1992). Cultural differences in health beliefs: Implications for social work practice in health care settings. *Social Work in Health Care, 17*(3), 81–96.

Conrad, A. & Joseph, V. (Nov., 1996). *A model for ethical problem solving: A process for resolving questions and quandaries.* Presentation at the Annual NASW Conference, Cleveland, OH.

Cooper, T. (1990). *The responsible administrator: An approach to ethics for the administrative role* (3rd Ed.). San Francisco: Jossey-Bass.

Corcoran, K. & Winslade, W. (1990). Eavesdropping on the 50-minute hour: Managed mental health care and confidentiality. *Behavioral Science and the Law, 12*(2), 351–365.

Cornos, F. (1989). Involuntary medication and the case of Joyce Brown. *Hospital and Community Psychiatry, 40*, 730–740.

Cumming, E. & Henry, W. (1961). *Growing old: The process of disengagement.* New York: Basic Books.

Dao, J. (1995). AIDS test data under accord. *New York Times,* Oct.10, pp. A1, B4.

Davidson, J. & Davidson, T. (1996). Confidentiality and managed care. *Health and Social Work, 21*(3), 208–215.

Dolgoff, R. & Skolnik, L. (1992). Ethical decision making, the NASW Code of Ethics and group work practice: Beginning explorations. *Social Work with Groups, 15,* 99–112.

Dolgoff, R. & Skolnik, L. (1996). Ethical decision making in social work with groups. *Social Work with Groups, 19*(2), 49–65

Dziech, B. & Weiner,L. (1990). *The lecherous professor: Sexual harassment on campus* (2nd Ed.). Urbana: University of Illinois Press.

Edelwich, J. & Brodsky, A. (1991). *Sexual dilemmas for the helping professionals.* New York: Bruner Mazel.

Fandetti, D. & Goldmeier, J. (1988). Social work as culture mediators in health care settings. *Health and Social Work, 13*(3), 171–179.

Fanshel, D. & Shinn, E. (1978). *Children in foster care: A longitudinal investigation.* New York: Columbia University Press.

Feiner, H. & Couch, E. (1985). I've got a secret: The student in the agency. *Social Casework, 66*(5), 268–274.

Field, M. (1990). Testing for AIDS: Uses and abuses. *American Journal of Law and Medicine, 16*(2), 33–106.

Garrett, K. (1994) Caught in a bind: Ethical decision making in schools. *Social Work in Education, 16*(2), 97–105.

Gechtman, L. (1989). Sexual contact between social workers and their clients. In G. Gabbard (Ed.), *Sexual exploitation in professional relationships* (pp. 27–38). Washington, DC: American Psychiatric Press.

Gelfand, D. & Yee, B. (1991). Trends and forces: Influences of immigration, migration, and acculturation in fabric of aging in America. *Generations, 15*(4), 7–10.

Gibelman, M. & Schervish, P. (1997). *Who are we: A second look.* Washington, DC: NASW Press.

Ginsberg, L. (1995). *Social work almanac.* Washington, DC: NASW Press.

Gleeson, J. & Philbin, C. (1994). *Current practices in kinship care: Supervisors' perspectives.* Chicago: Jane Addams Center for Social Policy and Research.

Goldstein, J., Freud, A., & Solnit, A. (1973). *Beyond the best interests of the child.* New York: Free Press.

Goldstein, J., Freud, A., Solnik, A., & Goldstein, S. (1986). *In the best interests of the child.* New York: Free Press.

Gordon, W. (1965). Toward a social work frame of reference. *Journal of Education in Social Work, 1,* 19–26.

Greenhouse, L. (1996). Justices recognize confidential privilege between therapist and patient. *New York Times,* June 14 (http://www.nytimes.com.96/14/6/front/scotus/privilege-html).

Gutheil, I. (1994). Introduction. *Working with older people: Challenges and opportunities* (pp. 1–5). New York: Fordham University Press.

Hairston, C. (1996). Foster care: Trends and issues. In P. Raffoul & C. McNeece (Eds.), *Future issues for social work practice.* Boston: Allyn and Bacon.

Hardman, D. (1975). Not with my daughter you don't. *Social Work, 20*(4), 278–285.

Hartman, A. & Laird, J. (1983). *Family centered social work.* New York: Free Press.

Hermann, D. (1991). AIDS and the law. In F. Reamer (Ed.), *AIDS and ethics.* New York: Columbia University Press.

Ho, M. (1991). The use of the ethnic sensitive inventory (ESI) to enhance practitioner skills with minorities. *Journal of Multicultural Social Work, 1*(1), 57–68.

Hogue, C. & Hargaves, M. (1993). Class, race, and infant mortality in the United States. *American Journal of Public Health, 83*(1), 9–12.

Horner, W. & Whitbeck, L. (1991). Personal versus professional values in social work: A methodological note. *Journal of Social Service Review, 14*(1/2), 21–43.

Huber, C. (1994). *Ethical, legal, and professional issues in the practice of marriage and family therapy.* New York: Merrill.

Jayartne, S., Croxton, T. & Mattison, D. (1997). Social work professional standards: An exploratory study. *Social Work, 42*(2), 187–199.

Joseph, V. (1983). The ethics of organizations: Shifting values and ethical dilemmas. *Administration in Social Work, 7*(3/4), 47–57.

Joseph, V. (1991). Standing for values and ethical action: Teaching social work ethics. *Journal of Social Work Education, 5*(2), 95–109.

Joseph, V. & Conrad, A. (1989). Social work influence on interdisciplinary decision making in health care settings. *Health and Social Work, 14*(1), 22–30.

Kadushin, A. (1992). *Supervision in social work* (3rd Ed.). New York: Columbia University Press.

Kagle, J. & Giebelhausen, P. (1994). Dual relationships and professional boundaries. *Social Work, 31*(2), 213–220.

Kagle, J. & Kopels, S. (1994). Confidentiality after Tarasoff. *Health and Social Work, 19*(3), 217–222.

Kaplan, M. & Krell–Long, L. (1993). AIDS, health policy and AIDS. *Affilia, 8*(20), 157–170.

Karls, J. & Wandrei, K. (1992). PIE: A new language for social workers. *Social Work, 37*(1), 80– 85.

Keith–Lucas, A. (1977). Ethics in social work. In *Encyclopedia of Social Work* (17th Ed.), pp. 350–355). Washington, DC: NASW.

Kirk, S. & Kutchins, H. (1992). The selling of DSM IV. New York: Aldine de Gruyere.

Konopka, G. (1978) The significance of social group work based on ethical values. *Social Work with Groups, 1*, 123–131.

Kreuger, L. (1997). The end of social work. *Journal of Social Work Education, 33*(1), 19–27.

Kurland, R. & Salmon, R. (1992). Self–determination: Its use and misuse in group work practice and graduate education. In D. Fike & B. Rittner (Eds.), *Working from strengths: The essence of group work.* Miami Shores, FL: Center for Group Studies.

Kutchins, H. (1991). The fiduciary relationship: The legal basis for social work responsibilities to clients. *Social Work, 36*(2), 106–113.

Lennon, T. (1995). *Statistics on social work education in the United States.* Alexandria, VA: CSWE.

Levy, C. (1973). The ethics of supervision. *Social Work, 18*(3), 14–21.

Levy, C. (1979). The ethics of management. *Administration in Social Work, 3*(3), 277–289.

Levy, C. (1983). *Guide to ethical decisions and actions for social service administrators: A handbook for managerial personnel.* New York: Haworth Press.

Lewis, H. (1972). Morality and the politics of practice. *Social Casework, 5*(3), 404–417.

Lewis, H. (1984). Ethical assessment. *Social Casework, 65*(4), 203–211.

Lewis, H. (1987). Teaching ethics through ethical teaching. *Journal of Teaching in Social Work, 1*(1), 3–14.

Lewis, H. (1988). Ethics and the management of service effectiveness in social welfare. *Social Work in Administration, 11*(3/4), 272–284.

Lockery, S. (1991). Caretaking among racial and ethnic minority elderly: Families and social supports. *Generations, 15*(4), 58–62.

Lowenberg, F. & Dolgoff, R. (1996). *Ethical decisions in social work practice.* Itasca, IL: Peacock.

Lowy, L. (1985). Values as context for work with the aging. *Social work with the aging: The challenge and promise of later years* (2nd Ed.). New York: Longman.

McGoldrick, M., Pearce, J. & Giordano, J. (1997). *Ethnicity and family therapy.* New York: Guilford Press.

McGowan, B. & Stutz, E. (1991). Children in foster care. In A. Gitterman (Ed.), *Handbook of social work with vulnerable populations* (pp. 382–415). New York: Columbia University Press.

Meinert, R. Pardek, J. & Sullivan, W. (1994). *Issues in social work: A critical analysis.* Westport, CT: Auburn House.

Morrison, M. (1995). Caseworkers' and social workers' definition of family in relationship to their decisions to place children in foster care. Ph. D. diss., Fordham University, New York.

Munson, C. (1996). Autonomy and managed care in clinical social work practice. *Smith College Studies in Social Work, 66*(3), 241–259.

National Association of Social Workers. (1984). *HIV/AIDS policy statement.* Silver Springs, MD: NASW.

National Association of Social Workers. (1993a). *Code of ethics.* Washington, DC: NASW.

National Association of Social Workers. (1993b). *End-of-life decisions: Delegate assembly policy statement.* Washington, DC: NASW.

National Association of Social Workers. (1995). *Social work role in managed care: Policy statement.* New York: NASW.

National Association of Social Workers. (1996). *Code of ethics.* Washington, DC: NASW.

Noble, D. & King, J. (1981). Values: Passing on the torch without burning the runner. *Social Casework, 62*(10), 579–584.

O'Neil, M. (1992). Ethical dimensions of nonprofit administration. *Nonprofit Management and Leadership, 3*(2), 199–213.

Perlman, H.(1975). Self-determination: Reality or illusion? In F. McDermott (Ed.), *Self-determination in social work* (pp. 65–89). London: Routledge and Kegan Paul.

Pine, B. (1987). Strategies for more ethical decision making in child welfare practice. *Child Welfare, 66*(4), 315–326.

Polowy, C. & Gilbertson, J. (1997). Social workers and subpoenas. *Currents* (June/July).

Pope, K. (1988). How clients are harmed by sexual contact with mental health professionals: The syndrome and its prevalance. *Journal of Counseling and Development, 67*, 222–226.

Proctor, E., Morrow–Howell, N. & Lott, C. (1993). Classification and correlates of ethical dilemmas in hospital social work. *Social Work, 38*(2), 166–177.

Pumphrey, M. (1959). *Teaching of values and ethics in social work education.* New York: Council of Social Work Education.

Raffoul, P. & McNeece, C. (1996). *Future issues for social work practice.* Boston: Allyn and Bacon.

Reamer, F. (1985). The emergence of bioethics in social work. *Health and Social Work, 10*(4), 271–281.

Reamer, F. (1987). Ethics committees in social work. *Social Work, 52*(3), 188–192.

Reamer, F. (1991). AIDS: The relevance of ethics. In F. Reamer(Ed.), *AIDS and Ethics* (pp. 1–25). New York: Columbia University Press.

Reamer, F. (1995a). Malpractice claims against social workers: First facts. *Social Work, 40*(5), 595–601.

Reamer, F. (1995b). *Social work values and ethics.* New York: Columbia University Press.

Reamer, F. (1997). Managing ethics under managed care. *Families in Society, 78*(1), 96–106.

Reisch, M. & Taylor, C. (1983). Ethical guidelines for cutback management: A preliminary approach. *Administration in Social Work, 7* (3/4), 59–72.

Rennie v. Klein (1983) 720 f 2 d 266 3rd Cir 1983 8 MPDLR 18.

Rhame, F. & Maki, D. (1989). The case for wider use of testing for HIV infection. *New England Journal of Medicine, 320*(19), 1242–1253.

Rhodes, M. (1992). Social work challenges: The boundaries of ethics. *Families in Society, 73*(1), 40–47.

Richardson, L. (1997). Program on AIDS brings movement for early detection and less secrecy. *New York Times,* Aug. 21, A1, B4.

Roberts, C. (1989). Conflicting professional values in social work and medicine. *Health and Social Work, 14*(3), 211–218.

Rock, B. & Congress, E. (1997). The new confidentiality for the 21st century. Unpublished manuscript.

Romano, K. & Zayas, L. (1997). Motherless children: Family interventions with AIDS orphans. In E. Congress, *Multicultural perspectives in working with families* (pp. 109–124). New York: Springer.

Rosenthal, E. (1993). Who will turn violent: Hospitals have to guess. *New York Times,* April 7, A1, C12.

Ross, W. (1992). Are social workers compromised? *Health and Social Work, 17*(3), 163–165.

Rothman, J. (1989). Client self-determination: Untying the knot. *Social Service Review, 63,* 598–612.

Russel, R. (1988). Role perceptions of attorneys and caseworkers in child abuse cases in juvenile court. *Child Welfare, 67*(3), 205–216.

Ryan, C. & Rowe, M. (1988). AIDS: Legal and ethical issues. *Social Casework, 69*(6), 324–333.

Saleebey, D. (Ed.). (1997). *The strengths perspective in social work practice.* New York: Longman.

Sands, R. (1991). *Clinical social work practice in community mental health.* New York: Macmillan.

Scarf, M. (1996). Keeping secrets. *New York Times Magazine,* June 16, pp. 38–40.

Shilts, R. (1987). *And the band played on.* New York: St. Martin's Press.

Shulman, L. (1992a). *The skills of helping individuals and groups* (3rd Ed.). Itasca, IL: Peacock.

Shulman, L. (1992b). *Interactional supervision.* New York: Columbia University Press.

Skolnik, L. & Attinson, L. (1978). Confidentiality in group work practice. *Social work with groups, 1,* 65–74.

Smith, S. & Meyer, R. (1988). *Law, behavior, and mental health.* New York: New York University Press.

Sontag, S. (1990). *Illness as metaphor: AIDS and its metaphor.* New York: Doubleday.

Specht, H. & Courtney, M. (1994). *Unfaithful angels: How social work has abandoned its mission.* New York: Free Press.

Stein, T. (1991). *Child welfare and the law.* New York: Longman.

Szasz, T. (1974). *The myth of mental illness.* New York: Harper and Row.

Tarasoff v. Board of Regents of University of California (1976). 17 Cal 3d 425.

Tepper, L. (1994). Family relationships in later life. In I. Gutheil (Ed.), *Working with older people: Challenges and opportunities.* (pp. 42–61). New York: Fordham University Press.

Thompson, R. (1990). *Ethical dilemmas in psychotherapy.* New York: Free Press.

Toseland, R. & Rivas, R. (1995). *Introduction to group work practice.* Boston: Allyn and Bacon.

Turnock, B. & Kelly, C. (1989). Mandatory premarital testing for HIV: The Illinois experience. *JAMA, 261*(23), 3415–3418.

U. S. Bureau of the Census. (1988). *Projection of population of U.S. by age, sex, and race: 1988–2080.* Current Population Reports (series P-25, no. 1018). Washington, DC: U.S. Government Printing Office.

U. S. Bureau of the Census. (1993). *Statistical abstract of the United States: 1993* (113th Ed.). Austin, TX: Reference Press.

U. S. House of Representatives. Select Committee on Aging. (1990). *Elder abuse: A decade of shame.* Washington, DC: U.S. Government Printing Office.

U. S. Senate (1988). *Developments in aging.* Vol. 1: *A report of special committee on aging.* Washington, DC: U.S. Printing Office.

Vandecreek, L., Knapp, S. & Herzog, C. (1988). Privileged communication for social workers. *Social Casework, 69,* 28–34.

Walden, T., Wolock, I. & Demone, H. (1990). Ethical decision making in human services. *Families in Society, 71*(2), 67–75.

Watson, K., Seader, M. & Walsh, E. (1994). Should adoption records be open? In E. Gambril & T. Stein (Eds.), Controversial issues in child welfare. Boston: Allyn and Bacon.

Wigmore, J. (1961). *Evidence in trials at common law* (Vol. 8), (McNaughton revision). Boston: Little, Brown.

Wilson, S. (1978). *Confidentiality.* New York: Free Press.

Wilson, S. (1980a). *Field Instruction.* New York: Free Press.

Wilson, S. (1980b). *Recording: Guidelines for social workers* (2nd Ed.) New York: Free Press.

Wilson, S. (1982). *Supervision.* New York: Free Press.

With cloning of a sheep, the ethical ground shifts. (1997). *New York Times,* Feb. 14, p. 8.

Wolf, R. & Pillemer, K. (1984). *Working with abused elderly: Assessment, advocacy, and intervention.* Worcester: University of Massachusetts Medical Center, Center on Aging.

Zawitz, M., Klaus, P. M., Bachman, R., Bastian, L., Debarry, M., Jr., Rand, M., & Taylor, B. (1993). *Highlights from 20 years of surveying crime victims: The National Crime Victimization Survey, 1973–92.* Washington, DC: U.S. Department of Justice, Bureau of Justice Statistics.

A

Abortion, 17
  easy access to, 63
Abramson, M., 69, 125, 132
Access to records, 164
Ackerman, Nathan, 92
Administration, 172–173
Administrators, 5
  and Code of Ethics, 11, 16
  cutback management, 143–144
  and distributive justice, 142–145
  ethics for, 141
  and HIV-positive employees, 138–139
Adolescents
  in family therapy, 91–92
  rights and privileges, 18
Adopted children, 63–67
Adoption Assistance and Child Welfare
      Act, 53
Adoption records, 64–65, 66
Adoptive parents, 63–67
Adult protective service programs, 99
Agency practitioners, fees, 48–49
Agency values, 18, 44
  and adoption, 65–66
  and AIDS confidentiality, 134–135
  and child welfare, 58–59
  on elder care, 101
  examining, 34–35
Aging, 5. *See also* Older people
AIDS, 5, 63, 119
  confidentiality issue, 132–137
  early detection, 132
  health care for patients, 137–138
  main issues concerning, 129
  number of victims, 129
  and oppressed population, 130–131
  treatment for, 70
AIDS-infected employees, 139
AIDS research, 138
AIDS testing, 131–132
Allen-Meares, P., 119
American Association of Group Workers,
      7
American Association of Medical Social
      Workers, 7
American Association of Psychiatric
      Social Workers, 7
American Association of Retired Persons,
      99
American Association of Social Workers,
      7

Americans with Disabilities Act, 129, 146
Assisted suicide
  ethics of, 74–76
  and Kervorkian, 74
  in the Netherlands, 73
Association for the Study of Community
      Organizations, 7
Attinson, L., 82
Attorneys, 121–125
Autonomy
  of clients, 42
  for older people, 100–103

B

Bartering arrangements, 36, 48
Beauchamp, T., 42
Beneficence, 30
Berkman, C., 130
Berman-Rossi, T., 117
Bial, M., 97
Biestek, F., 110
Billing, 172
Birth parents, 63–67
Black, C., 60
Blanket release form, 51–52
Borys, D., 106, 110, 112
Boyd-Franklin, N., 61
Brodsky, A., 109, 110
Brownell, P., 99
Bureau of the Census, 18, 20

C

Callahan, J., 74
Cantor, M., 96
Carolina Children and Families Service
      Agency, 2
Centers for Disease Control, 129
Chernesky, R., 97
Child abuse/neglect
  reporting, 54–56
  role of social problems, 54–56
Child Abuse Prevention and Treatment
      Act, 53
Children's Defense Fund, 56
Children with AIDS, 129
Childress, J., 42, 131, 132
Child welfare, 4
  adoption, 63–67
  attorney-social worker collaboration,
      121–125
  cases, 54–55, 56, 57–58, 64–65
  in ETHIC model, 58–63
  permanency planning, 53, 58, 63–67

placement decisions, 60
protective services, 56–63
reporting abuse/neglect, 54–56
Child welfare agencies, 18
Client autonomy, 42
Client records, 172
Clients
in attorney-social worker collaboration,
121–122
blanket release form, 51–52
commitment to, 159–160
competence, 43
in dual relationships, 110–113
impact of managed care, 40
lacking decision-making capacity, 166
needs of, 146
privileged communication, 86
refusal of treatment, 42
right to records, 50–51
self-determination, 21, 87–89
sexual relationships with, 105–107
vulnerability, 45
Client transfer, 172
Client values, 18–19
and adoption, 65–66
and AIDS confidentiality, 134–135
and child welfare, 58–59
on elder care, 101
examining, 34–35
Cloning, 69–70
Code of Ethics. *See* National Association
of Social Workers Code of Ethics
Coerciveness, 43
Cohen, B., 149
Cohen, C., 56, 82, 97
Colleagues
consulting, 33, 37–38
consulting on adoption, 67
consulting on AIDS confidentiality,
136–137
consulting on child welfare, 62–63
consulting on confidentiality, 45–46
consulting on elder care, 102
disputes involving, 168
impaired, 10–11, 15–16, 107–110,
169–170
incompetent, 10–11, 15–16, 170
respect due to, 167–168
unethical conduct of, 170–171
Collopy, B., 97
Commitment to employers, 173–174
Community care, 100–103

Compensation-based oppression, 142
Competence, 49
of clients, 43
in Code of Ethics, 160, 174–175
Confidentiality, 2–3
in attorney-social worker collaboration,
122–125
cases, 82–84, 85, 133–134
in Code of Ethics, 162–164
Code of Ethics on, 81–82
and colleagues, 168
diligence in, 154
and ETHIC model, 43–46
in family work, 10, 14, 82–86, 92-93
in group work, 10, 14, 82–86
guidelines, 85–86
with HIV/AIDS clients, 132–137
impact of technology on, 9–10, 40-41
in interdisciplinary teams, 118–119
limits to, 9, 43
in managed care, 10
principle of, 30
reasons for breaking, 14
and subpoenas, 124–125
task groups, 84–86
and technology, 15
Conflicting professional values, 125
Conflict of interest, 161–162
Congress, Elaine P., 11, 19, 20, 30, 33, 71,
77, 85, 91, 97, 103, 107, 110, 117,
119, 141, 149, 150, 154
Conrad, A., 19, 31, 33, 69, 71, 117, 125
Consequences
examining, 30
hypothesizing about, 32
Consultation, 168–169, 171
Continuing education, 173
Contribution principle, 142–143
Cooper, T., 141
Corcoran, K., 154
Cornos, F., 42
Couch, E., 149
Council of Social Work Education, 20
Courses of action, 36–37, 45
in adoption cases, 66–67
and AIDS confidentiality, 135–136
on child welfare, 59–60
in elder care, 101–102
Courtney, M., 47
Credit, acknowledging, 176
Croxton, T., 36, 112, 151, 153, 154
Cultural competence, 10, 14

and American diversity, 152
  in Code of Ethics, 160–161
Cultural diversity, 119–120
  among older people, 103–104
  in family treatment, 91–92
  guidelines on, 77–79
  and health care, 76–79
  in schools, 119–120
Cultural sensitivity, 20–21
Cummings, E., 95
Cutback management, 143–144

D

Dao, J., 132
Davidson, J., 40
Davidson, T., 40
Deception, 175
Deinstitutionalization, 42
Demone, H., 30, 31, 154
Deontological model, 30
Derogatory language, 166
Diagnosis, 13, 41–42
Diagnostic and Statistical Manual (APA)
  diagnoses from, 153
  use of, 41–43
Dignity, 25–26
Discrimination, 175
Dishonesty, 175
Distributive justice
  case, 144
  in health care system, 70–71
  principles of, 71, 142–145
  and supervisors, 146–147
Diversity
  of American society, 152
  valuing, 20–21
Dolgoff, R., 7, 8, 17, 31, 82, 136
Do-not-resuscitate orders, 73
Downsizing, 143–144
Drug abuse, 63
DSM-IV. *See Diagnostic and Statistical Manual*
Dual relationships, 1–2, 5, 35–36
  avoidance of, 10, 14
  cases, 110–111, 112–113, 114
  ethics of, 110–113
  with former clients, 112–113
  guidelines for, 115
  with students, 11, 112
  with supervisors, 114–115
  supervisor-supervisee, 150
Dubler, N., 97
Dziech, B., 107

E

Edelwich, J., 109, 110
Education, 11, 49, 171
Educators, 117–120
Elder abuse, 97–100
Elder care, 100–102
Emery, A., 139
Employee Assistance Programs, 108
End-of-life decisions, 4, 72–74
  assisted suicide, 74–76
  guidelines for, 75–76
English Poor Law, 130
Equality, principle of, 142, 146
Ethical dilemmas
  of advanced technology, 4
  cases, 1–2, 34–38
  DSM-IV use, 41–43
  and ETHIC model, 31–34
  guiding principles, 30
  in health care, 69–71
  in home care, 97
  hospital committees for, 126–127
  in managed care, 4
  over confidentiality, 44–46
  resolving, 29–31
Ethical issues, shift in, 1–3
Ethical principles
  in Code of Ethics, 157–158
  kinds of, 19
Ethical standards
  case, 35–36
  in Code of Ethics, 158–179
ETHIC decision-making model
  and adoption, 65–67
  and AIDS confidentiality, 133–137
  application of, 33–34
  child welfare, 58–63
  client confidentiality, 43–46
  definition, 31–33
  for elder care, 100–102
  and private practitioners, 47
  steps, 4
Ethics committees, in hospitals, 126–127
Ethics Review Committee, 63
Euthanasia, 73
Evaluation and research, 177–178

F

Family values, 90–91
Family work/therapy
  cases, 90, 91, 92–93
  confidentiality, 10, 14, 82–86, 92–93
  cultural diversity and, 91–92

ethical challenges, 89–91
ethical dilemmas, 81–84
ethical issues, 4–5
Fandetti, D., 78
Fanshel, D., 53
Federal Trade Commission, 8
Fees
    of agency practitioners, 48–49
    bartering arrangements, 36, 48
    in Code of Ethics, 166
    policy in setting, 48–49
Feiner, H., 149
Fewell, C., 107
Field, M., 131
Flexner Report, 7
Former clients
    in dual relationships, 112–113
    in sexual relationships, 106–107
Foster care, 56–63
    negative effects of, 53
Fraud, 175
Freud, A., 61, 121
Freud, Sigmund, 152

G
Garland, B., 96
Garrett, K., 117
Gay disease, 130
Gechtman, L., 106
Gelfand, D., 103
Genetic counseling, 69–70
Gibelman, M., 8, 41, 47, 152
Giebelhausen, P., 106, 110, 112
Gilbertson, J., 46
Gingrich, Newt, 53
Ginsberg, L., 45, 53, 72, 81
Giordano, J., 78
Gleeson, J., 61
Goldmeier, J., 78
Goldstein, J., 61, 121
Goldstein, S., 121
Gordon, W., 1
Grand narratives, collapse of, 152
Greenhouse, L., 46, 124
Group work/therapy
    cases, 82–84, 85, 86, 87, 88, 89
    confidentiality, 10, 14, 82–86
    ethical dilemmas, 81–84
    ethical issues, 4–5
    informed consent, 87
    mutual aid model, 88
    privileged communication, 86
    self-determination, 87–89

social control versus respect for
    individual, 89
task groups, 84–86
Gummer, B., 141
Gutheil, I., 96

H
Hairston, C., 61
Hardman, D., 19
Hargraves, M., 72
Hartman, A., 81
Health care
    and assisted suicide, 73–76
    cases, 69–70, 74–76, 77
    cloning issue, 69
    cultural differences, 76–79
    distributive justice in, 70–71
    end-of-life decisions, 72–74
    ethical dilemmas, 69–71
    ethical issues, 4
    genetic counseling, 69–70
    for HIV/AIDS patients, 137–138
    HIV/AIDS testing, 131–132
    life expectancy, 72, 131
    managed care, 79–80
    Medicaid, 80
    premature infants, 72
    renal dialysis, 70
Health care professionals, 125–128
Henry, W., 95
Hermann, D., 129
Herzog, C., 46, 47, 86
Hierarchical model, 31
HIV, 5, 63, 129
    confidentiality issue, 132–137
    health care for patients, 137–138
HIV-positive employees, 138–139
HIV Prevention Act, 132
HIV testing, 131–132
Ho, M., 78
Hogue, C., 72
Home care, 97
Homophobia, 130
Homosexual population, 129–131
Horner, W., 19
Hospitals, ethics committees, 126–127
Huber, C., 92
Huntington's chorea, 69
Hypothesizing
    about adoption, 66–67
    about confidentiality, 45
    about consequences, 32
    and AIDS confidentiality, 135–136

on child welfare, 59–60
on elder care, 101–102

I
Illinois, AIDS testing in, 132
Immigrant children, 119–120
Impaired colleagues, 10–11, 15–16,
    107–110
    behavioral patterns, 107–108
    in Code of Ethics, 169–170
    physical signs, 107
Incompetent colleagues, 10–11, 15–16
    in Code of Ethics, 170
Information
    released to other agency, 51–52
    sharing of, 51
Informed consent, 42, 87
    Code of Ethics on, 81, 159–160
Integrity of profession, 176–177
Interdisciplinary collaboration, 117
Interdisciplinary consultation, 5
Interdisciplinary teams, 117
    cases, 118–120, 122–123, 126–127
    in Code of Ethics, 168
    educators and social workers, 117–120
    guidelines for, 127–128
    social workers and attorneys, 121–125
    social workers and health care profes-
        sionals, 125–128
Interruption of services, 166
Intravenous drug users, 130

J
Jayartne, S., 36, 112, 151, 153, 154
Johns, M., 103
Joseph, V., 19, 31, 33, 69, 71, 117, 125,
    141

K
Kadushin, A., 149
Kagle, J., 43, 106, 110, 112
Kaplan, M., 129, 130–131
Karls, J., 41
Keith-Lucas, A., 32
Kelly, C., 132
Kervorkian, Jack, 74
King, J., 19
Kinship placement, 56–63
    merits of, 61–62
Kirk, S., 42
Knapp, S., 46, 47, 86
Konopka, G., 82
Kopels, S., 43
Krell-Long, L., 129, 130–131

Krueger, L., 152
Kurland, R., 82, 88
Kutchins, H., 21, 42

L
Labor-management disputes, 174
Laird, J., 81
Law, and sexual relationships, 105–106
Legal procedures, 46–47
Lennon, T., 152
Levy, C., 141, 149
Lewis, H., 21, 32, 136, 141, 150
Life expectancy, 72
    of women with AIDS, 131
Living will, 73
Lockery, S., 96–97
Lott, C., 69
Louisiana, AIDS testing in, 132
Lowenberg, F., 7, 8, 17, 31, 136
Lowry, L., 78
Lynn, M., 20, 33, 85, 119
Lyons, B., 71, 77

M
Mack, J., 139
Maki, D., 131
Managed care, 13, 79–80
    confidentiality in, 10
    impact on service to clients, 40
    Medicaid, 80
Mantle, Mickey, 71
Marx, Karl, 152
Mattison, D., 36, 112, 151, 153, 154
McGoldrick, M., 78
McGowan, B., 53, 54
McNeece, C., 152, 153
Medicaid, 80
Meinert, R., 1
Mental health
    cases, 39, 48, 49
    DSM-IV use, 41–43
Mental health field, 153
Misrepresentation, 175–176
Morrison, M., 53, 90
Morrow-Howell, N., 69
Munson, C., 40, 154
Mutual aid model, 88

N
National Association of School Social
    Workers, 7
National Association of Social Workers
    Committee on Inquiry, 109
    development of current code, 7–11

on end-of-life decisions, 4
first code of ethics, 7
Insurance Trust, 46
Medicaid recommendations, 80
origin of, 7
peer consultation services, 108
National Association of Social Workers
Code of Ethics, 1, 3-4, 5, 35
on abandoning clients, 48–49
on access to care, 40
on administrative ethics, 141
and adoption, 66
and AIDS confidentiality, 135
on bartering, 36
changed from earlier codes, 9–11
on client needs, 146
on client's comprehension, 52
on clients' cultures, 77
on competence, 49
on confidentiality, 124
on dual relationships, 2, 110
on elder care, 101
ethical standards, 31–32
on group/family work, 81–82
on homophobia, 130
on impaired colleagues, 107
on informed consent, 87
on interdisciplinary collaboration, 117
limits of confidentiality, 43, 44, 133
limits to self-determination, 70
main purposes, 9
provisions, 157–179
purpose, viii
on record keeping, 49–50
on release of records, 50–51
on resolving ethical dilemmas, 29–31
on self-determination, 87–88
on setting fees, 48
on sexual relationships, 105–106
status of, 151
on supervisor responsibilities, 149
on unethical conduct, 109
values described in, 20–21
on volunteerism, 153
on vulnerable people, 136, 139, 143
on working with older people, 96
National Association of Social Workers
Delegate Assembly, 72
on end-of-life decisions, 74
on vulnerable people, 142
Need, principle of, 142
Netherlands, euthanasia in, 73

New York, AIDS testing in, 132
New York Times, 130
Noble, D., 19
Nonmalfeasance, 30
Nonprofit agencies, 153

O
Older people
assistance in child care, 96–97
autonomy/community care, 100–103
cases, 95–96, 98–99, 100, 103–104
culturally diverse, 103–104
diversity of needs, 96–97
elder abuse, 97–100
home care, 97
percent of population, 96
O'Neill, M., 141
Oppressed population, 130–131
Organ transplants, 71
Orphanages, 53

P
Pardek, J., 1
Parens patriae doctrine, 118
Passive euthanasia, 73
Patient Self-Determination Act, 73
Pearce, J., 78
Peer consultation services, 108
Performance evaluation, 172
Permanency planning policy, 53
adoption, 63–67
and agency values, 58
Personal impairment, 175
Personal values, 18
and adoption, 65–66
and AIDS confidentiality, 134–135
and child welfare, 58–59
on elder care, 101
Person in Environment, 41
Philbin, C., 61
Phillips, M., 82
Physical contact, 10, 15, 165
Pillmer, K., 98
Pine, B., 54
Poddar, Prosenjit, 43
Political action, 179
Polowy, C., 46
Pope, K., 106, 110, 112
Premature infants, 72
Preventive medicine, 77
Privacy, 162–164
Private agencies, 153
Private conduct, 175

Private practice, 47, 153–154
  fees, 48–49
Privileged communication, 46–47, 86
Pro bono service, 48–49
Proctor, E., 69
Professional codes, need for, 7
Professional responsibilities, 174–176
Professional values
  and adoption, 65–66
  and AIDS confidentiality, 134–135
  and child welfare, 58–59
  conflicting, 125
  on elder care, 101
  examining, 34–35
  kinds of, 19
Prognosis, 13
Public emergencies, 179
Public participation, 179
Pumphrey, M., 3, 19

R
Raffoul, P., 152, 153
Rahme, F., 131
Rawls, John, 31
Reamer, F., 29, 31, 40, 46, 69, 71, 106,
  126, 127, 137
Reasonable person standard, 42
Record keeping, 49–50
Records, 172
  access to, 164
  blanket release form, 51–52
  clients' right to, 50–51
Referral services, 169
Reisch, M., 32, 136, 143
Renal dialysis, 70
Rennie v. Klein, 42
Research, 177–178
Respect due to colleagues, 167–168
Respect for individuals, 89
Return to birth parents, 56–63
Rhodes, M., 110
Richardson, L., 129, 132, 133, 138
Richmond, Mary, 7
Rich-poor gap, 154–155
Rivas, R., 85, 88
Roberts, C., 33, 125
Rock, B., 154
Romano, K., 129
Rosenthal, E., 44, 124
Ross, W., 69
Rossi, P., 117
Rowe, M., 134
Russel, R., 121

Ryan, C., 134

S
Saleebey, Dennis, 3, 32
Salmon, R., 82, 88
Sands, R., 42
Schervish, P., 8, 41, 47, 152
Seader, M., 64
Self-determination, 21, 25–26, 35
  in Code of Ethics, 158
  in group work, 87–89
  limits to, 70
  and mental health, 41, 42
  for older people, 97
Self-determination principle, 30
Service
  cutting back on, 143–145
  interruption of, 166
  social triage model, 142
  termination of, 166–167
  unitary model, 143
Sexual harassment, 10, 15
  in Code of Ethics, 165
  and colleagues, 169
Sexual relationships, 10, 15
  in Code of Ethics, 164–165
  and colleagues, 169
  with former clients, 106–107
  in law and ethics, 105–106
Shilts, R., 130
Shinn, E., 53
Shulman, L., 87, 88, 149
Sibling groups, 57
Skolnik, L., 82
Social action, 179
Social control, 89
Social diversity, 10
Social justice, 20
Social triage model, 142
Social welfare, 179
Social work
  assessment tools, 41–43
  cases, 17–18
  changing environment, 154
  competence in, 21
  confidentiality in, 2–3
  cutting service, 143–145
  deontological model, 30
  dual relationship issue, 1–2
  ETHIC model, 31–33
  future of, 152–155
  hierarchical model, 31
  need for professional code, 7

teleological model, 30
Social workers
  challenges facing, vii
  collaborating with attorneys, 121–125
  collaborating with educators, 117–120
  collaborating with health care
    professionals, 125–128
  commitment to service, 20
  and confidentiality, 9–10
  cultural competence, 10
  and distributive justice, 142–145
  dual relationship guidelines, 115
  and dual relationships, 10
  education and training, 11
  family/group work, 4–5
  family values of, 90–91
  guidelines for task groups, 85–86
  guidelines on cultural diversity, 77–79
  and impaired colleagues, 10–11,
    107–110
  impartially based practice, 153–154
  and incompetent colleagues, 10–11
  in managed care, 79–80
  in private practice, 153–154
  professional responsibilities, 174–176
  relationships with supervisors, 147–150
  release of information, 51–52
  reporting child abuse/neglect, 54–56
  resolving ethical dilemmas, 29–31
  responsibilities in practice, 171–174
  responsibilities to profession, 176–178
  responsibilities to society, 179
  setting fees, 48–49
  and sexual harassment, 10, 15
  sexual relationships, 10, 15, 105–107
  sharing information, 51
  working with other professionals, 117
  from younger age group, 152–153
Social work ethics, 3
  for administrators, 141
  and distributive justice, 142–145
  and dual relationships, 110–113
  environment, vii
  future of, 151–155
  and legal procedures, 46–47
  limited literature on, 141
  and premature infants, 72
  and private practice, 47
  sexual relationships, 105–106
  of supervisors, 145–147
  supervisor-supervisee relationships,
    147–150

Social work field instructor, 148–149
Social Work Research and Abstracts, 141
Social Work Research Group, 7
Social work values, 1, 3
Societal responsibilities, 179
Societal values, 18
  and adoption, 65–66
  and AIDS confidentiality, 134–135
  and child welfare, 58–59
  on elder care, 101
Solicitations, 176
Solnit, A., 61, 121
Sontag, Susan, 130
Specht, H., 47
Staff development, 173
Stein, T., 60, 118, 121
Student relationships, 112
Stutz, E., 53, 54
Subpoenas, 124–125
Sullivan, W., 1
Supervision, 171
Supervisors, 5
  administrative tasks, 146–147
  case, 146–147, 148–149
  consulting, 33, 37–38
  consulting on adoption, 67
  consulting on AIDS confidentiality,
    136–137
  consulting on child welfare, 62–63
  consulting on confidentiality, 45–46
  consulting on elder care, 102
  and dual relationships, 114–115
  ethical choices, 33
  ethical dilemmas, 145
  and HIV-positive employees, 138–139
  relations with supervisees, 147–150
Szasz, Thomas, 43

T
Tarasoff, Tatiana, 43
Tarasoff v. Board of Regents of the
    University of California, 43, 133
Task delineation, 121
Task groups, 84–86
Taylor, C., 32, 136, 143
Technology, impact on confidentiality,
    9–10, 15, 40–41, 154
Teleological model, 30
Tepper, L., 96, 97
Termination of services, 166–167
Thompson, R., 41, 42
Toseland, R., 85, 88
Training, 11, 49, 171

Trustworthiness, 21
Truth telling, 26
Turnock, B., 132

U
Unitary model of service delivery, 143
United States Supreme Court, on
        privileged communication, 46–47, 86

V
Values, 1
    assessing, 22–27
    in child welfare cases, 58–59
    competence, 21
    definition, 17–18
    described in Code of Ethics, 20–21
    dignity, 25–26
    diversity, 20–21
    examining, 34–35, 44
    respecting dignity, 20–21
    self-determination, 25–26
    strengthening relationships, 21
    trustworthiness, 21
    truth telling, 26
    types of, 18–19
Vandecreek, L., 46, 47, 86
Volunteerism, 153
Vulnerable people, 45
    in adoption cases, 67

and AIDS confidentiality, 136
    in child welfare system, 62
    older people, 102

W
Walden, T., 30, 31, 154
Wandrei, K., 41
Watson, K., 64
Weiner, L., 107
Welfare Reform law, 137
Welsh, E., 64
Whitbeck, L., 19
Wigmore, J., 46
Wilson, S., 122–125, 149
Winslade, W., 154
Wolf, R., 98
Wolock, I., 30, 31, 154
Worker power, 146
Workers' needs, 146

Y
Yee, B., 103

Z
Zawitz, M., 45
Zayas, L., 129
Zinberg, G., 130
Zuckerman, C., 97